def	Define your terms.
det	Add specific details. (page 14)
div	Divide a word only between syllables.
dm	Revise the sentence so the dangling modifier has something to modify. (page 117)
emph	Rewrite to strengthen emphasis. (page 125)
ex	Add an example. (page 14)
fig	Revise the figure of speech to make it more effective. (page 129)
frag	Make this fragment into a complete sentence. (page 131)
fs	Revise this fused sentence. (page 163)
glos	See the glossary in Chapter 4 for the word marked.
hy	Add hyphen. (page 135)
id	Change to appropriate idiomatic usage. (page 136)
ital	Underline to indicate italics. (page 186)
logic	Rethink this passage. (page 138)
lc	Use a lowercase letter. (page 91)
mng?	Clear up the meaning. (page 113)
mm	Put misplaced modifier where it belongs. (page 141)
mix	Rewrite to get rid of the mixed construction. (page 113)
no punc	Don't use punctuation here. (page 143)
¶	Indent for a new paragraph here. (page 145)
¶ dev	Develop this paragraph more fully. (page 186)
paral or ‖	Make these elements parallel in form. (page 86)
pass	Change passive voice to active. (page 149)
quot	Use quotation marks correctly. (page 154)
ref	Make pronoun reference clear. (page 159)
rep	Get rid of careless repetition. (page 162)
run-on	Revise this run-on sentence. (page 163)
semi	Insert a semicolon where needed. *Or:* correct the misuse of the semicolon. (page 165)
shift	Revise to correct the shift in tense or person. (page 170)
sm	Correct the squinting modifier. (page 174)
sp	Correct the misspelled word. (page 380)
sub	Correct the faulty subordination. (page 176)
t	Correct the error in use of tense. (page 179)
trans	Make a smooth, clear transition. (page 184)
trite	Revise trite expression or cliché. (page 185)
und	Underline to indicate italics. (page 186)
un	Unify: stick to the thesis idea. (page 187)
usage	Check dictionary or Chapter 4 for standard usage.
vb	Correct the verb form. (page 181)
w	Tighten up this wordy expression or passage. (page 188)
ww	Revise for tone, meaning, or effectiveness, to get rid of the wrong word. (page 120)
x	Correct the careless error.

The Writer's Handbook

SECOND EDITION

Elizabeth McMahan
Illinois State University

Susan Day
Illinois State University

McGRAW-HILL, INC.
New York   St. Louis   San Francisco
Auckland   Bogotá   Caracas
Lisbon   London   Madrid   Mexico
Milan   Montreal   New Delhi
San Juan   Singapore
Sydney Tokyo Toronto

THE WRITER'S HANDBOOK

This book is printed on acid-free paper.

67890   DOC/DOC   9987654

ISBN   0-07-045432-9

This book was set in Caledonia by Bi-Comp, Inc.
The editors were Emily Barrosse, Allan Forsyth, and Curt Berkowitz;
the designer was Joan Greenfield;
the production supervisor was Diane Renda.
The drawings were done by Wellington Studios, Ltd.
R. R. Donnelley & Sons Company was printer and binder.

Library of Congress Cataloging-in-Publication Data

McMahan, Elizabeth.
 The writer's handbook/Elizabeth McMahan, Susan Day.—2nd ed.
   p.   cm.
 Includes index.
 ISBN 0-07-045432-9
 1. English language—Rhetoric—Handbooks, manuals, etc.
2. English language—Grammar—1950—Handbooks, manuals, etc.
I. Day, Susan.   II. Title.
PE1408.M3948 1988   87-24160
808'.042—dc19   CIP

About the Authors

ELIZABETH McMAHAN grew up in College Station, home of the "Fightin' Texas Aggies," where her father taught physics at Texas A & M University. Her B.A. and M.A. degrees in English are from the University of Houston; her Ph.D. (in American literature) is from the University of Oregon, where she enjoyed the benefits of an NDEA Fellowship. While still in graduate school, she wrote her first text, *A Crash Course in Composition*, now in its third edition, published by McGraw-Hill. Since then she has embraced the joys of collaborative writing with Susan Day. They have published the following texts with McGraw-Hill: *The Writer's Rhetoric and Handbook, The Writer's Handbook,* and *The Writer's Resource: Essays for Composition.*

She considers herself most fortunate in having a husband who is a feminist; three cats (one crazy); two fat, white geese; one small, rotund dog; and a house on Lake Bloomington where she composes on an IBM PC.

SUSAN DAY got her profession genetically: she comes from a whole family of English teachers. The alarming decline of language skills in America has been dinner-table conversation for as long as she can remember, though she hasn't noticed the discourse of her loved ones getting any less forceful or precise. Susie got her education as a sales clerk, sign painter, traveler, student at Illinois State University (BS in English Education and MS in English), go-go dancer, tutor, editor, and organizer. For 15 years she has been a writer and artist for the nation's oldest community-based alternative newspaper, the *Post Amerikan*. She also currently works as a career counselor, tutor of business writing, teacher trainer, photographer's assistant, freelance writer, teacher of writing to adult learners and college freshmen (since 1973), and computer jockey. In her spare time she paints and converses.

In loving memory of Sally Smith (1894–1987)

Contents

Preface

WE HAVE TRIED to follow our own advice in this book and write in a tone and style appealing to students, our primary audience. The content is traditional, and instructors who are accustomed to such a text will feel at home with this one. We rely mainly on approaches that have proved successful in our own teaching, and we aim at a level of competence which should be possible for most students to achieve: to write standard English that is clear, coherent, and economical.

PRACTICAL APPROACHES TO TRADITIONAL MATERIAL

The Writer's Handbook outlines the rules of standard English grammar and usage. We limit our discussion of grammar to the concepts applicable to writing. Drawing on the most useful concepts from traditional, structural, and transformational grammar, we explain the system as simply as possible and illustrate the principles with sentence diagrams—a useful tool which lets students see how sentence elements function. Gaining this knowledge is important for student writers because learning how to punctuate correctly depends upon understanding the function of sentence elements.

We call the chapter on mechanics, punctuation, and style the "Revising Index" because it contains—conveniently alphabetized for easy reference—all the advice necessary for revising and editing a paper. The "Revising Index" is keyed to the correction symbols inside the covers of this book.

The "Glossary of Usage" reflects current standard English usage and relies mainly on the research of Robert Pooley's *The Teaching of English Usage*, Roy H. Copperud's *American Usage: The Concensus*, Theodore Bernstein's *Dos and Don'ts and Maybes of English Usage*, several current collegiate dictionaries, and a stack of widely used composition textbooks. We urge instructors to look through the usage chapter since we often found ourselves surprised by recent changes.

Exercises are interspersed throughout the book. There are two diagnostic exercises—one on mechanics and style at the end of the "Revising Index," and one on usage at the end of the "Glossary of Usage."

SPECIAL SKILLS SECTION

Part 2 of *The Writer's Handbook* includes several practical chapters which do not necessarily have to be studied in class in order to prove useful to students.

Chapter 5 on study skills, entitled "Reading and Writing in College Classes," contains helpful advice on how to read textbooks, take notes, budget time, and pass tests—including essay examinations. We have now added additional instruction on how to become a good reader.

Chapter 6, "Researched Writing," covers library resources, precis writing, paraphrasing, and quoting from sources. It also provides complete information for following both the new MLA documentation style as well as the increasingly popular APA style.

Chapter 7, "Practical Career Writing," offers advice for writing effective job application letters and résumés—an important skill for every college graduate. We have increased the number of model resumes in order to illustrate how the form can vary according to content and purpose.

THE APPENDIXES

We have added a new appendix offering tips on using computers in writing—generic advice that will prove helpful in achieving maximum efficiency from any word processing software. The other appendix makes spelling rules simple and suggests alternate paths to improvement for those who cannot remember the rules.

INSTRUCTOR'S MANUAL

We've written the Instructor's Manual as a resource book. Beyond suggesting answers for exercises and discussion questions, the *Instructor's Manual* offers further suggestions for classroom activities and a set of duplicating or transparency masters that provide extra samples of student writing for in-class criticism. We've also included masters for the diagnostic exercises on grammar, mechanics, and usage.

ACKNOWLEDGMENTS

We want to extend thanks to the many people who have helped us survive the writing of this book: our friends and loved ones—Dan LeSeure, Mark Silverstein, Sue LeSeure, and David X. Lee; and our colleagues and critics who critiqued the manuscript: Dennis Baron, University of Illinois; Frederick Becker, Illinois Central College; Charles Beirnard, University of Alaska; Earle V. Bryant, University of New Orleans; Louie Edmundson, Chattanooga State Technical Community College; Jerry Fishman, Sacramento City College; Alice Forer, University of Michigan at Flint; Loris D. Galford, McNeese State University; Norma L. Gaskey, Jefferson Community College; Susan Jhirad, North Shore Community College; Joseph Johnson, Ramapo College; Jane Katims, Middlesex County College; John Lamiman, Guilford College; Steven Mainville, Shaw University; JoAnna S. Mink, University of Southwestern Louisiana; Susan Schiller, Sacramento City College; Evelyn T. Silliman, Alice Lloyd College; Lawrence J. Skinner, St. Louis Community College; Donald L. Stewart, Kansas State University; Margaret Taylor, Cuyahoga Community College; Gary Wilhardt, Monmouth College; and James L. Willis, Charles S. Mott Community College. We owe thanks to Bill Mullaney and Charlotte Smith of McGraw-Hill for their research assistance. And to our invaluable editors—Emily Barrosse and Curt Berkowitz—our warm gratitude.

Elizabeth McMahan
Susan Day

Part One

Just Your Basics

Chapter One
The Writing Process

This first, brief chapter explains more or less step-by-step the process you will go through in writing a paper. But, of course, if you have written anything lately, you know that writing is not as neat and tidy as we make it sound.

You sometimes add ideas in the middle of writing your first draft. Or you may rearrange your plan when you suddenly discover a better way to get your point across. Or perhaps you will take out ideas that no longer seem important. In the heat of composing you may generate a totally new main idea or a better approach to the idea you started with. You will almost certainly stop and change a word when a better one flashes into your mind or scratch out a sentence and write an improved version as you read back over a paragraph you have just written. If you compose on a word processor, you make these changes neatly with the touch of a key and a leap of words on the screen. If you write by hand, you can see by glancing at your first draft just how messy the composing process really is.

So do not feel that you must necessarily follow the advice given here as if it came down the mountain with Moses. We offer only guidelines describing in general the processes that most composition instructors recommend to their students. If you decide to follow these instructions, try not to get so rushed that you have to skip any part of the process. Good writing involves multiple drafts. That means writing and then *re*writing and sometimes rewriting even more. This diligent revising is what makes the difference between good writing and merely passable or poor writing. And remember that you can ruin the effect of even the best essay by neglecting the editing stage—the crucial process of proofreading and then correcting typos and careless mistakes in grammar and punctuation. Writing well involves hard work, but satisfying results will more than repay your efforts.

START WITH THE ESSENTIALS

Before you begin to write, you need to consider three things:

1. *Your thesis:* What am I going to write about?
2. *Your purpose:* Why am I writing?
3. *Your audience:* Who am I writing for?

These questions are equally important, and your answer to one will often affect your response to the others. For purposes of discussion, let's consider them one by one.

Find a Thesis

The first question involves choosing (or being assigned) a subject of some sort to write about. In composition class you may be allowed to choose your topic. In history class you are more likely to be told the topic. On the job you will probably be required to report in writing on a certain subject. Once you have chosen or been assigned a topic, you need to find an approach that allows you to cover the subject in an appropriate number of pages. Then, try to focus on the main idea that you want to get across—your *thesis*—and write it out in a single sentence, if possible.

Your thesis should clearly state the point you want to make about your subject. If, for instance, your topic is conservation, you need to narrow it considerably for a short paper. Try to think of some problem concerning conservation. You might decide to write just about the need for protecting wildlife. But even that is too broad an idea to cover in a brief essay. You could then limit yourself to seals. But now, ask yourself, what *about* seals? What is the problem? What is the point you want to make? You could assert that seals should be protected from industry by international treaty. Or you could insist that people should not buy any product made of sealskin in order to keep industry from finding the slaughter profitable.

Remember: **Your thesis should contain a verb to say something about your subject.**

Unsuitable thesis:	Drugs
Unsuitable thesis:	Drug abuse
Workable thesis:	Drug abuse can occur with perfectly legal prescription drugs.
Workable thesis:	Excessive use of alcohol constitutes the number-one drug abuse problem in the United States.

Determine Your Purpose

As you work out your thesis, you need also to ask yourself what your purpose is. *Why* are you exerting all this energy and straining your brain to do this piece of writing? Because your teacher or your boss told you to may be an honest answer, but not a useful one. Think beyond that immediate response to the reason that makes writing worthwhile. What do you hope to accomplish? Are you writing *to inform* your readers? Do you hope *to persuade* your readers to change their minds about some issue? Perhaps you simply want *to entertain* them. Or you may be keeping a journal or writing in a diary just *to express* yourself.

Your purpose affects your whole approach to writing: how you begin, whether you state or imply your thesis, what specific details you choose, how you organize the material, how you conclude, as well as what words you select for each sentence. You must give thought to your purpose before you begin.

Consider Your Audience

You cannot successfully determine why you are writing without also considering the final question: Who is going to read what you write? Your audience may be a single person—your boss, perhaps, your history professor, your senator. Or you may sometimes wish to reach a larger audience—your city council, your composition class, the readership of some publication like your campus or city newspaper, *Time* magazine, or *Rolling Stone*.

If your purpose, for instance, is to inform, you need to think about how to present your information to your specific audience most effectively. You can see at once that the larger your audience, the more touchy the problem. If you are writing a letter to the editor of your local newspaper explaining the appeal of reggae music, you will be addressing people of all ages with assorted dispositions and prejudices. You need to choose your words carefully and present your information calmly, or you may end up with next to no readers at all.

If you are writing that letter to the editor of *Rolling Stone*, though, your verbal tactics would be different. Since your audience would be primarily people who know a lot about popular music, you would omit background information explaining how reggae originated. You would write in a more conversational manner, using current slang and even music jargon, since your audience could be expected to understand the jargon and not be offended by the slang.

Think carefully about both purpose and audience as you formulate your thesis. Continue to keep all three in mind as you write. Consider them again as you revise. These three concepts are crucial to the effectiveness of your writing.

EXERCISE   1-1

Some of the numbered sentences below are workable thesis statements for an essay of about 500 to 700 words, but some need to be made more specific. Pick out the successful ones, and try to tell what went wrong with the losers. See if you can make every one into a reasonably good thesis. Here are five workable thesis statements to inspire you:

A. Many Americans spend so much time in front of the television that they never really experience their own lives. (In the introduction of your paper, this thesis might appear in a livelier form, like, "Turn off the TV and turn on to life!")

B. I think that college students and teachers would be happier with education if people didn't enroll in college before the age of twenty-five.

C. On a sunny summer morning last year, I realized that I was ultimately alone.

D. The perfect omelet is fluffy, light, delicately browned, and even attainable if the cook follows five practical guidelines.

E. In Shakespeare's *Hamlet,* Ophelia's insanity and suicide represent what might have happened to Hamlet had he been female.

Now try to whip these into shape:

1. Television commercials are an outrage.
2. Freedom and independence carry with them responsibilities and consequences.
3. I'm going to describe the dying flowers and yellowing leaves outside my window.
4. My dog and my boyfriend are much alike.
5. I learned not to worry when I was sixteen.
6. Thousands of Americans go through the vicious cycle of eating until they are overweight and then dieting until they reduce.
7. The predominant views on capital punishment are very controversial.

8. The purpose of this paper is to compare and contrast the Catholic schools and the public schools.
9. Do you feel cheated because you can't grow a beard?
10. Making a lemon pie is easy.

DEVISE A PLAN

Once you have established your thesis, your purpose, and your audience, you must decide what to say. What major points will you present? In what order? What specific details will you use? To structure all this information, you need some sort of plan.

Start by Brainstorming

As you are working out your thesis, jot down every idea that comes to mind pertaining to your subject. After you have come up with a workable thesis, continue searching your mind—and maybe a few magazine articles or books—for more information. Write down every notion, whether it seems exactly to the point or not. You can easily scratch out things you do not need, and you may end up altering your thesis slightly to suit the available facts.

Let's assume that you have been assigned a five-page type-written paper in horticulture class on home gardening. Since you are not interested in growing flowers, you narrow the topic to home vegetable gardening. That's still a subject more suited to a book than a short essay. How about organic vegetable gardening? Better, but five pages is not much. You need to narrow the topic some more. What are some of the problems involved in organic gardening? Making compost; keeping the bugs under control. How about fighting bugs organically? That might work.

Now, what *about* fighting bugs organically? Your thesis: *Fighting bugs organically allows home gardeners to avoid the dangers of pesticides.* What points can you think of that might prove useful in such an essay? After thinking for a while, you may end up with a jumbled list something like this:

> Some insects eat garden pests.
> Soapy water kills some insects but not most plants.
> Slugs like beer—will drown themselves in it, given the chance.
> Can buy useful insects, mail order.
> Praying mantises like to eat caterpillars and mites.
> Ladybugs zap aphids.
> Milky spore disease kills Japanese beetles.
> Cabbage worms zonked by *bacillus thuringiensis*.
> Pick off insects by hand—drown or suffocate them in a jar.
> Birds eat insects.
> Laying aluminum foil on the ground will drive aphids to suicide.
> Green lacewings eat mealybugs like crazy.

A Plan Brings Order out of Chaos

You now need three or four main ideas—in this case, methods of controlling insect pests—to serve as the major points you want to make in developing your thesis. Keep looking over your list to see if you can discover patterns. Try to determine which are major ideas and which would better serve as supporting details.

Note that "some insects eat garden pests" is a major idea. You have several examples to support it. Perhaps you need to rephrase the idea to suit your thesis: *Bring in natural enemies to kill pests.* As supporting evidence you can mention praying mantises, ladybugs, and green lacewings (plus the specific insects they control) and note that these useful insects can be purchased by mail. That's plenty for one paragraph.

You may detect several supporting details that are similar and need only to have a major heading added. Notice in your list that these three items all share a common trait:

> Putting out beer for slugs.
> Laying down aluminum foil for aphids.
> Squirting soapy water on plants.

These methods all use products found usually in the kitchen. You could group these three under the heading, *Try safe and easy household remedies.*

Two other items on the list clearly belong together: milky spore disease and *bacillus thuringiensis.* Since these remedies work by introducing diseases fatal to insects but harmless to plants and people, you could label this section, *Introduce insect diseases to destroy pests.* By the way, you discover such unusual remedies through research—in this case, by reading Laurence Sheehan's "Garden Club Notes: Fighting Bugs Organically," in *Harper's,* April 1979, which we used as a model for organizing this imaginary paper.

Only two items in the brainstorming list remain unused: picking insects off by hand and encouraging birds to come to your garden. Probably picking bugs by hand is too tiresome to be a practical suggestion. And enticing birds may hurt more than help. Birds eat bugs indiscriminately—the ladybugs along with the aphids—and are exceptionally fond of many garden vegetables as well. You might better let those leftover ideas go, unless you decide to mention in your conclusion that if all else fails, the dedicated gardener can always pick off the beastly bugs by hand.

Arrange Your Points

After you have discovered the main ideas and supporting details for your paper, the last step is deciding in what order to present your ideas. Since there is no chronology, or time order, involved in this case, you should begin with a fairly strong and interesting point to get your readers' attention. End with your strongest point to leave the readers feeling that you have said something worthwhile. With this pest-control paper, you could almost flip a coin. But since the household remedies are the cheapest and most entertaining to describe, you might wisely begin there. Save the section on natural enemies for the end, since it sounds like a dramatic and effective solution.

Tidy Your Plan

If that piece of paper on which you began brainstorming is now too messy to follow, you may want to take a fresh sheet and jot down the plan you worked out before it gets away from you. Some exceedingly neat people even like to make formal outlines, which look impressive but probably are not necessary for most writing tasks. If you ever do encounter the need to construct a formal outline, it should look something like the one which follows.

Sample Outline

Thesis: Fighting bugs organically allows home gardeners to avoid the dangers of pesticides.

   Introduction

I. Try safe and easy household remedies.
   A. Set out trays of beer to attract slugs, which drown in it.

      B. Spray soapy water (not detergent) on hardy plants.
      C. Spread aluminum foil under plants to disorient aphids, luring them to their doom.

   II. Introduce insect diseases to destroy pests.
      A. Milky spore disease kills larvae of Japanese beetles.
      B. *Bacillus thuringiensis* sprayed on soil is deadly to cabbage worms.
      C. Both remedies are available at garden stores.

  III. Bring in natural enemies to fight pests.
      A. Praying mantises devour caterpillars and mites.
      B. Ladybugs consume quantities of aphids.
      C. Green lacewings feed on mealybugs.
      D. These useful insects can be ordered by mail.

    Conclusion

In his essay, Laurence Sheehan uses more imaginative but less informative headings:

I.	Hand-to-hand combat	(for "Household remedies")
II.	Biological warfare	(for "Insect diseases")
III.	Hired-guns approach	(for "Natural enemies")

In writing your paper you might want to employ such colorful language, but good organization is more important at this stage. In your plan, set your ideas down in a clear and orderly fashion. When you revise your first draft, you can then make the phrasing witty and entertaining, if it suits your purpose.

Check Your Plan

    Since the unity and coherence of your paper depend largely on the way you order your ideas—that is, on how well you have arranged your plan—you should take a few minutes to go over it after you finish. Check these points carefully.

1. Make sure every major idea relates to your thesis.
2. Make sure every major idea has adequate supporting details.
3. Make sure every supporting detail relates to its major idea.
4. Do not let any major point get buried as a supporting detail or any minor points get elevated as major headings.
5. Do not allow any careless repetition of ideas anywhere.

FOLLOW YOUR PLAN AS YOU WRITE

Once you have a suitable plan, you can relax and write. Pay particular attention to *clarity*. As Quintilian advises, "The writer should so write that the reader not only may, but must, understand."

Develop Each Paragraph Fully

Each major idea in your plan should contain enough supporting material to produce at least one and perhaps several well-developed paragraphs, which usually run from about 75 to 150 words. Introductions and conclusions are often much shorter. For additional information, look up *Paragraph* in Chapter 3, the "Revising Index," which is alphabetized for easy reference.

Use Topic Sentences.　Each major idea in your plan will probably become the topic sentence of a paragraph in your paper. Like the thesis sentence for an essay, a topic sentence states the controlling idea for the paragraph. All details within that paragraph will support, illustrate, amplify, or explain that idea. If you follow a unified plan, you will automatically write unified paragraphs. But if you have to dredge up more details while actually writing the paper, be sure these additions are to the point.

Include Concrete Details. Whenever possible, use examples that your readers can visualize. If you say that motorcycle riding can be dangerous, mention the crushed noses, dislocated limbs, splintered teeth, cracked skulls. Be as concrete and specific as possible. You cannot avoid abstractions, of course, but try to follow abstract words—like *dangerous*—with concrete illustrations—like *broken bones*. For further advice, consult *Underdeveloped Paragraphs* in Chapter 3.

Notice in the following example how many concrete details Laurence Sheehan uses in developing the "Hired-Guns Approach" section of his essay, which is section III of our sample outline. (We have used boldface type for his topic sentence.)

> **Continuing our "warfare" analogy, this method refers to using natural enemies of the unwanted intruders.** Ladybugs can be purchased by mail order for less than $1 per thousand. They devour forty to fifty aphids per day. The down side is you may have to buy in *aphids* come August, to keep your ladybugs fat and happy. Green lacewings are excellent against scale insects and mealybugs. They lay eggs at night and their babies look like tiny alligators when they hatch. It is impressive to see them tearing through a mealybug infestation. Praying mantises make another good gardener's ally, as they will destroy any and all caterpillars or mites that you "mite" have in the garden.

Work for Coherence. Since your plan will be structured in a logical or chronological manner, with each point naturally following the preceding one, your paper will have built-in *coherence*—it will hold together. Occasionally, though, you will still need to use transitions to signal readers that you are taking up a new idea, making a contrast, adding a qualification, or coming to a conclusion.

In the paragraph we just quoted, the opening phrase—*continuing our "warfare" analogy*—is a transition to help readers move smoothly from one paragraph to the next. In the last sentence, the word *another* is a transition to introduce the final example.

You will find several kinds of transitions explained in Chapter 3. Look up *Transitions* and study the entry. Then remember to refer to that section whenever you need help in making your ideas flow easily.

Choose Your Words Carefully. If your writing is colorless and boring, try to select lively verbs and vivid adjectives. Mark Twain's advice about the adjective still goes: "When in doubt, leave it out." If you sprinkle them all over, they lose impact. But an occasional, well-chosen adjective can be effective.

Using animated words helps keep your readers reading. James Thurber, in his essay "Sex Ex Machina," speaks of a "world made up of gadgets that *whir* and *whine* and *whiz* and *shriek* and sometimes *explode*." (Emphasis added.) The force of the verbs conveys the feeling of anxiety produced by living in the machine age. In his essay "A Hanging," George Orwell describes a dog that "came *bounding* among us with a loud volley of barks, and *leapt* around us *wagging* its whole body, *wild* with glee at finding so many human beings together." (Emphasis added.) The verb *leapt*, plus the italicized verbal adjectives, enable readers to visualize the energy and excitement of the dog. Similar vibrant word choices can add energy and excitement to your own writing.

Advice about Introductions

An effective introduction should state your thesis, capture your readers' interest, and set your tone, that is, convey your attitude toward what you are writing—satirical, serious, light, humorous, or neutral, to name a few.

Stating your thesis is the most important consideration in introducing informative and persuasive essays. Narrative essays, which tell a story in order to make a point, and descriptive essays, which describe in order to produce an effect, are usually more successful if the thesis is only implied. Even in informative and persuasive writing, you may want to make your thesis statement less blunt and straightforward in your introduction than it was during the planning stage.

Consider the thesis of our sample outline: *Fighting bugs organically allows home gardeners to avoid the dangers of pesticides.* You could write a sentence or two denouncing pesticides and describing their deadly effects, and then state that exact thesis. You would have a perfectly serviceable introduction. In order to make it a shade more interesting, though, you might convey this same thesis idea more subtly, as Sheehan does in his essay:

> A vegetable garden is a lovesome thing, said the poet, but what about bugs and pests? How can we protect our bounty from invaders without resorting to using the pesticides and insecticides that ravage soil and spring leaks in our ozone layer? There are many effective non-chemical-company methods of de-bugging the garden. Some are new, some old, but all are safe and sane and may be used without fear of upsetting Nature's balance.

This introduction begins with a quotation of sorts to catch our interest, conveys the thesis clearly, and also establishes the mildly humorous tone ("ravage soil," "spring leaks," "de-bugging," "non-chemical-company methods").

Advice about Conclusions

Work particularly hard on your conclusion. Its effectiveness will influence the way your readers react to your paper. If you trail off at the end, they will sigh and feel let down. Try to write a first-rate final sentence that will leave a positive psychological effect. For help in constructing an impressive sentence, look up *Balanced Sentences* in Chapter 3.

Sometimes you may be able to write a concluding paragraph in which you propose a solution to the problem discussed, suggest alternatives, or simply call for some action. But if your paper is short, only two or three typed pages, you may find that a concluding sentence is enough.

Try to summarize briefly your main idea using different phrasing from that of the introduction. Here is the way Laurence Sheehan ends his essay on organic pest control.

> Until researchers come up with something new, we must depend on the various pest-management methods previously discussed to keep garden and conscience clear during the growing season.

That's not a dazzling conclusion, by any means, but it serves its purpose. You can easily do as well.

Add a Title

If you have trouble coming up with a suitable title, consult *Title Tactics* in Chapter 3.

RELAX, THEN REVISE

After you finish the first draft, set it aside and relax for a while so that you can approach the revising process with renewed vigor. If you have not yet hit upon a good introduction or conclusion, now is the time to apply yourself to that task.

The most important thing in revising is to make sure that you have said what you intended to say in the best possible way. Make sure that the material is organized as effectively as it can be. As you reread your paper, make sure that you have written fully developed paragraphs with clear transitions between ideas. Be sure that you have not strayed from your plan on any little side trips or digressions which have only a passing relationship to your thesis. Now is the time also to look up word meanings and spellings in doubtful cases.

Most important, be sure that the whole essay makes sense—that each sentence is clear, not just to you but to anyone who happens to read the paper. If possible, get someone else to read what you have written to be sure that it makes sense. Make certain that each sentence really *is* a sentence, not a fragment, unless you have used a fragment deliberately for stylistic purposes. And if you are not sure what a sentence fragment is, look up *Fragment* in Chapter 3.

Revising Checklist

A number of other revising strategies are explained in various entries in Chapter 3. After reading your paper, your instructor will refer you to specific items in case you make errors. But you can save yourself difficulty by consulting the following entries as you revise:

1. Write in active, not passive voice: see *Passive Voice*.
2. Stay in the same tense: see *Shifts in Tense and Person*.
3. Consider your word choice carefully: see *Diction, Triteness, Wordiness, Connotation and Denotation, Figures of Speech, Repetition,* and also *Levels of Usage* at the beginning of Chapter 4.
4. Use subordination wisely: see *Subordination*.
5. Make sure the whole paper is logical: see *Logic*.

If you are at all uncertain about the fine points of grammar and syntax, you should also take these final precautions:

1. Be sure you have no sentence fragments: see *Fragments*.
2. Be sure you have no comma splices: see *Comma Splice*.
3. Be sure your pronoun reference is clear: see *Reference of Pronouns*.
4. Be sure your pronouns are in the proper case: see *Case of Pronouns*.
5. Be sure all pronouns and antecedents agree: see *Agreement (Pronoun-Antecedent)*.
6. Be sure all subjects and verbs agree: see *Agreement (Subject-Verb)*.
7. Be sure all modifiers are used effectively: see *Dangling Modifier, Misplaced Modifier,* and *Squinting Modifier*.
8. Be sure your verb tenses are correct: see *Tense*.
9. Be sure each word is spelled right: see Appendix B.

DON'T FORGET TO EDIT

After you have typed your revised paper, force yourself to reread it one more time to pick up typos.

Proofreading Tips

Most people have difficulty in proofreading their own writing because they *know* what they wanted to say and thus do not notice that they have not said it correctly. They get caught up in the content and fail to see the errors. If you have this trouble, try reading the sentences from the bottom of the page to the top, out of order, so that you do not get interested in what you are saying. Force yourself to read slowly, word by word. If possible, find someone to proofread for you.

Proofreading Checklist

Pay no attention to content this time. Read for mechanical errors to make certain that you have

1. No words left out or carelessly repeated
2. No words misspelled (or carelessly spelled—**use to** for **used to**)
3. No plurals left off
4. No apostrophes omitted in possessives or in contractions
5. No periods, dashes, commas, colons, or quotation marks left out
6. No confusion of **to/too, their/they're/there, its/it's, then/than, your/you're, effect/affect**

Remember that a neatly typed paper has a psychological advantage. It suggests to your readers that time and effort went into the preparation—that this paper wasn't just dashed off at the last minute. Make corrections neatly and retype any pages that look like disaster areas.

IDEAS FOR WRITING

Topics for Writing Descriptive Papers

Short practice items:

1. Describe as thoroughly as possible in one sentence how cat's fur feels, how modeling clay feels, how soft rain feels, how a hangover feels. Or describe in a sentence how a snake moves, how a cat walks, how a dog greets you; or how a vampire looks, or a werewolf, or a visitor from outer space.
2. Describe a food you hate or love with as much sensory detail as possible.

Longer paper topics:

3. Describe something you know more about than most people.
4. Describe the place in which you feel most at peace—or most ill at ease.
5. Describe a place (like a classroom, a cafeteria, a bar, your teacher's office) and try to convey your attitude toward it through use of specific details.

Topics for Writing Narrative Papers

1. I learned _____ the hard way.
2. Think of a conflict situation between two people: teacher/student, parent/child, employer/employee, man/woman. Describe the conflict first as though you were one person and then as though you were the other.
3. Write an account of your initiation into some facet of the adult world which you were unaware of as a child: violence, hypocrisy, prejudice, or sexuality.
4. Write the story that your older relatives most often tell about something you did as a child.
5. Tell about the first time you remember being punished at school or at home.

Topics for Writing Process Papers

1. How to train an animal—dog, parrot, rabbit, or turtle.
2. How to get rid of a bad habit: nail biting, smoking, or interrupting others.
3. How to say "no" to a persistent child (man) (woman).
4. How to get rid of the blues.
5. How to change a flat tire, repair a light switch, grow African violets, transplant seedlings, or barbeque a chicken.

Topics for Writing Definition Papers

1. Think of a word that you use a lot, and then define what you mean by it in different situations.
2. Define your own best qualities—or those of someone you admire.
3. Define a slang term and discuss its possible origins and significance.
4. Define a certain type of person—the perfectionist, the intellectual, the slob, the egomaniac, the male chauvinist, the life of the party— and tell how you respond to this type.
5. Think of a word whose sound is at variance with its meaning—like **temerity, melanoma, fulsome**—and tell what you think it should mean.

Topics for Writing Classification Papers

1. What different types of heroes have you had in your life?
2. Contemplate some magazine advertisements. What types of emotions and thoughts are they designed to appeal to?
3. How would you classify the types of people you can find in your classroom, at your workplace, in your favorite pub?
4. If you have ever been a salesperson or a waiter or waitress, how would you classify your customers?
5. What types of TV shows are the most popular this season? Tell why you think each type is popular.

Topics for Writing Comparison and Contrast Papers

1. Discuss one or more illusions that are presented as reality on television and compare the illusion with the reality as you have experienced it.
2. Compare two lifestyles you have observed, the work of two artists, two films, a film and the novel it was based on, two cars you have driven, two TV characters.
3. Compare how you perceived some person, place, or situation as a child with how you perceive the same thing today.

4. Compare a woman's emotions on a first date with a man's (or vice versa).
5. Compare two popular magazines, one written for men, the other for women.

Topics for Writing Cause and Effect Papers

1. Discuss the probable cause of any situation, practice, law, or custom that strikes you as unfair.
2. Imagine that a close friend tells you that she or he is homosexual. The friend is the same sex you are. What are your reactions? Why should you have these reactions?
3. All school attendance has just been declared voluntary. How will this change the schools?
4. A group of extraterrestrial beings visits Earth. On their planet people are neither male nor female: each person is both (androgynous). Explain how their society is different from ours.
5. Explain the causes (or effects) of any drastic change of opinion, attitude, prejudice, or behavior you have undergone in your life.

Topics for Writing Persuasive Papers

1. Partners in marriage should/should not write their own detailed marriage contracts.
2. College teachers should/should not be evaluated by their students each term.
3. Watching television in the United States has/has not been harmful to individuals, families, and the society.
4. Think of one of our popular maxims—like "Early to bed, early to rise, makes a man healthy, wealthy, and wise," or "Love is never having to say you're sorry," or "Home is where the heart is." Write about whether you consider the message truth or propaganda—and why.
5. Assume that half the world's population is going to be exterminated. Persuade the exterminators that you should be in the saved half.

Chapter Two
Background in Grammar

The ideal grammar of English would explain how human beings produce and understand the millions of utterances that they actually do produce and understand daily. That is a tall order, involving study of language history, physiology, brain functions, gesture, tone, emphasis—and even silence—as well as words and sentences.

WHAT YOU NEED TO KNOW

But you do not need a complete and thorough theory of grammar in order to write well. You do need a basic vocabulary, shared by you and your teachers and other writers, in which you can talk about sentences. Learning the terminology of traditional grammar can help you identify and correct sentence fragments, comma splices, and run-on sentences. It can help you decide where to put commas and semicolons. It can help you untangle sentences that are marred by dangling modifiers, misplaced modifiers, or pile-ups of prepositional phrases. It can help you perk up your style as you cultivate sentence variety and weed out ineffective use of the passive voice.

In this chapter, we avoid the right-and-wrong rules that many people mistakenly associate with the study of grammar. We are more interested in describing how English sentences do work than in showing how persons of refinement should speak: that is a much more slippery subject, called *usage*, which we take on in the glossary in Chapter 4 of this book. We have used the traditional aid of the sentence diagram so you can see the system we describe. Like many teachers of English, we have developed an eye for the beauty of this system. Maybe you will too. At least you will benefit from the order it shows underlying a seemingly unruly subject.

IN THE BEGINNING WAS THE WORD: PARTS OF SPEECH

You have probably grappled before with sorting words into parts of speech or word classes. This time, remember that you can classify a word dependably only if it is in a sentence, since many words in English act as more than one part of speech.

A. He will *line* his denim jacket with the blue plaid fake fur.
       verb

B. Clarissa told the team to stand with their toes on the white *line*.
       noun

C. Ed did a clever *line* drawing of Sue's feet.
       adjective

A group of words—a phrase or clause—can act as a single part of speech in a sentence too.

D. Claude said that he required fresh orange juice *in the morning*.
       preposition adj. n.
       —— *adverb* ——

The phrase *in the morning* modifies *required*, and thus acts like an adverb even though none of the words in the phrase is an adverb.

pronoun vb. infinitive

E. Rita replied that he had better find a girlfriend | ***who likes to squeeze***
└────── *adjective* ──────

n.
oranges.

The clause modifies *girlfriend*, and thus plays the part of an adjective.

If you feel lost—if everything you ever knew about phrases and clauses seems to have fallen out of a hole in your head—stay with us. We will explain phrases and clauses right after we explain the eight parts of speech. As you read about them, try to think of parts of speech as roles words can play within sentences. You can see relationships among words in sentence diagrams, which we will offer throughout this chapter. You can also use tests to find out what part a word is playing, just as you test to find out what chemicals are in a solution. We will show you how. Nouns, verbs, and adjectives are the easiest parts of speech to pin down, so let's start with those.

For each part of speech, we will give you (1) a definition, (2) examples of the roles it plays in sentences, (3) categories within that part of speech, and (4) diagrams.

Nouns

n

A noun names a person, place, thing, quality, idea, condition, or activity. Yes, the list has gotten longer since you were in the fourth grade, but the definition still lacks precision.

To find out whether a word is acting as a noun in a sentence, try either (or both) of these tests.

Test 1. Can you substitute a personal pronoun for the

word in a sentence? (Personal pronouns are *he, she, it, I, me, you, him, her, we, us, they, them.*)

A. **Sue** nailed up **lath** so **Andrea** could plaster the **walls**.

  ↓   ↓   ↓   ↓

 she   **it**   **she**   **them**

By no stretch of the imagination could you reasonably substitute a personal pronoun for *nailed, up, so, could plaster,* or *the,* so you know they are not acting as nouns.

Test 2.   Can the word be used after one or more determiners within or outside a particular sentence? (*Determiners* are adjectives that classify: *a, an, the, this, these, that, those, some, any, no, his, her, its,* and other possessives, *seven, four,* and other numbers.)

B. **Tests** are a good **way** to sort **parts** of **speech**.

the tests, those tests
some way, no way, one way
seven parts, these parts
a speech, her four speeches

These four words sound natural with determiners, so you know they are nouns.

Roles Nouns Play.   The most familiar role a noun plays in a sentence is that of *subject.*

      subject of sentence
C. The **submarine** leaked.

          subject of clause
D. The captain, whose **knees** shook violently, installed screen doors.

A prepositional phrase has a noun as its object.

        subj.   *object of prep.*
  E. The **sea** flowed through the **screen**.

(A noun that serves as the object of a preposition can never also serve as the subject of the sentence.) Nouns also act as *complements* (see Figure 2-1 on page 57).

        subj.   *direct object of verb*
  F. The **submarine** followed **sharks**.

                   indirect
      subj.   *object* *d. obj.*
  G. The **leaks** gave the **crew trouble**.

        subj.   *d. obj.*   *obj. of prep.*
  H. The **crew** threw the **captain** to the **sharks**.

        subj.   *predicate nominative (refers to subj.)*
  I. The **submarine** was a **hazard**.

               objective complement (refers to d. obj.)
  J. We thought Claudius a **bore**.

An *appositive*, which renames a noun preceding it, contains a noun.

  K. Mr. Bly, the **captain**, was nervous.

Nouns act as terms of *direct address*.

  L. **Ishmael**, please don't slam that screen door.

Noun Categories. Sometimes justifiably and sometimes as a result of a neurotic need for order, we classify nouns into different groups like the following:

Abstract nouns: justice, flippancy, Darwinism, boredom, reality, habit

Concrete nouns (in contrast to abstract nouns): heliotrope, hammer, aardvark, elbow, hangnail

Collective nouns: audience, crowd, committee, group, collective

Proper nouns: Ishmael, Idaho, Lucy, Mr. Bill, Vegematic, Yellowstone Park, English

Common nouns (in contrast to proper nouns): violet, moss, stone, shoelace, mathematics

Mass nouns: water, lasagna, rice, population, salt

Count nouns (in contrast to mass nouns): person, helicopter, egg, bullet

Another important category is the *nominal*, which substitutes for a noun in a sentence by filling one of its roles. A nominal can be one word or a group of words.

Nominals include two kinds of verbals. *Verbals* are words that come from verbs, but act like other parts of speech. One verbal noun is the *gerund*, the *-ing* form of a verb, which passes the tests for a noun in these sentences:

M. *Dancing* is a form of self-expression.
↓
It

(Test 1, role: subject of the sentence.)

N. After his conviction, he had to wait a month for *sentencing*.
his sentencing, *a* sentencing, *the* sentencing

(Test 2, role: object of a preposition.)

An *infinitive*, which is another kind of verbal, sometimes acts as a noun in a sentence. An infinitive is the simple form of a verb beginning with *to:* to walk, to jump, to levitate.

> **O.** His first idea was ***to disappear****.*

In this sentence, *to disappear* is the name of an idea. Role: predicate nominative.

> **P.** ***To stay*** out of trouble was not his main goal.

In this sentence, *to stay* is the name of an activity. Role: subject of the sentence. Phrases and clauses are nominals sometimes, too, as you will see in the discussion at the end of this chapter, pages 55–65.

Verbs

A verb describes the action, existence, or occurrence of a subject. Here are two tests to help you identify verbs in sentences.

Test 1.   Can you put it in the past tense?

> **A.** Anyone who ***goes*** to that saloon ***is looking*** for disaster.
>   ↓   ↓
>   ***went***   ***was looking***

You are not likely to mistakenly identify *salooned, fored,* or *disastered* as natural English words.

Test 2.   Can you conjugate it in first, second, and third person?

B. Whenever I **walk** in there, I **see** a fight.

I walk, you walk, he walks   I see, you see, she sees

Although *fight* can be conjugated, it is easy to see that it acts as a noun in the sentence above: it has a determiner before it, and thus clearly passes noun test 2.

Roles Verbs Play.   The verb in a sentence tells what a subject is or does. A complete sentence always has a main verb.

main vb.

C. Charmaine **decorates** her apartment beautifully.

A sentence is likely to include verbs in dependent clauses as well.

vb. in dependent clause   *main vb.*

D. Even if she **is staying** only a month, Charmaine **decorates** her apartment beautifully.

Besides showing action and being, the verb in a sentence expresses the time of the action. You can express twelve different time relations with these different verb forms:

Present:	He delays
Past:	He delayed
Future:	He will delay
Present perfect:	He has delayed
Past perfect:	He had delayed
Future perfect:	He will have delayed
Present progressive:	He is delaying
Past progressive:	He was delaying
Future progressive:	He will be delaying
Present perfect progressive:	He has been delaying
Past perfect progressive:	He had been delaying
Future perfect progressive:	He will have been delaying

The verb also shows whether the subject is acting or being acted upon, because it can be in *active* or *passive* voice.

E. She shot. (*active*)   She was shot. (*passive*)

Passive voice adds twelve more possible verb forms to our list, although some of them sound unlikely.

Present:	He is delayed
Past:	He was delayed
Future:	He will be delayed
Present perfect:	He has been delayed
Past perfect:	He had been delayed
Future perfect:	He will have been delayed
Present progressive:	He is being delayed
Past progressive:	He was being delayed
Future progressive:	He will be being delayed
Present perfect progressive:	He has been being delayed
Past perfect progressive:	He had been being delayed
Future perfect progressive:	He will have been being delayed

Finally, the verb indicates the manner of expression: the *mood.* Three moods exist:

Indicative, for ordinary statements or questions about facts:

F. I'll eat at four. When will you eat lunch?

Imperative, for making requests:

G. Eat your zucchini.

Subjunctive, for expressing wishes or statements contrary to fact:

H. If I were rich, I would eat pizza every night.

The subjunctive mood has all but vanished from informal usage: look up *Subjunctive Mood* in Chapter 3 to get the full story.

Verb Categories.   Every verb has an *infinitive* and three *principal parts*, which are used alone or combined with auxiliary verbs to form the various tenses. An infinitive can act as a noun, as we explained earlier, and also can fill the role of an adjective or adverb, as we will explain later. The three principal parts are *present*, *past*, and *past participle*.

Infinitive	Present	Past	Past Participle
to jump	jump	jumped	jumped
to fight	fight	fought	fought
to lose	lose	lost	lost
to see	see	saw	seen
to be	am	was	been

Verbs that form the past and past participle simply by adding a suffix of *-d*, *-ed*, or *-t* are *regular verbs*, like *jump* and *lose* above. *Fight, be* and *see* are *irregular verbs* because they form the past and past participle in an odd way. In Chapter 3, under *Tense*, we list some common irregular verbs.

Verbs also have present participles, which are formed by adding *-ing* to the present. Present participles are verbals, sometimes used as gerunds (see *Nouns*, page 29); sometimes used as adjectives, as in "She felt she had reached a *turning* point in life"; and sometimes used in progressive tenses to show future time ("I am *going* to Denver in March") or continuing action ("I've been *asking* too many questions for my own good.")

Auxiliary verbs are used in combination with other verbs to signal the tense of or add meaning to the other verbs. Two kinds of auxiliaries exist: The plain auxiliaries are *be, do,* and *have:*

I. I *am* trying to keep Lenin the cat out of the philodendron.   (be)
I *do* want a few leaves left this spring.   (do)
She *has* nibbled the edges of every one.   (have)
I *have been* politely advising her to stop this destructive habit.
    (have, be)

When plain auxiliaries are used as main verbs, they have definite meanings of their own:

J. I *am* a writer.
I *have* three philodendrons.
I *do* yoga exercises every morning.

The modal auxiliaries are *can, may, might, must, should:*

K. You *can* learn yoga too.   (are able to)
You *should* practice every day.   (ought to)
I *may* teach you some exercises.   (possibly will)

Modal auxiliaries affect the meaning of the main verb when they are used as auxiliaries, but they are never used by themselves as main verbs. Short answers are exceptions: Do you have any brick cheese left? We *should.* Does Sheila intend to make dinner tonight? She *may.*

Linking verbs show the relationship between the subject of the sentence and a nominal or adjective in the predicate. They connect the subject to a word that renames or describes it.

```
   subj.   linking vb.  pred. adj.
    ↓          ↘          ↘
```
L. His ***costume looked outrageous.***

```
   subj.   linking vb.   pred. nom.
    ↓        ↙             ↙
```
M. The ***hat was*** a watering ***can*** covered with blue glitter.

Common linking verbs are *appear, be, become, seem, taste, smell, feel, look,* and *sound.*

Transitive verbs have objects which complete their meaning.

```
   vb.  obj.    d. obj
```
N. We ***gave him*** first ***prize*** in the costume contest.

Intransitive verbs make sense without objects.

```
   intransitive vb.
```
O. His eyes ***sparkled*** with joy.

Most verbs work both ways.

```
   transitive
   vb.              d. obj.
```
P. I ***ate*** pistachio ***cheesecake*** for breakfast.

```
   intransitive
   vb.
```
Q. I ***ate*** unconventionally this morning.

How It Looks. Sentence diagrams show the relationships among words in a sentence. The diagram is a visual representation of what words fill what roles in the sentence. Nouns and the verbs that describe them are diagrammed as follows (we will ignore other parts of speech for now):

subj.   vb.
R. Charla runs.

subj.   vb.   d. obj.
S. Charla runs a drill press.

subj.   vb.   i. obj.   d. obj.
T. The company gave Charla a raise.

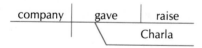

subj. vlk.*   *pred. nom.*
U. Charla is a dependable worker.

| Charla | is | \ worker |

---

* *vlk.* is the abbreviation for *linking verb.*

Adjectives

adj

Adjectives describe or limit nouns or noun substitutes. Here are two tests for identifying an adjective:

Test 1.   Can it be used between a determiner and a noun?

A. Sonia's *lazy* boss lives in a *prestigious* suburb

    ↓   ↓

   the lazy boss   ***that prestigious suburb***

and drives a *flashy* Mercedes.

    ↙

  one flashy Mercedes

B. Sonia is not *envious*, because her boss is *unhappy*.

     ↓   ↙

   the envious clerk   ***seven unhappy dwarfs***

Test 2.   Can degrees of the word (changes in form to show comparative quality or quantity—like "good, better, best") be shown?

C. The *unhappy* boss gets no pleasure from his *big* house,

  ↙   ↙

unhappier, unhappiest   ***bigger, biggest***

his *plush* furniture, or his *selfish* children.

    ↓   ↘

plusher, plushest   ***more selfish, most selfish***

Roles Adjectives Play.   The most easily identified role of an adjective is to describe a noun or pronoun.

       adj.   *n.*   *adj.*   *n.*
D. That ***sensational*** headline is a ***perfect*** example of
  adj.   *n.*
shoddy journalism.

In the sentence above, the words *that* and *a* are also adjectives. Their role is to ***limit;*** that is, they point out which one or how many or whose. Adjectives sometimes show degrees of comparison.

           adj.   *n.*
E. I'll take the ***cheapest*** harmonica you have.

You usually think of adjectives as coming before the words they modify, but sometimes they spring up later in the sentence. A *predicate adjective* comes after a linking verb and describes the subject of the sentence:

      n. *pred. adj.* *pred. adj.*
F. Dan's hair is ***thick*** and ***beautiful.***

An *objective complement* comes after an object and modifies it.

                                         obj. comp.
G. This harmonica costs only $10, but I think I can find one ***cheaper.***

Adjective Categories. Other than the basic descriptive adjectives, two kinds of adjectives occur often. *Determiners* limit nouns and are usually thrown in with adjectives even though they do not always pass the adjective tests. The determiners are:

Articles:	a, an, the
Demonstratives:	this, that, these, those
Possessive adjectives:	his, her, its, their, our, my
Question words:	which, what, whose
Numbers:	one, seven, five, *etc.*
Others:	no, whichever, whatever, all, some

Remember that these words are determiners only when they modify nouns, not when they stand by themselves in a sentence.

determiner
H. **Which** child has the measles?

pron.
I. The measles are contagious, **which** means all three children will get them.

det.
J. **That** illness should last only four or five days.

pron.
K. **That** is no great comfort to me.

Verbals are sometimes adjectives, too. Here is an infinite used as an adjective:

inf.
L. I want a good book **to read.**

(modifies **book**)

And present and past participles can act as adjectives:

participle
M. ***Tired*** of his meaningless existence, the boss

↘

modifies ***boss***

part.
stared into his ***swimming*** pool.

↘

modifies ***pool***

How It Looks. In sentence diagrams, adjectives usually hang down on slanted lines from the nouns they modify. Predicate adjectives go on the main line of the diagram after the verb and are separated from it by a slanted line, like predicate nominatives.

adj. subj. vb. d. obj.
N. Lazy bosses make trouble.

adj. adj. subj. vb.
O. Many impatient employees quit.

vlk.
adj. subj. pred. adj.
P. My boss is lazy.

Adverbs

adv

Adverbs modify verbs, adjectives, other adverbs, or whole clauses. You can identify an adverb by its function in the sentence because all adverbs answer one of these questions:

How?	Where?
To what degree?	Why?
When?	True or False?

A. Dierdre had ***completely*** forgotten about the test.

     ↓
    To what degree?

B. Her mind was ***soon*** confused as she wandered the ***almost*** deserted

     ↓   ↓
    When?   *To what degree?*

hallways.

C. When she ***successfully*** found the classroom, everyone inside

     ↓
    How?

turned ***slowly*** and stared ***balefully*** at her.

 ↓   ↓
How?   *How?*

D. She was ***not*** wearing shoes or a coat in midwinter; ***consequently,***

  ↓   ↓
True or false?   *Why?*

she looked strange.

E. As she ***slowly*** walked ***inside,*** she realized that she was ***surely***

    ↓   ↓   ↓
  How?   *Where?*   *True or false?*

dreaming.

Roles Adverbs Play.   Adverbs have so much power that if
you cannot for the life of you figure out what part of speech a
word in a sentence is, you are probably safest calling it an
adverb. In fact, an adverb modifies any word or group other
than a noun or pronoun.
Adverbs modify verbs:

        adv.   *vb.*
F. Leta **quickly** chased the villain.

Notice that the adverb can move to several places in the sen-
tence and still make sense: *Quickly*, Leta chased the villain.
Leta chased the villain *quickly*.
Adverbs modify adjectives.

                    adv.   *adj.*
G. The villain's mustache looked **especially** sinister.

Adverbs modify other adverbs.

H. When he saw Leta approaching, the villain
        vb.   *adv.*   *adv.*
    retreated **very cautiously**.

Adverbs modify whole clauses.

        adv.
I. **Finally,** he admitted his folly.

Adverbs modify verbals.

    participle adv.
J. Sinking **slowly** to the ground, he wept.

In any of these roles, adverbs can show degree.

              adv.   *adv.*

K. Leta forgave him ***more quickly*** than he expected. ***Most thoughtfully,*** she even provided a handkerchief.

Adverb Categories.   One group of adverbs does not modify verbs—just adjectives or adverbs. This group of *intensifiers* makes the words that follow (or sometimes precede) stronger or weaker.

> ***much*** more confused
> ***very*** strange
> no one ***at all***
> ***too*** deserted
> ***quite*** uplifting

Adverbials are other parts of speech or word groups that fulfill the role of adverbs in sentences. Sometimes an *infinitive* is an adverbial.

L. I went to Virginia ***to collect samples of American dialect.***

The infinitive answers the question *Why?*

Some sentences use *prepositional phrases* (see *Prepositions*, page 48) as adverbials.

M. ***At this point,*** I feel ***like giving up.***

At this point answers the question *When?* and *like giving up* answers the question *How?*

Nouns can be adverbials when they express time, place, degree, or manner.

   N. Clyde left **Sunday.**
   O. Sylvia worked a **year** as a bartender.

An *adverb clause* includes a noun and verb and answers questions about the main clause of the sentence.

   P. **Before Ann became a farmworker,** she was a veterinarian's assistant.

The clause answers the question *When?*

   Q. She acts **as if she likes her new job.**

The clause answers the question *How?*

How It Looks.   Adverbs, like adjectives, hang down on slanted lines from whatever they modify.

   subj. vb.   adv.
   R. They stared balefully.

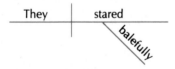

   adj. adv.   adj.   subj.   vb.   adv.
   S. The almost deserted hallways echoed eerily.

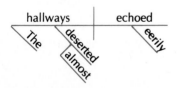

FUNCTION WORDS

The next three parts of speech—pronouns, prepositions, and conjunctions—are different from nouns, verbs, adjectives, and adverbs, and are sometimes called *function words*. This term signifies that their meaning is not as concrete and visual as the meanings of nouns, verbs, adjectives, and adverbs (*form words*). Just try to visualize—or even define—the meanings of *of* and *that* (in contrast with, say, *sinister* and *chocolate cream pie*).

Function words serve to show the relationships among the other words in a sentence. They are basically there for their grammatical function, not for their inherent lexical (vocabulary) meaning. And since the basic grammar of English sentences does not change much, new function words do not appear in the language. In contrast, new nouns are invented and added to our language all the time—monorail, leisure suit, disco, quark.

Pronouns

A pronoun takes the place of a noun. Therefore, a

pronoun is a nominal (see *Nouns*, page 29). Sometimes the words in the group including nouns and pronouns are called *substantives*.

Roles Pronouns Play. Pronouns substitute for nouns when nouns would be too awkward or repetitious in a sentence. The noun that a pronoun substitutes for is its *antecedent*.

A₁. *With pronouns:*   Ann offered to lend Mark ***her*** socket set after she finished using ***it***.

A₂. *Without pronouns:*   Ann offered to lend Mark her socket
                          set after Ann finished using the socket set.
B₁. *With pronouns:*   ***He*** had fallen into a deep depression
                          which got worse with every step ***he***
                          took.
B₂. *Without pronouns:*   Arthur had fallen into a deep depres-
                          sion. Arthur's depression got worse
                          with every step Arthur took.

Pronoun Categories.   There are six important kinds of pronouns.

Personal pronouns substitute for the names of animate and
inanimate things and indicate their number and sex: *he, she,
it, I me, you, him, her, we, us, they, them.*

C. Did **we** hear **you** say that **he** told **her** to give **it** to **them?**

Demonstrative pronouns take the place of things being
pointed out: *this, these, that, those.*

D. **Those** are my favorite blue jeans.

Reflexive pronouns occur in sentences in which the doer
and receiver of the action are the same: *myself, herself, himself, yourself, themselves, itself, oneself, ourselves.*

E. Marcella caught **herself** grinding her teeth again.

Possessive pronouns refer to a belonging: *his, hers, mine,
yours, ours, theirs.* (But *her, my, your,* which go before nouns,
are adjectives.)

F. **Mine** is funkier than **hers**.
G. Your Chevy runs, but **ours** flies.

Indefinite pronouns refer to nouns that you cannot quite pin down: *anybody, someone, everyone, many, neither, no one, others, several, all, another, little.*

H. *Others* may say I'm insane.
I. *Everyone* agreed that we must choose, but *many* felt that the choices were too limited.

Relative pronouns refer to people and objects. When a relative pronoun is the subject of a clause, the entire clause acts like an adjective (see *Dependent Clauses*, page 61). *Who, that, which, whose, whom* are relative pronouns.

J. The woman ⎪**who** wants to be a homemaker⎪ must have many inner resources.
K. The kitten ⎪*that* I want⎪ is unusually friendly.

How It Looks.   In a sentence diagram, a pronoun is placed where the noun it substitutes for would be.

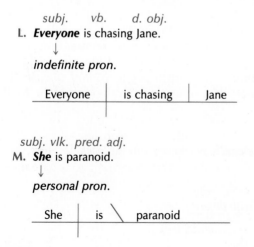

```
      subj.     vb.      d. obj.
L. Everyone is chasing Jane.
       ↓
   indefinite pron.
```

| Everyone | is chasing | Jane |

```
   subj. vlk. pred. adj.
M. She is paranoid.
     ↓
   personal pron.
```

| She | is \ paranoid |

subj. subj. vb. adv. vb. d. obj.
N. Jane, ***who*** runs fast, eats granola.
        ↓
      rel. pron.

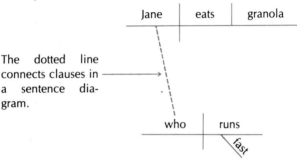

The dotted line connects clauses in a sentence diagram.

![prep] **Prepositions**

Prepositions are function words that act as *connectors:* they show relationships between certain parts of a sentence.

Roles Prepositions Play. Prepositions are followed by nominals (see *Nouns,* page 29), and these nominals are called the *objects* of the prepositions. A preposition, its object, and the object's modifiers make up a *prepositional phrase.* The preposition connects the object to another word or to the whole sentence.

                    vb.   *prep. obj.*
A. Dynsdale accidentally swallowed a fly │ ***at lunch***. │

        adj. prep.   obj.
B. He was sick │ ***with disgust***. │

n. prep.   obj.

C. The restaurant owner soon felt the wrath │ *of his favorite customer.* │

In A, the prepositional phrase relates to a verb, and therefore acts as an adverb. In B, the prepositional phrase relates to an adjective, also acting as an adverb. In C, the prepositional phrase relates to a noun, and therefore acts as an adjective.

Prepositions most commonly show relationships of *space* (a fly *in* his potato soup), *time* (an incident *during* lunch), or *possession* (the anger *of* the customer).

Preposition Categories. Some of the most common single-word prepositions are *about, above, across, after, against, at, before, below, between, by, down, during, except, from, in, into, like, of, off, on, outside, since, through, till, to, until, up, upon, with.*

Some prepositions are made up of more than one word and are therefore called *compound prepositions.* Some familiar ones are: *according to, because of, except for, in back of, in front of, in spite of, instead of, out of.*

How It Looks. In a sentence diagram, prepositions hang off whatever they modify on slanted lines. The objects go on flat lines, with modifying words hanging down.

subj. vb. prep. adj. obj.

D. I will go in the morning.

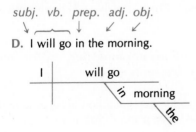

Conjunctions

$conj$

Conjunctions, like prepositions, are *connectors*. A preposition, however, can relate only a nominal to another word in a sentence. A conjunction, on the other hand, can join many different sentence elements.

Roles Conjunctions Play. A conjunction can link single words within a sentence.

> A. I brought food **and** nails.

Or it can link phrases.

> B. I figure we'll need the food **either** during our project **or** after it.

A conjunction can also connect clauses. (A *clause* is a string of words with both a noun and a verb, plus the related modifiers. See pages 59–65.)

> C. **Unless** we're done early, my husband will make us sandwiches **while** we work.
> D. Claudia likes avocado and walnut sandwiches; **however,** I would prefer avocado and sprouts.

Conjunction Categories. Four kinds of conjunctions exist.

The **coordinating conjunctions** are *and, but, or, for, nor, yet,* and *so.* They often join two sentences.

> E. Clovis knows how to mix plaster, **but** I know how to put up drywall.
> F. He has the right tools, **and** I have plenty of patience.

We put commas before the coordinating conjunctions when they separate two sentences: He has the right tools. I have plenty of patience. Coordinating conjunctions also link pairs or groups of nouns, verbs, phrases, and dependent clauses.

         n.   *n.*
G. Hand me the hammer **and** nails.

    vb.   *vb.*
H. Clovis stepped on the edge of the drywall panel **and** ruined it.

                       ┌─ *prep. phrase* ─┐
I. We put drywall tape │between the panels│ **and**

┌──── *prep. ph.* ────┐
│along the inside corners│ of the room.

                          │*dependent clause*│
J. Let's try to keep our minds on │what we're doing│ **and**

┌──── *dep. cl.* ────┐
│how we're doing it.│

Subordinating conjunctions also relate two clauses, but they make one clause *depend* on the other clause to complete its meaning.

They define relationships of time, manner, cause, or result between the clauses. Thus, a dependent clause introduced by a subordinating conjunction is often an *adverb clause* (see *Adverbs*, page 44). Some common subordinating conjunctions are

after	before	so as	till	whereas
although	if	so far as	unless	while
as, as if	only	so that	until	
because	since	though	when, whenever	

K. *If* you want a smooth joint between pieces of drywall, you must use a six-inch taping knife.
L. Don't try to get by with your little putty knife **because** the goop will ooze out from under it and make ugly ridges.
M. *As* you try to smooth out one ugly ridge, the putty knife makes a bump in another place.

Notice that when the subordinating conjunction and its clause come first in the sentence, we separate the clauses with a comma (K and M). Also, notice that putting a subordinating conjunction before a clause makes it sound incomplete as a sentence by itself:

As you try to smooth out one ugly ridge.
If you want a smooth joint between pieces of drywall.

Conjunctive adverbs are adverbs used as conjunctions or transitional words.

The most common ones are *however, thus, therefore, consequently, indeed, furthermore.* Conjunctive adverbs do *not* make the clauses that follow them dependent as subordinating conjunctions do. A conjunctive adverb is often preceded by a semicolon, although a period would be fine too.

N. He used the wrong nails to put up the drywall; **thus,** the nails popped right out when spring came.
O. His daughter had told him to use special nails; **however,** he hated to follow her advice.

Sometimes a conjunctive adverb simply interrupts one independent clause. In such a case, do not put a semicolon before it.

P. *Wrong:* The nails; therefore, popped out of the wall.
   Right: The nails, therefore, popped out of the wall.

Correlative conjunctions are coordinating conjunctions that are used in pairs to relate two parallel sentence elements (two phrases, two adjectives, two nouns, and so on).

Common correlative conjunctions are *either . . . or, neither . . . nor, not only . . . but also, both . . . and.*

Q. Clovis should *either* hold up the drywall *or* get out of the way.

R. *Not only* does he constantly complain, *but* he *also* continually loses our tools.

How It Looks.   In diagrams, conjunctions appear on dotted lines between the sentence elements they connect.

                           coordinating
                           conjunction
adj. subj.   vb.   d. obj.   ↓   d. obj.
S. My husband made sandwiches and lemonade.

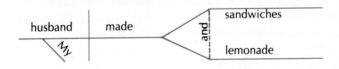

         coord.
subj. vb. conj. subj. vb.
T. I worked, but Clovis loafed.

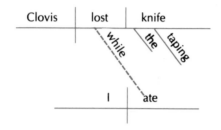

subordinating
conjunction
subj. vb. adj. adj. d. obj ↓ subj. vb.
U. Clovis lost the taping knife while I ate.

Interjections

int

    Interjections are not strictly classifiable as either form or function words. They are grammatically independent of sentence structure. They can be sounds (*oh, ah*), profanity, or other parts of speech used to express a strong emotion (*fiddlesticks!*). Interjections attract the attention of the listener, express a general strong emotion on the speaker's part, or inject themselves into speech as a habit.

    A. *Wow,* what a great concert!
    B. *Oh,* I didn't think it was that great.
    C. *Well,* wasn't it terrific when the band smashed up all their equipment and threw it out the window?
    D. *Hey,* I think that was pretty decadent.

How It Looks. Because interjections are not related to sentence structure, they are placed on a line separate from the rest of the sentence diagram.

int. subj. adv. vb. adv.
E. Hey, you finally got here!

Hey

you | got
finally here

PUTTING THE WORDS TOGETHER

Isolated words, as we have pointed out, often mean very little.
What does someone mean, for example, by the word *set?*
Bridge players, tennis buffs, china collectors, and math teachers no doubt have certain concepts in mind when they use the
word—concepts that are superficially unrelated to each other.
Only through considering the words around it and the social
situation in which it's used can anyone decide with certainty
what the word means.

Because words depend on context for meaning, we have
already had to bring up the terms *phrase* and *clause,* even
though we tried not to. We found that we could not discuss
prepositions outside of prepositional phrases, and we could
not write about conjunctions without mentioning the clauses
they connect. Now we will look more closely at phrases and
clauses and how they work.

Phrases

ph

A phrase is a string of related words that does *not*
include a subject and verb combination. As a unit, a phrase
acts as a part of speech in a sentence. First we will quickly list

the seven kinds of phrases and then show how they act as nouns, adjectives, and adverbs within sentences.

Kinds of Phrases

1. **Noun phrase:** a noun plus its modifiers

   the six-foot submarine sandwich

2. **Prepositional phrase:** a preposition, its object, and the object's modifiers

   with dill pickles

3. **Infinitive phrase:** a plain verb with *to* before it plus its modifiers and complements (See Figure 2-1 for examples of complements.)

   to eat the six-foot submarine sandwich

4. **Gerund phrase:** an *-ing* word derived from a verb plus its modifiers and complements (called a gerund phrase only when used as a noun)

   eating the six-foot submarine sandwich

5. **Participial phrase:** an *-ing* or *ed* word derived from a verb plus its modifiers and complements (called participial only when used as an adjective)

   having studied grammar
   bored with life

6. **Verb phrase:** an action or being verb plus the related auxiliary verbs

   have been
   should be willing
   will dance

Subject	Verb	Complement
		d. obj.
A. Raythel	made	a cherry cheesecake.
		i. obj. d. obj.
B. He	fed	George a slice.
		pred. adj.
C. The cheesecake	was	creamy.
		pred. nom.
D. Raythel's cooking	was	a success.
		adv.
E. Unfortunately, I	was	here.
		Where? (*adverb of place*)

Figure 2-1 The Flattering Complement. A *complement* is the last part of a garden variety English sentence (and is included in the term *predicate*). It is an adjective, nominal, or adverb of place that completes the meaning of a verb or verbal.

7. **Absolute phrase:** a word group that modifies another part of the sentence or all of it, but is not related to it with a conjunction or relative pronoun. An absolute phrase usually consists of a nominal and a participle.

> ***All told,*** the situation is grim.
> ***His life ruined,*** Jake smiled bravely.

Roles Phrases Play. Every phrase, short or long, acts like a single part of speech within a sentence.

1. **Phrases used as nouns:**

   A. The best place to spend Sunday afternoon is in bed.

In bed is a prepositional phrase acting like a noun, in this case the predicate nominative.

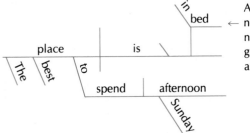

A phrase used as a noun appears in the noun's place in a diagram, drawn on a stilt above the main line

B. To read anything complicated is unwise.

To read anything complicated is an infinitive phrase acting as a noun, the subject of the sentence.

C. I enjoy drowsing off in midpage.

Drowsing off in midpage is a gerund phrase used as the direct object of *enjoy*.

2. **Phrases used as adjectives:**

D. Most of the newspaper is too grim to read for fun.

Of the newspaper is a prepositional phrase used as an adjective modifying *most*.

A phrase used as an adjective hangs down from the nominal it modifies. →

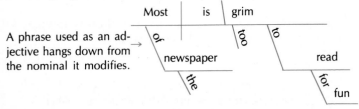

E. The best thing to read in bed is a Sherlock Holmes story.

To read in bed is an infinitive phrase used as an adjective modifying *thing*.

F. Tired of reading, I can depend on Holmes to solve the murder without me.

Tired of reading is a participial phrase used as an adjective modifying *I*.

3. **Phrases used as adverbs:**

G. I slumber peacefully until suppertime.

Until suppertime is a prepositional phrase used as an adverb modifying the verb *slumber*.

A phrase used as an adverb hangs down from → the verb, adjective, adverb, or verbal it modifies.

H. I am lucky to have Sundays free.

To have Sundays free is an infinitive phrase used as an adverb modifying the adjective *lucky*.

Clauses

Clauses contain both subjects and verbs plus all their related modifiers and complements (see Figure 2-1). The two kinds of clauses are *independent* (sometimes called *main*) and *dependent* (sometimes called *subordinate*).

Independent Clauses.   Independent clauses are complete sentences. Their usual pattern is

Subject + verb

or

Subject + verb + complement
$$\downarrow$$
d. obj.
d. obj. plus i. obj.
pred. nom.
pred. adj.
adv. of place

Here are some labeled independent clauses.

      subj.   *vb.*
A. Her tires squealed.

                  complement
       subj. vb.   *d. obj.*
B. Flying gravel hit | the sidewalk. |

                     comp.
       subj.   *vb.*   *i. obj.*   *d. obj.*
C. Shana's driving gave | her father the creeps. |

                comp.
   subj. vb.   *pred. nom.*
D. He was | her driving teacher. |

```
                   comp.
   subj. vb.  |       pred. adj.
E. He was | usually terrified. |
```

```
                      comp.
   subj.  vb.  adv. | adv.
F. Shana was rarely | here. |
```

Dependent Clauses. Dependent clauses do not sound like complete sentences when they are spoken or written by themselves. They *depend* on an independent clause to complete their meaning. The word that makes all the difference is the subordinating conjunction or relative pronoun that introduces the clause. For instance, suppose a stranger walked up to you and said

I eat blue bananas.

You would understand those words as a complete, though odd, utterance. In contrast, suppose the stranger said

Since I eat blue bananas,

or

That I eat blue bananas,

or

After I eat blue bananas.

You would think this even more unusual: you would want the stranger to finish the sentence. The words *since, that,* and *after* make the clauses dependent.

Like phrases, dependent clauses act as single parts of speech within a sentence. They can function as nouns, adjectives, or adverbs.

Noun Clauses.   You can tell when a dependent clause is functioning as a noun by making up another sentence in which you substitute a single noun or pronoun for the clause.

$$\overset{\text{— n. cl. —}}{\overset{\textit{subj. vb.}}{\boxed{\textit{\textbf{What you told me}}}}}$$

A. |***What you told me***| will remain locked in my heart.

Your ***secret*** will remain locked in my heart.

The boldface parts act as the subject of each sentence.

B. Send letters to |***whoever fills out the coupon.***|

with label: *n. cl.* / *subj.   vb.*

Send letters to ***everyone***.

The boldface parts are both objects of the preposition *to*.

Besides acting as subjects and as objects of prepositions, noun clauses can be direct objects and predicate nominatives. Here are some sentences with noun clauses diagrammed on two-legged stilts above the main line.

C. |***Whoever ate that banana***| is in trouble.

with label: *n. cl. (subj.)*

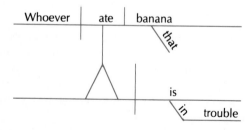

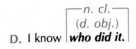

D. I know │ *who did it.* │

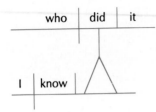

EXERCISE   2-1

Find the noun clauses in the following sentences. Underline each one and label it *subject, direct object, predicate nominative,* or *object of the preposition*.

1. I remember what you told me.
2. Which way he turned was their major disagreement.
3. Sheila asked when she could go.
4. What you see is what you get.
5. The question about why housewives leave home was never considered.

Adjective Clauses. An adjective clause is introduced by a relative pronoun (who, which, that, whose, whom) and usually follows the noun or pronoun it modifies. In the following diagrams, we connect the adjective clause to the rest of the sentence by drawing a dotted line between the relative pronoun and the word it relates to.

E. The price, │**which was outrageous,**│ included state tax.
    ┌────── *adj. cl.* ──────┐

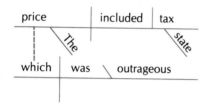

F. The lawyer │**whose donut you ate**│ is famous.
             ┌────── *adj. cl.* ──────┐

EXERCISE   2-2

Identify the adjective clauses and the nouns or pronouns they modify in the following sentences.

1. She was the only student whose favorite subject was philosophy.
2. Her teachers liked having a student who was so enthusiastic.
3. These were memories that gave her pleasure.
4. She disliked Nietzsche, whom she considered depressing.
5. R. D. Laing's views were the ones that seemed realistic to her.

Adverb Clauses. Like an adverb, an adverb clause answers the following questions: How? When? Where? Why? To what degree? True or false? It modifies a verb, an adjective, or another adverb. Here are some examples.

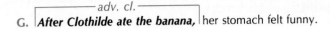

G. **After Clothilde ate the banana,** her stomach felt funny.
—— adv. cl. ——

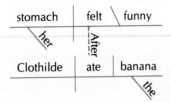

H. The banana was blue **because it was a mutation.**
——— adv. cl. ———

I. It was so bright **that we carried it in a cardboard box.**
——————— adv. cl. ———————

J. Everyone was surprised **that Clothilde ate all of it.**
——— adv.cl. ———

EXERCISE   **2-3**

Identify the adverb clauses in the following sentences.

1. If you learned grammar in seventh grade, this exercise should be easy.
2. When you study a foreign language, you will find your knowledge of English grammar useful.
3. Transformational grammar is so unfamiliar that many students are frustrated by it.
4. Transformational grammar, however, is fascinating to some people because it challenges them.
5. Grammarians are welcome at parties because they are lively and eccentric.

COMPREHENSIVE EXERCISE   2-4

Label parts of speech, independent and dependent clauses, and phrases.

1. Many cures for insomnia exist.
2. Drinking warm milk is a common home remedy for sleeplessness.
3. Milk contains calcium, which is a natural tranquilizer.
4. When you heat the milk, you make the calcium in it easier for your body to absorb.
5. The warm milk cure does not work for everyone.
6. Some people believe in counting sheep.
7. This boring activity quickly makes them drowsy.
8. Others claim that long nineteenth-century novels will produce sleep efficiently.
9. Alarmed at such barbarism, nineteenth-century fiction scholars are frantically trying to find alternative sedatives.
10. Their most recent work, which is now in experimental stages, involves Wordsworth's *Prelude*.

Chapter Three
Revising Index

We do not expect you to sit down and read this chapter straight through. But before you begin writing, it may help you to read the sections that pertain to the writing process: *Unity, Coherence, Transitions, Logic, and Thesis Statement,* for example. After that, use this alphabetized index to get quick advice during your revising process. For the convenience of both you and your instructor, the entries are keyed to common theme correction symbols. Table 3-1 presents a punctuation guide as a quick reference for determining correct punctuation.

Our advice covers current standard English, the language used by educated people in our society. While standard English is not necessarily any better than the language you may hear at the grocery store or in your local tavern (it may, in fact, be less vigorous and colorful), standard English is the language required of college students and in the business world.

We have also included exercises so you can get some practice on especially knotty problems. If you want to identify some of your difficulties before you begin to write papers, try the comprehensive exercise on pages 188–190. Your instructor has the answers and can direct you to entries in this index which will help you correct your mistakes.

Table 3-1 Quick Punctuation Guide*

Between two whole sentences	Between a phrase or dependent clause and a whole sentence	In a whole sentence interrupted by a phrase or dependent clause	In a list or series
(:) usually	(,) if the phrase or dependent clause comes first and is long (see p. 103)	(○〰○) no punctuation if the interrupter limits the meaning of the word before it (see p. 103)	(,) between each parallel item (see p. 106)
(,) if connected by *and, but, or, nor, yet, so, for* (see p. 104)	(○) no punctuation if the whole sentence comes first followed by a phrase or clause	(,〰,) if the interrupter simply adds information or detail (see p. 102)	(;) between all items when one of the items already has a comma in it (see p. 167)
(;) if they are closely related in meaning (see p. 165)		(〰) to play down interrupter (see p. 146)	
(:) if the second one restates the first (see p. 100)		(—〰—) to stress interrupter (see p. 119)	
(;) if followed by a conjunctive adverb (like *however, thus, nevertheless*) (see p. 165)			

* A glance at this table will solve most of (but not all) your punctuation quandaries. Decide which one of the four situations given in the column headings has you baffled and find the appropriate solution in the table.

Abbreviation

$a\!\ell$

1. Abbreviate only the following terms in formal writing.

A. **Personal titles:** Mr., Ms., Mrs., Dr.
   Abbreviate doctor only before the person's name: Dr. Dustbin—
   but never "The dr. removed my appendix."
   By the same token: St. Joan—**but:** "My mother has the patience of
   a saint."

B. **Academic degrees:** Ph.D., M.D., D.V.M., R.N., M.S., or all can
   be written without periods.

C. **Dates or time:** 1000 B.C. or AD 150 (periods are optional here)
   10:00 a.m., 3 p.m., or 10 A.M., 3:00 P.M.
   (**but not:** "Sylvester succumbed to exhaustion in
   the early a.m.")

D. **Places:** Washington, D.C. or DC, the U.S. economy (**but not:**
   "Ringo flew to the U.S. on a jumbo jet.")

E. **Organizations:** IRS, FBI, ITT, UNICEF, YWCA.
   Many organizations are commonly known by their abbreviations
   (usually written in capital letters without periods). If you are not
   certain whether your readers will recognize the abbreviation, write
   the name out the first time you use it, put the initials in parentheses
   following it, and use only the initials thereafter.

F. **Latin expressions:** e.g. (for example); i.e. (that is); etc. (and so
   forth)—but do not use *etc.* just to avoid thinking of other examples.

2. In "Works Cited" listings for papers that use sources, abbreviate the following.

A. The month (except for March, April, May, June, and July)
B. The names of publishers (Yale UP is Yale University Press)
C. The names of states, if cited (Boston, MA)
D. The words *editor* (ed., eds.) and *volume* (vol., vols.)

3. **Avoid using symbols (%, #, &).**

In scientific papers, however, you are expected to use both numerals and symbols.

See also *Numbers*.

4. **The abbreviations for states mandated by the U.S. Postal Service are listed on p. 350.**

Active Voice See *Passive Voice*.

adv	**Adverb/Adjective Confusion**

1. **Adverbs usually end in *-ly*.**

Adjective	Adverb
beautiful	beautifully
rapid	rapidly
mangy	mangily

Naturally there are exceptions—adjectives that end in *-ly* like *sickly, earthly, homely, ghostly, holy, lively, friendly, manly*—but these seldom cause difficulty. Also, there are adverbs that do not end in *-ly*—*now, then, later, there, near, far, very, perhaps*—but hardly anybody messes these up either.

2. **Adverbs modify verbs, adjectives, and other adverbs.**

                      subj.   *vb.*   *adv.*

A. *Standard:* The car was vibrating badly.

                      subj.   *vb.*   *adj.*

  Faulty: The car was vibrating bad.

```
               subj.   vb.    adv.        adv.
```
B. *Standard:*   The car was moving really rapidly.

```
               subj.   vb.    adj.       adv.
```
Faulty: The car was moving real rapidly.

```
             subj.  vb.  adv.     adj.
```
C. *Standard:*   The car was badly damaged.

```
             subj.  vb.   adj.      adj.
```
Faulty: The car was damaged bad.

3. **Adjectives modify *nouns* or *pronouns*.**

```
   n.  vb.  adj.    n.
```
A. Fido is a frisky pup.

```
pron.  vb.   adj.
```
B. She looks frisky.

4. *Adjectives* **also follow** *linking verbs* **(*to be, to feel, to appear, to seem, to look, to become, to smell, to sound, to taste*) and refer back to the noun or pronoun subject.**

```
 subj.  vlk.  adj.
```
A. Fido feels bad.

```
 subj.  vlk.   adj.
```
B. Fido smells bad.

Notice that a verb expressing action requires an adverb in what appears to be the same construction, but the adverb here modifies the verb:

```
   subj.  vb.   adv.
```
C. Fido eats messily.

```
   subj.   vb.        adv.
```
D. Fido scratches frequently.

5. Some short adverbs do not need the -*ly* ending in informal writing.

Drive slowly!   Drive slow!
Yell loudly.   Yell loud.

6. The distinction between *good* and *well.*

Good is an adjective: it can be compared (*good, better, best*). *Well* can be an adverb (as in "Kevin writes well.") or an adjective (as in "Carla is well now.") What you want to avoid, then, is using *good* as an adverb.

A. *Wrong:*   Kevin writes **good.**
   Right: Kevin writes **well.**
B. *Wrong:*   Carla's job pays **good.**
   Right: Carla's job pays **well.**

Remember, though, that the linking verbs take predicate adjectives, so you are right to say:

      linking pred.
  subj. *vb.* *adj.*
C. Kevin looks good.

        linking pred.
    subj. *vb.* *adj.*
D. Carla's attitude is good.

E. I feel good.

If in doubt, find a more precise expression.

Kevin looks healthy (or happy or handsome).
Carla's attitude is positive (or cooperative or hopeful).
I feel frisky (or energetic or great).

EXERCISE 3-1

In the following sentences choose the correct form to use in writing standard English.

1. Tony certainly dances (good, well).
2. The candidate talked too (loud, loudly).
3. Larry responds to requests (lazy, lazily).
4. Onion soup tastes (yummy, yummily).
5. Sodium nitrite reacts (dangerous, dangerously) in your stomach.
6. Joseph had been arguing (extreme, extremely) (loud, loudly).
7. Be (careful, carefully)!
8. Martha appears to be (good, well).
9. Rhinoceroses seldom move very (quick, quickly).
10. (Rippling, ripplingly), the stream flowed through the park.

Agreement (Pronoun and Antecedent)

agr

1. **Pronouns should agree in number with their antecedents (the words they stand in for).**

A. Charlene shucked **her** sweater.
B. Charlene and Susie shucked **their** sweaters.
C. Neither Charlene nor Susie shucked **her** sweater.

Some indefinite pronouns can be singular or plural, depending on the construction.

D. **All** my money is gone.
E. **All** my pennies are spent.
F. **Some** of this toast is burned.
G. **Some** of these peas are tasteless.

2. Some *indefinite* pronouns *sound* plural but have been decreed grammatically singular.

anybody	none	someone	neither
anyone	no one	everyone	either

Consider, for instance, the logic of these grammatically correct sentences:

> Because everyone at the rally spoke Spanish, I addressed him in that language.
>
> Everyone applauded, and I was glad he did.
>
> After everybody folded his paper, the instructor passed among him and collected it.

Robert C. Pooley points out in *The Teaching of English Usage* that grammarians since the eighteenth century have been trying to coerce writers into observing this arbitrary, often illogical, distinction. Professor Pooley, in summarizing his findings on current usage, reports:

> It may be concluded, then, that the indefinite pronouns *everyone, everybody, either, neither,* and so forth, when singular in meaning are referred to by a singular pronoun and when plural in meaning are referred to by a plural pronoun. When the gender is mixed [includes both females and males] or indeterminate [possibly includes both sexes] the plural forms *they, them, their* are frequently used as common gender singulars.[1]

Thus, we may now write in standard English,

> A. ***Everyone*** should wear ***their*** crash helmets.

---

[1] Pooley, *The Teaching of English Usage,* 2nd ed. (Urbana, IL: National Council of Teachers of English, 1946, 1974): 83–87.

B. *Neither* of the puppies has *their* eyes open yet.
C. *None* of those arrested will admit *they* were involved.

That takes care of what used to be a really troublesome problem with pronoun agreement. But you should realize that there are still plenty of people around who will look askance at this usage. Many people who learned standard English, say, twenty years ago will declare you wrong if you write *everyone* followed by *their*. If you prefer to avoid ruffling such readers, you can easily observe the old rule and consider these pronouns as always singular: *anybody, anyone, someone, everyone, none, neither, either.* Unless you are discussing a group that's entirely female, you will write

D. *Everyone* should wear *his* crash helmet.
E. *Neither* of the informers escaped with *his* life.
F. *None* of those arrested will admit *he* was involved.

There remains, too, the sticky problem of what pronoun to use if your indefinite pronoun is strictly singular in meaning. This dilemma occurs frequently because we are programmed to write in the singular. Many people would write

G. *Each* student must show *his* permit to register.

Just as effectively, you can write

Students must show *their* permits to register.

or, try this:

Each student must show a permit to register.

The meaning remains the same, and you have included both sexes.

Occasionally you may need to write a sentence in which you emphasize the singular:

    H. *Each* individual must speak *his* own mind.

But the sentence will be just as emphatic if you write it in this way:

    Each one of us must speak *our* own minds.

Try to break the singular habit and cultivate the plural. You can thus solve countless agreement problems automatically.

For more tips on avoiding sexist language, see *he or she* and *man/person* in Chapter 14.

EXERCISE   **3-2**

In the following sentences, select one or more words suitable for filling the blank in a nonsexist way. If you cannot think of such a word, revise the sentence.

1. Everyone on the plane should fasten _____ seat belts.
2. Anyone living outside of town should leave _____ job early to avoid getting _____ car stuck in a snow drift.
3. A good student does _____ homework.
4. Someone has left _____ car lights on.
5. Our dog has lost _____ collar.
6. The writer must consider _____ audience.
7. Everyone must present _____ ID at the door.
8. Anyone wishing to improve _____ tennis game should work on _____ backhand.
9. After listening the the patient's heartbeat, the doctor removed _____ stethoscope.
10. Each person must cast _____ own vote.

Agreement (Subject and Verb)

agr

1. **Subjects and verbs should agree in *number* (singular or plural).**

     plural   plural
     subj.   vb.
A. <u>Artichokes</u> <u>are</u> a struggle to eat.

     singular singular
      subj.   vb.
B. An <u>artichoke</u> <u>is</u> a struggle to eat.

Note: **The *to be* verb (*am, was, were, being, been,* etc.) agrees with the subject (a noun before the verb), not the predicate nominative (a noun following the *to be* verb).**

          subj. pred. nom.
C. My favorite <u>fruit</u> <u>is</u> preaches.

    subj.   *pred. nom.*
D. <u>Peaches</u> <u>are</u> my favorite fruit.

2. **Most nouns add -*s* to form the plural.**

    snips and snails and puppy dogs' tails

But with most verbs, the singular form ends in -*s* and you drop it to form the plural.

    one squirrel gnaws, several squirrels gnaw

3. **Do not let intervening modifiers confuse you.**
    Sometimes a modifier gets sandwiched in between subject and verb to trip the unwary, like this:

         subj.   *vb.*
A. *Wrong:*   The full <u>extent</u> of his crimes <u>have</u> now <u>been</u> <u>discovered</u>.

"Crimes have been discovered" sounds fine, but *crimes* is *not* the subject of that sentence. The actual subject is the singular noun *extent*, with *crimes* serving as object of the preposition *of.* The sentence should read:

          subj.   *vb.*
Right: The full <u>extent</u> of his crimes <u>has</u> now <u>been</u> <u>discovered</u>.

Here are more correct examples of sentences with intervening modifiers.

      subj.
B. The <u>bother</u> of packing clothes, finding motels, and searching for
               vb.
restaurants <u>takes</u> the joy out of vacation.

      subj.
C. <u>Pictures</u> showing nude women and men having sexual con-
        vb.
tact <u>are</u> shocking.

      subj.   *vb.*
D. <u>Books</u> full of adventure <u>are</u> what Lucy likes.

4. Singular subjects connected by *and* require a plural verb.

      1   +   *1*   = *plural*
A. The <u>pitcher</u> and the <u>catcher</u> <u>are</u> both great players.

But sometimes we complicate matters by connecting singular subjects with *correlative conjunctions* (*not . . . but, not only . . . but also, neither . . . nor, either . . . or*) instead of *and.*

Then the verb should be singular, although the idea may still come out plural:

B. Not only the pitcher but the catcher also is getting tired.
C. Neither the pitcher nor the catcher is still frisky.
D. Either the pitcher or the catcher is slowing down.

5. **Compound *plural* subjects connected by *or* require a plural verb.**

Fleas or ticks are unwelcome.

6. **In the case of subjects joined by *or* or *nor*, if one subject is plural and the other singular, the verb agrees with the subject closest to it.**

A. Leather or hubcaps remind me of you.

B. Hubcaps or leather reminds me of you.

Warning: **Some constructions appear compound but really are not. Singular subjects followed by words like *with, like, along with, as well as, no less than, including, besides* are still singular because these words are prepositions, not coordinating conjunctions. The idea in the sentence may be distinctly plural, but be advised that the subject and verb remain singular.**

C. My cat, as well as my parakeet, is lost.

D. Seymour, together with his St. Bernard, his pet alligator, and his piranha fish, is moving in with us.

E. Claudia, no less than Carlyle, is responsible for this outrage.

7. **Always find the grammatical subject, and make the verb agree.**

We do not always follow the usual subject-followed-by-verb sentence pattern:

         vb.   *subj.*   *vb.*
A. Where <u>have</u> all the <u>flowers</u> <u>gone</u>?

If the sentence is longer, you may have trouble:

B. *Wrong:* Where has all the hope, gaiety, yearning, and excitement gone?

Note: **The adverb *where* can never be the subject of a sentence, so you must look further. The actual subject is compound: "hope, gaiety, yearning, and excitement," which means the verb should be *plural.***

Right: Where <u>have</u> all the <u>hope</u>, <u>gaiety</u>, <u>yearning</u>, and <u>excitement</u> <u>gone</u>?

We often invert subject and verb for stylistic reasons.

                                      vb.   *subj.*
C. *Right:* In poverty, injustice, and discrimination <u>lies</u> the <u>cause</u> of Juan's bitterness.

          vb.   *subj.*   *subj.*
D. *Right:* Here <u>are</u> my friend <u>Seymour</u> and his cousin <u>Selma</u>.

Like the adverbs *here* and *where*, the word *there* often poses alluringly at the beginning of a sentence, looking for all the world like the subject. Do not be deceived. *There* can never be the subject; it is either an adverb or an *expletive* (a "filler" word that allows variety in sentence patterns). So before you automatically slide in a singular verb after *there*, find out what the subject really is.

              vb.   *subj.*

E. *Right:* There is great hope for peace today.

              vb.   *subj.*

F. *Right:* There are two great hopes for peace today.

The pronoun *it* can also be an expletive, but unlike *there*, it can be the subject of a sentence and always takes a singular verb, even when functioning as an expletive.

G. *Right:* It is a mile to the nearest phone.

H. *Right:* It is miles to the nearest phone.

8. Collective nouns can be singular or plural.

Some words in the language (like *group, staff, family, committee, company, jury*) can be either singular or plural, depending on the context. To suggest that the members are functioning together as a single unit, you can write

A. The office staff is working on the problem.

B. The jury has agreed on a verdict.

Or to suggest that individual members are functioning separately within the group, you can write

C. The office staff are debating that proposal.

D. The jury have not yet agreed on a verdict.

EXERCISE 3-3

In the following sentences choose the correct word.

1. There (is, are) my cousin Ralph and his friend Rudolph, jogging in the rain.
2. Where (has, have) the toothpaste and the hairbrush gone?
3. Not only adults but also children (has, have) problems.
4. Bananas and peanut butter (make, makes) a tasty sandwich.
5. Caffeine or cigarettes, in quantity, (cause, causes) damage to the body.
6. Cigarettes or caffeine, in quantity, (cause, causes) damage to the body.
7. The impact of these statistics (has, have) not yet been fully analyzed.
8. Movies packed with violence (is, are) still a favorite with the public.
9. In great poetry (lie, lies) many great truths.
10. Our family (is, are) in disagreement about where to spend our vacation.

Analogy

An *analogy* is a form of comparison, either brief or extended.

A brief analogy will be a metaphor or simile. (See *Figures of Speech.*) An extended analogy provides a more thorough comparison and can be a means of organizing a paragraph, perhaps even a whole essay. You use something familiar to explain something unfamiliar. Geologists, for instance, often describe the structure of the earth's crust by comparing the strata to the layers of an onion. Sometimes writers use analogy in an attempt to persuade, as advocates of legalizing marijuana are likely to argue that the present laws are as ineffective and unnecessary as prohibition laws in the twenties. Although analogy is not purely logical, you can certainly use analogy persuasively—so long as your analogy is indeed persuasive.

Antecedent See *Agreement* (*Pronoun and Antecedent*).

Apostrophe

apos

,

1. **The apostrophe signals possession (except for the possessive pronouns, which do not need apostrophes: *ours, yours, its, theirs*).**

> Clarence's car
> the Joneses' junk
> Yeats's yearnings or Yeats' yearnings

2. **An apostrophe signals that some letters (or numbers) have been left out.**

> we've (for ***we have***)
> something's (for ***something has*** or ***something is***)
> mustn't (for ***must not***)
> class of '75 (for ***class of 1975***)
> o'clock (for ***of the clock***)

3. **The *its*/*it's* confusion.**
Use the apostrophe only for the contraction. *It's* = *it is* or *it has*. If you use the apostrophe to form the possessive of *it* and write

> That dumb dog chomped it's own tail.

you have really said

> That dumb dog chomped it is own tail.
> That dumb dog chomped it has own tail.

And your readers may wonder about you as well as the dog. Make a mental note to check every *its* and *it's* when you proofread if you tend to be careless about apostrophes.

> *Remember:* **its** = "of it"—possessive (**The dog chomped its tail.**)
> **it's** = "it is"—contraction (**It's not an intelligent dog.**)

4. Apostrophes are optional in forming the plural of numbers, titles, letters, and words used as words.

> The 1970's [or 1970s] proved quieter than the 60's [or 60s].
> We hired two new Ph.D.'s. [or Ph.D.s]
> Seymour makes straight A's. [or As]
> Those two **and**'s [or **and**s] are ineffective.
> You are learning the dos and don'ts of English usage.
> Horace rolled three consecutive 7's [or 7s].

But no apostrophe in

> Horace rolled three consecutive sevens.

EXERCISE 3-4

Choose the correct word in the following sentences.

1. The (Cox's, Coxes) will be gone for two weeks.
2. That donkey is not known for (it's, its) docility.

3. The (begonia's, begonias) have finished blooming.
4. Some lucky (dogs', dogs) houses are as warm as toast.
5. Mind your (ps and qs, p's and q's).
6. We want to be home before (its, it's) dark.
7. Steve smashed up Bill (Smiths', Smith's) car.
8. Melvin is learning the (ins and outs, in's and out's) of computer programming.
9. Marcia's children are already in their (teens, teens').
10. Harold has gone to see the (Harrises', Harris's, Harris') new house

Appositive

An appositive is a word or phrase that comes directly after a noun and identifies or supplements it. Appositives should have commas on both ends.

> Stella, *the older sister,* was quite intelligent, while Blanche, *the younger sister,* was courageous.

Also see *Case of Pronouns*, number 3.

Article

Articles are words used to limit or identify nouns: *a, an, the.*

Auxiliary Verb See *Verbs*, page 34.

Bafflegab See *Diction*, number 4.

Balanced Sentence

1. **A sentence that has balanced (or *parallel*) structure includes a series or pair of elements that are grammatically similar:**

A. **Series of prepositional phrases**

> The juggler tosses ninepins over his head, behind his back, and under his knee.

B. **Series of three adjectives**

> Ignorant, sullen, and mean-spirited, the young man did not seem to be a promising father.

C. **Pair of clauses**

> She hoped that she argued the case well and that she achieved justice quickly.

2. **Make items in series parallel.**

Most of the time, similar grammatical constructions pair up naturally, but sometimes they get jumbled. You must then decide what grammatical construction you want and make the items in the series or pair fit that construction.

> A. *Jumbled:* She never got used to the drudgery, depression, and being so ill-paid for her work at the nursing home.

That example has two nouns and a gerund phrase.

> *Improved:* She never got used to the drudgery, depression, and low pay of her work at the nursing home.

Now all are nouns.

B. *Jumbled:*   This new kind of therapy promises to make you happy, to improve your love life, and that it will make your hair shiny.

This one has two infinitive phrases and a clause.

Improved: This new kind of therapy promises to make you happy, to improve your love life, and even to make your hair shiny.

Now all three items are infinitive phrases.

C. *Jumbled:*   The bell was about to ring, the students closed their books, and watched the clock anxiously.

The third item is not a clause.

Improved: The bell was about to ring, the students closed their books, and everyone watched the clock anxiously.

Now all the items are independent clauses.

3. **Balance sentences for effect and emphasis.**
Practice writing parallel constructions for their beauty and impact. These qualities shine in the conclusion of a review of Dee Brown's *Bury My Heart at Wounded Knee*, a book detailing the deplorable treatment of American Indians by white Americans who desired their land. The paragraph is effective for several reasons, but mainly because of the balanced structure:

The books I review, week upon week, report the destruction of the land or the air; they detail the perversion of justice; they reveal national stupidities. None of them—not one—has saddened me and shamed me as this book has. Because the experience of reading it has made me realize for once and all that we really don't

know who we are, or where we came from, or what we have done,
or why.

—Geoffrey Wolff, *Newsweek,* 1 Feb. 1971.

4. All items in a formal outline should be parallel (or balanced).

All should be complete sentences or all should be meaningful fragments (or topics).

EXERCISE   3-5

Put items in the following sentences into parallel constructions. Revise as much as you like.

1. The first part of the Bus Stop, a disco dance, consists of three steps backward, a touch step, and then stepping forward three times.
2. The dancer should remember to act unruffled, self-composed, and as though the steps came naturally.
3. After the dancer repeats the first part, a sideways two-step is executed, and the dancer two-steps back into the starting position.
4. Experienced dancers say that the hops and touches in the third part of the Bus Stop are the most exciting and also hard to teach to others.
5. The final step is executing a ninety-degree kick-turn and to start the pattern over from the beginning.
6. Patti knows all about how to pack a suitcase and finding clothes that wash easily.
7. Roommates are told everything from grades to who went out with whom the night before.
8. Fred's designs are simple in pattern and bold colors.
9. Mainly poor people, retired people, and those who have lost their jobs are protesting.
10. Horace leaps to his feet, runs upstairs, grabs his tennis racquet, and then is unable to find a partner.

Brackets

[ ]

Use brackets as a signal for readers in the following cases.

1. To change verb tenses in a quotation.

Usually you can adjust your phrasing to suit a quotation, but if the quotation is past tense and you are writing in present tense (or vice versa), it is considerably easier to change the verb in the quotation than to rewrite your paper. If you want to make a past tense quotation about H. L. Mencken fit your present tense essay, do it like this:

Original in past tense:

"He defended prostitution, vivisection, Sunday sports, alcohol, and war."[2]

Changed to present tense:

"He defend[s] prostitution, vivisection, Sunday sports, alcohol, and war."[2]

2. To clarify any word in a quotation.

"In those days [the early 1940s] until the post-war repression set in, the [Communist] Party was a strange mixture of openness and secrecy."[3]

3. To enclose *sic.*

When you quote a passage that contains an error, you must

---

[2] William Manchester, *H. L. Mencken: Disturber of the Peace* (New York: Collier, 1962): 79.

[3] Jessica Mitford, *A Fine Old Conflict* (New York: Knopf, 1977): 67.

copy the error. The word *sic* ("thus" in Latin) means, "Honest, it really was written that way."

> "The correspondent, as he rowed, looked down as [sic] the two men sleeping underfoot."[4]

4. **To enclose parenthetical material that is already within parentheses.**

Use brackets this way only if you cannot avoid it, as in a scholarly aside, like this one:

> (For an informed appraisal of her relationship with the Rev. Mr. Wadsworth, see Richard B. Sewall, *The Life of Emily Dickinson* [New York: Farrar, Straus, and Giroux, 1974]. 2:444–462.)

You may not have keys for brackets on your typewriter. Do *not* substitute parentheses. If you use parentheses, your readers will assume that the material appeared in the original quotation and may become either hopelessly confused or endlessly annoyed. All you need to do is skip two spaces as you type; then neatly write in the brackets later with a pen. Or you can make brackets with the slash and underscore keys, like this:

$$\lfloor \qquad\qquad \rceil$$

---

[4] Stephen Crane, *The Red Badge of Courage and Selected Prose and Poetry*, ed. William M. Gibson, 3rd ed. (New York: Holt, 1950): 285.

Capitalization

cap

1. **Begin each sentence with a capital letter, including sentences you quote.**

lc

> Ambrose Bierce says that "Diplomacy is the patriotic art of lying for one's country."

2. **Begin each line of poetry with a capital letter only if the poet has used capitals.**

> Candy
> Is dandy
> But liquor
> Is quicker.
>
> —Ogden Nash.

> God has a brown voice,
> as soft and full as beer.
>
> —Anne Sexton.

3. **Always capitalize the pronoun *I*.**

4. **Use caution in capitalizing words to express emphasis or personification (Truth, Justice, Beauty), unless you are writing poetry.**

5. **Capitalize proper nouns—the names of specific persons, places, historical events and periods, organizations, races, languages, teams, and deities.**

Lowercase	Capitalized
the town square	Washington Square
go to the city	go to Boston
our club secretary	the Secretary of State

traveling east	visiting the Far East
a historical document	the Monroe Doctrine
reading medieval history	studying the Middle Ages
taking Latin, chemistry, and math	Latin 100, Chemistry 60, Math 240
an industrial town	the Industrial Revolution
a political organization	Common Cause
an ethnic group	an American Indian
our favorite team	the Galveston Gophers
buttered toast	French toast
the gods	Buddha, Allah, Zeus

6. **Most people capitalize pronouns referring to the Christian God or Jesus.**

Our Father, Who art in heaven, hallowed be Thy name . . .

In His name, Amen.

7. **When in doubt, consult your dictionary.**

If the word is capitalized in the dictionary entry, you should always capitalize it. If you find a usage label, like "often cap." or "usually cap.," use your own judgment. Occasionally a word will acquire a different meaning if capitalized:

Abraham Lincoln was a great democrat.

Lyndon Johnson was a lifelong Democrat.

The Pope is Catholic.

Carla's taste is catholic (all-encompassing).

8. **Capitalize the *first* and *last* words of titles; omit capitals on articles and on conjunctions and prepositions of fewer than five letters.**

If you are unable to tell an article from an artichoke or a preposition from a pronoun, see our Chapter 2, "Background in Grammar."

Pride and Prejudice
Gone with the Wind
Shakespeare Without Tears
Been Down So Long It Looks like Up to Me
One Flew Over the Cuckoo's Nest

9. Capitalize after colons.
Always capitalize the first word following the colon in a title.

Problems of Urban Renewal: A Reconsideration

A capital letter on the first word after a colon in a sentence is optional—unless a question or quotation follows; then capitalize.

Case of Pronouns

case

1. Pronouns change form with function.
Although nouns do not change form to show case when they move from being subjects to objects, pronouns do. We can write

A. Martha resembles my sister.
B. My sister resembles Martha.

But with pronouns, alas, we must use a different form for subjects and objects.

C. **She** resembles my sister.   D. My sister resembles **her.**

The case forms are easy:

Subjective	Objective	Possessive
I	me	mine
he	him	his
she	her	hers
you	you	yours
it	it	its
we	us	ours
they	them	theirs
who	whom	whose
whoever	whomever	whosever

Most of the time the possessives give no trouble at all, except for the confusion of the possessive *its* with the contraction *it's* (see *Apostrophe*, section 2). But problems like the following do come up.

2. When the subject or object is compound, drop the noun momentarily to decide which case to use.

A. *Faulty:* Sylvester and **me** went to a lecture.
   Preferred: Syvester and **I** went to a lecture.
B. *Faulty:* Martha sat with Sylvester and **I**.
   Preferred: Martha sat with Sylvester and **me**.

If in doubt about which pronoun to choose, drop the noun momentarily and see how the pronoun sounds alone:

I went?   *or*   **me** went?
Martha sat with **me**?   *or*   Martha sat with **I**?

Your ear will tell you that "me went" and "sat with I" are not standard constructions.

Remember that although prepositions are usually short words (like *in, on, at, by, for*), a few are deceptively long (like *through, beside, among, underneath, between*). Long or short, prepositions always take the objective pronoun:

between Homer and *me*
among Homer, Martha, and *me*
beside Martha and *me*.

3. **When pronouns are used with appositives, drop the noun momentarily to decide.**

   A. *Faulty:*   *Us* cat lovers are slaves to our pets.
     Preferred: *We* cat lovers are slaves to our pets.
   B. *Faulty:*   Spring is a delight for *we* hedonists.
     Preferred: Spring is a delight for *us* hedonists.

Once more, if in doubt about which pronoun to choose, drop the noun and your ear will guide you: "*We* are slaves to our pets," not "*Us* are slaves to our pets"; "Spring is a delight for *us*," not "Spring is a delight for *we*."

4. **When pronouns are used in comparisons, finish the comparison in your mind.**

   Faulty: Demon rum is stronger than me.
   Preferred: Demon rum is stronger than I.

These comparisons are incomplete (or *elliptical*). If you finish the statement—at least in your mind—you will eliminate any problem. You would not be likely to write, "Demon rum is stronger than *me* am." Naturally, "stronger than *I* am" is standard English. How about "Henrietta's husband is ten years younger than her"? Younger than *her* is? No, younger than *she* is.

5. **When the choice is between *who* and *whom*, substitute *he* or *she* to decide the proper usage.**
   Colloquial usage now allows *who* in all constructions be-

cause when we begin a sentence in conversation, we scarcely know how it's going to come out.

But in writing you can always see how your sentence comes out, so you need to know whether to use *who* or *whom*. When the choice occurs in midsentence, you can fall back on substitution. Replace the prospective *who* or *whom* with *she* or *her* in the following sentence, and your ear will tell you whether to choose the subjective or objective form.

Kate Chopin was a superb writer (who, whom) literary critics have neglected until recently.

Ask yourself

Critics have neglected *she?*

or

Critics have neglected *her?*

We would all choose *her*, naturally. Since *her* is objective, the sentence needs the objective *whom:*

Kate Chopin was a superb writer whom literary critics have neglected until recently.

There is also a sneaky way to avoid the choice. If you are writing an exam and have no time to think, try using *that:*

Kate Chopin was a superb writer *that* literary critics have neglected until recently.

Although many people still find this usage distasteful, it is now standard English. But do not ever substitute *which* for *who* or *whom*. Standard usage still does not allow *which* to refer to people.

Preferred: the woman ***whom*** I adore
Acceptable: the woman ***that*** I adore
Faulty: the woman ***which*** I adore

EXERCISE   3-6

Choose the correct pronoun in each sentence.

1. You can't win if you run against Coreen and (she, her).
2. At the next meeting Sherman and (I, me) are going to present a modern morality play.
3. For too long (we, us) taxpayers have been at the mercy of Congress.
4. Monty Python's Flying Circus is the group on (whom, who, which) I base all hope for humor on television.
5. (Who, Whom) is going to deliver the keynote address?
6. You will never persuade the people (who, whom, that) you need the most to go along with your proposal.
7. The very person (who, whom, that) you are trying to help is the least likely to accept your plan.
8. If you will agree to see us tomorrow, Sedgewick and (I, me) will go home now.
9. Stanley and (I, me) are planning to become transcendentalists.
10. The public should be spared commercials (who, whom, that, which) are an insult to our intelligence.

Clauses and Phrases

A *clause* is a group of words that has both a subject and a verb; a *phrase* does not have both.

Clauses: after I lost my head

            I lost my head

            that I lost my head

Phrases: having lost my head
to lose my head
after losing my head

Infinitive and gerund phrases can have a subject but will not have a finite verb:

[The <u>negatives</u> to be developed] <u>are</u> on the desk.

[The <u>film</u> being shown] <u>is</u> a classic.

Each bracketed phrase functions as the subject of its sentence. The subject within the phrase is underlined.

For a complete explanation of clauses and phrases, including their many functions, see pages 55–65 in Chapter 2.

Cliché See *Triteness.*

coh **Coherence**

Good writing must have *coherence*—a logical relationship among the parts. In short, it must *hang together.*

1. Organize your ideas before you begin.

Each point should clearly follow the one before it. Make sure that all points pertain to the idea contained in your *thesis*, or main idea. (See also *Unity.*)

2. Keep your audience in mind.

In order not to lose your readers when you move from one example to the next (between sentences) or from one main idea to the next (between paragraphs), you must provide *tran-

sitions—words like *for example, for instance, namely, next, besides, finally, otherwise, but, since, thus, therefore.* (See also our lists of subordinating conjunctions and conjunctive adverbs, pages 51–52.)

3. Use plenty of specific, concrete examples.

You cannot expect your readers to read your mind. Whenever you make a *generalization* (a general statement, a main point), be sure to follow it with specific examples or precise explanations to make sure that your readers can follow your thinking.

Collective Noun   See *Agreement (Subject and Verb)*, number 8.

Colloquial   See page 192.

Colon

colon

:

For quick advice, see our handy punctuation chart on page 68.

1. Use a colon to introduce lists of things: single words, phrases, or subordinate clauses.

A. A hawk sometimes catches small animals: chickens, rabbits, moles, and mice.
B. "It is by the goodness of God that in our country we have those three unspeakably good things: freedom of speech, freedom of conscience, and the prudence never to practice either of them."
—Mark Twain.

2. Use a colon to connect two independent clauses when the second enlarges on or explains the first.

A. The students had an inspired idea: they would publish a course guide.
B. Only later did the truth come out: Bumper had gambled away his inheritance, embezzled the company funds, and skipped town with the manager's daughter.

If the second clause poses a question, begin with a capital letter.

The main question is this: What are we going to do about the nuclear arms race?

3. In most cases, a colon should be used only after a complete sentence.

A. My favorite animals are the following: lions, tigers, aardvarks, and hippopotamuses.

Many people, though, will stick in a colon without completing the first independent clause

B. *Faulty:*   My favorite animals are: lions, tigers, aardvarks, and hip-popotamuses.

Careful writers would eliminate the colon in that sentence.

Right: My favorite animals are lions, tigers, aardvarks, and hippo-potamuses.

4. Use a colon (or a comma) to introduce a direct quotation when your lead-in is a complete sentence.

Camus puts the matter strongly: "Without work all life goes rotten—but when work is soulless, life stifles and dies."

5. Use a colon to separate numerical elements.

Time   9:35
Biblical chapter and verses: Revelations 3:7–16 *or*
                                     Revelations III:7–16

Act and scene: II:2
Act, scene, and line: IV:iii:23–27 *or*
                             IV, iii, 23–27

6. Use a colon after the salutation of business letters.

Dear Mr. Shuttlecock:
Dear Credit Manager:

7. Use a colon between the title and subtitle of a book or article.

American Humor: A Study in the National Character
"The Money Motif: Economic Implications in *Huckleberry Finn*"

Note: **When typing, leave two spaces after colons, except in biblical references, between hours and minutes, and between volume and page numbers in some documentation styles (5:47–49).**

Combine Sentences for Fluency

comb

If your sentences tend to be fairly simple and monotonous in structure, combine one or two of them.

Say you are writing too many repetitious sentences like these:

Cucumber beetles begin their life cycle as white larvae. These larvae are hatched from yellowish eggs. The eggs are deposited in the soil around the cucumber plants.

What you need to do is combine the three ideas there into a single sentence, like this:

Cucumber beetles, which begin their life cycle as white larvae, are hatched from yellowish eggs deposited in the soil around the plants.

Or, if you want to emphasize instead the larval stage, you could combine the material this way:

Cucumber beetles, which are hatched from yellowish eggs deposited in the soil around the plants, begin their life cycle as white larvae.

For other material about combining ideas, see *Subordination and Coordination, Emphasis,* and *Overburdened Sentence.* And for a more thorough discussion of sentence combining, see pages 176–177.

Comma

comma

See also *Comma Splice.*

, For quick advice, see the handy punctuation chart on page 68.

c/ **1. Use commas to set off interrupters (nonrestrictive modifiers).**
A word, phrase, or clause that interrupts the normal flow of the sentence *without changing the meaning* is nonessential or *nonrestrictive.* You need a comma both *before* and *after* the interrupter.

A. Magnum Oil Company, our best client, canceled its account.
B. Our instructor, who usually dresses conservatively, wore jeans and a headband today.
C. "Being merciful, it seems to me, is the only good idea we have received so far."
—Kurt Vonnegut.

2. Do not use commas around restrictive modifiers.

c2

A. *Restrictive:*   Students who can't swim must wear life jackets on the canoe outing.
B. *Nonrestrictive:* Melvin, who can't swim, must wear a life jacket on the canoe outing.

Notice that "who can't swim" is essential to the meaning of the first example (it *restricts* the subject) but can easily be left out in the second without changing the basic meaning. Thus in sentence B the modifier "who can't swim" is nonrestrictive and is set off by commas. But commas around "who can't swim" in sentence A would mislead readers. The difference in meaning between restrictive and nonrestrictive modifiers should be clear in these two sentences:

C. *Restrictive:*   Students who are lazy should be closely supervised.
D. *Nonrestrictive:* Students, who are lazy, should be closely supervised.

3. Use a comma for clarity.

c3

After any longish introductory element (like a dependent clause or a long phrase), a comma makes the sentence easier to read.

A. Since we've run out of lemons, we'll have to make do with limes.
B. After all the trouble of sneaking into the movie, Arnold didn't like the film.

Once in a while you may write a sentence that needs a comma simply to make it easier to read, like this one:

> The main thing to remember is, do not light a match.
> Smoking permitted, the passengers all lit up.

Do not write unclear sentences, though, and depend on a comma to make them intelligible. If in doubt, rewrite the sentence.

| *Ct* | 4. **A comma precedes a coordinating conjunction (*and, but, or, for, nor, yet, so*) that connects two complete sentences (*independent clauses*).** |

A. Myrtle splashed and swam in the pool, but Marvin only sunned himself and looked bored.

Notice, there are three coordinating conjunctions in that example, but a comma precedes only one of them. The *and*s connect compound verbs (splashed *and* swam, sunned *and* looked), not whole sentences the way the *but* does. Thus, a comma before a coordinating conjunction signals your readers that another complete sentence is coming up, not just a compound subject or object. Here are two more examples:

B. Curtis adores coconut cream pie, yet three times he has suffered ptomaine poisoning from eating it.

C. Harvey went to the library, so he may well be lost in the stacks.

| c5 | 5. **Use a comma to separate independent clauses if they are *short* and *parallel in structure*.** |

A. "We shall fight on the beaches, we shall fight on the landing grounds, we shall fight in the fields and in the streets, we shall fight in the hills; we shall never surrender."

—Sir Winston Churchill.

B. "It was the best of times, it was the worst of times. . . ."

—Charles Dickens.

6. Use a comma before a phrase or clause tacked on at the end of a sentence.

c6

A. "The universal brotherhood of man is our most precious possession, what there is of it."

—Mark Twain.

B. I just failed another math exam, thanks to Rob's help at the local tavern.

Note: **You can use a dash instead of a comma for greater emphasis.**

C. I just failed another math exam—thanks to Rob's help at the local tavern.

7. Use a comma to separate a direct quotation from your own words introducing it—if you quote a complete sentence.

c7

A. F. L. Lucas observes, "Most style is not honest enough."

Omit the comma if you introduce the quotation with *that* or if you quote only a part of a sentence.

B. F. L. Lucas observes that "Most style is not honest enough."
C. F. L. Lucas observes that in writing we are often "not honest enough."

If your introduction interrupts the quotation (as sometimes it should, for variety), you need to set off your own words with commas as you would any other interrupter:

> D. "Most style," observes F. L. Lucas, "is not honest enough."

c8 | **8. Use commas to set off nouns of direct address and other purely introductory or transitional expressions.**

A. **Direct address**

> Dr. Strangelove, your proposal boggles the mind.
> Your proposal, Dr. Strangelove, boggles the mind.
> Your proposal boggles the mind, Dr. Strangelove.

B. **Introductory and transitional words**

> Well, anywhere you go, there you are.
> Yes, we are now hopelessly lost.
> My, how the child has grown.
> In the first place, we must clean up the environment.
> We must, however, consider one thing first.
> We must first consider one thing, however.

c9 | **9. Use commas to separate elements in series.**

> A. Gertie ordered tomato juice, bacon and eggs, pancakes, and coffee with cream.

B. Some of the old moral values need to be revived: love, pity, compassion, honesty.

Note: **For variety you can omit the *and*, as we did in sentence B. In sentence A the comma before *and* is now optional.**

Another option: For emphasis, replace the commas with *and*s.

> C. Some of the old moral values need to be revived: love and pity and compassion and honesty.

10. Use a comma to separate adjectives in series before a noun if you can insert *and* between them. | *c10*

Suppose you want to write

> Tigers have thick short orange and black striped fur.

Can you say *thick and short?* You can. Can you say, *short and orange?* Yes. What about *orange and and?* No way. *And and black?* Surely not. *Black and striped?* Sure. *Striped and fur?* No. So you need only three commas:

> Tigers have thick, short, orange and black, striped fur.

11. Use commas to separate numerals and place names and to set off names of people from titles. | *c11*

> A. Eudora, who was born November 15, 1950, in Denver, Colorado, moved to Dallas, Texas, before she was old enough to ski.
> B. You may write to Laverne at 375 Fairview Avenue, Arlington, TX 20036.
> C. My friend Laverne lives in Arlington, Texas.
> D. Arthur Schlesinger, Jr. writes intelligently and persuasively.
> Or: Arthur Schlesinger, Jr., writes intelligently and persuasively.
> E. The committee chose Lola Lopez, attorney-at-law, to present their case.

See also *No Punctuation Necessary* for advice about where *not* to use a comma.

EXERCISE 3-7

Try your hand at putting commas in the following sentences, if needed.

1. Your new hairstyle is stunning Selma.
2. Oh I'll finish the job all right but it won't be because you inspired me.
3. My point however must not be misunderstood.
4. In the first place Heathcliff should never have taken the job.
5. Heathcliff should never have taken the job in the first place.
6. Although Irving takes his studies seriously he still flunks math regularly.
7. I said you made a slight miscalculation not a mistake.
8. The tall willowy red-haired girl with the short squinty-eyed long-haired dog is Jocasta.
9. Before getting all excited let's find out if the money is real.
10. He intends to help you not hinder you.
11. The principal without a shred of evidence accused Leonard of inciting the riot.
12. If you go out please get me some cheese crackers pickles and a quart of ice cream.
13. "Whatever you do" begged Florence "don't tell Fred."
14. Percy had a fearful time talking his way out of that scrape yet two days later he was back in trouble again.
15. Barbara's new address is 1802 Country Club Place Los Angeles CA 90029.

Comma Splice

A comma splice (or *comma fault* or *comma blunder*) occurs when a comma is used to join ("splice") two independent clauses together, instead of the necessary semicolon or colon.

1. Use a semicolon or possibly a colon—*not a comma*—to separate closely related independent clauses.

These sentences are correctly punctuated:

A. Morris has been listless all day; he appears to have a cold.
B. It's tough to tell when Morris is sick: he just lies around all day anyway.
C. Tonight he skipped dinner; Morris must be sick if he misses a meal.

If you end up with comma splices, you are probably not paying attention to the structure of your sentences. You are writing complete sentences (independent clauses) without realizing it. Study the section on independent clauses in our "Background in Grammar" chapter to be sure you know what constitutes a simple sentence.

2. Conjunctive adverbs cannot connect sentences.

There's another devilish complication that can produce comma splices. Conjunctive adverbs—transitional words like *indeed, therefore, nevertheless, however*—sound for all the world like coordinating conjunctions, *but they are not*. They cannot connect two independent clauses with only a comma the way coordinating conjunctions can. The solution to this seemingly baffling difficulty is to memorize the coordinating conjunctions: *and, but, or, for, nor, yet, so*. Then all you have to do is remember that all those other words that *sound* like pure conjunctions really are not; hence you need a semicolon.

A. It's tough to tell when Morris is sick; indeed, he just lies around all day like a rug.

One final word of warning: try not to confuse the conjunctive adverbs (listed on page 165) with subordinating conjunctions (listed on page 51). A subordinating conjunction at the beginning of a clause produces a *dependent*, not an independent, clause. Thus, you do not need a semicolon in the following sentence because there is only one independent clause.

B. It's tough to tell when Morris is sick because he just lies around all day anyway.

If you know you have difficulty with comma splices, slip a bookmark into your text to mark the list at page 51, and another at page 165. Get into the habit of checking your punctuation when you revise.

3. Independent clauses (except short, balanced ones) must be separated by something stronger than a comma.
You have all these options:

A. **Use a semicolon.**

Morris feels better today; he's outside practicing chip shots.

B. **Use a period.**

Morris feels better today. He's outside practicing chip shots.

C. **Use subordination to eliminate one independent clause.**

Morris apparently feels better today since he's outside practicing chip shots.

D. **Use a comma plus a coordinating conjunction.**

Morris feels better today, so he's outside practicing chip shots.

E. **Use a semicolon plus a conjunctive adverb.**

Morris feels better today; indeed, he's outside practicing chip shots.

EXERCISE 3-8

Correct any comma splices in the following sentences. Just to increase the challenge, we have included one that is already correct.

1. We just passed Clark Kent, he was changing his clothes in a telephone booth.
2. Doris says she doesn't want to live on a cannibal isle, she'd be bored.
3. Once a week I go out into the country and fill my lungs with clean air, this outing gives me a chance to remember what breathing used to be like.
4. Henrietta spent a grim half hour shampooing Bowser to get rid of fleas, Bowser probably preferred to keep them.
5. Hunched over her typewriter, Flossie doggedly pecks out her term paper, it isn't even due until Monday.
6. Monroe complains that his history class offers little intellectual challenge, yet he never even reads the textbook.
7. This paper is due at nine o'clock in the morning, thus you'll have to go swimming without me.
8. You can't control your temper, Throckmorton, you shouldn't be teaching a Carnegie course.
9. Seymour's a polite young man, so far as I know, he never swears.
10. My opinion of Orville is not high, because he has a closed mind, I doubt that he'll be a good teacher.

Common Noun See *Proper Noun.*

Comparison, Degrees of See *Adjectives* and *Adverbs.*

Comparisons, Incomplete or Illogical

comp

1. Comparisons must involve at least two things being compared.

A. *Incomplete:* Calculus is the hardest course.
   Improved: Calculus is the hardest course I've ever taken.
B. *Incomplete:* Eloise has fewer inhibitions.
   Improved: Eloise has fewer inhibitions now that she's Maybelle's roommate.

While the comparison in "improved" sentence B is still only implied, the meaning is easy to understand. But if you want to avoid all possibility of confusion, state the comparison flat out, like this:

   Better: Eloise has fewer inhibitions than she did before becoming Maybelle's roommate.

2. The second element of any comparison must not be ambiguous, vague, or illogical.

   Illogical: A passionate kiss is Scarlett O'Hara and Rhett Butler in *Gone with the Wind.*
   Improved: A passionate kiss is one like Rhett Butler gives Scarlett O'Hara in *Gone with the Wind.*

3. Do not compare words that denote absolutes, like *unique, omnipotent, infinite.*

   Illogical: Clovis came up with a very unique design.
   Improved: Clovis came up with a unique design.

Complement See pages 28 and 57.

Complex Sentence   See *Sentence Types.*

Compound-Complex Sentence   See *Sentence Types.*

Compound Sentence   See *Sentence Types.*

Conciseness   See *Wordiness,* page 188.

Concrete Examples   See *Coherence,* number 3.

Confused Sentence

Take care that every sentence you write makes sense.

```
mng?
```

Be careful not to begin a sentence one way, lose track in the middle, and finish another way.

A. *Confused:*   The first planned crime will tell how well a boy has learned whether or not he is caught to become a juvenile delinquent.

   Improved: Whether or not a boy is caught in his first planned crime may determine whether he will become a juvenile delinquent.

B. *Confused:*   When frequently opening and closing the oven door, it can cause a soufflé to fall.

   Improved: Frequently opening and closing the oven door can cause a soufflé to fall.

Usually such sentences result from sheer, unpardonable carelessness. You should catch them when you revise. *Do not forget to proofread.*

EXERCISE   3-9

Try to straighten out the following confused sentences. Some of them are not easy to patch up. You will need to back off and begin again in a different way.

1. The second qualification for my ideal roommate would have to be easy going.
2. Prison, bringing deprivation and degradation, is many hardships.
3. By driving too fast on the freeway, it can lower your gasoline mileage.
4. A political tone is dominant through reference to economic hardship.
5. People who are continually placed in a certain category, especially a dehumanizing one, in order to achieve an appropriate self-image.
6. We often treat strangers better than how we relate to those in our own families.
7. The difficulty in achieving goals can be determined early in an individual's development of a problem personality.
8. The flooding gets really serious and will be difficult to keep emergency vehicles running.
9. Whether a person makes the choice to go to college or not has both its problems and rewards.
10. The judge ruled that the plaintiff, even though failing to appear since ill, she could not challenge the decision.

Conjunctions, Coordinating   See *Comma Splice*, number 2.

Conjunctions, Correlative   See *Agreement (Subject and Verb)*, number 4.

Conjunctions, Subordinating

See *Comma Splice*, number 2.
See *Comma*, number 3.
For a list of subordinating conjunctions, see *Fragment*, number 2.

Conjunctive Adverb

See *Comma Splice*, number 2.
For a list of conjunctive adverbs, see *Semicolon*, number 2.

Connotation and Denotation

Words are symbols that often carry two meanings:

1. Denotative meaning—the actual person, thing, or abstract quality referred to; the term *mother*, for instance, denotes a woman who gives birth to and cares for a child.

2. Connotative meaning—those feelings usually associated with the word; the term *mother* suggests to most of us warmth, love, security, comfort, apple pie.

Whether you choose to refer to the President as a *statesman* or as a *politician* may well reveal your political sympathies. Consider, for example, Frederick Lewis Allen's description of Woodrow Wilson as a "Puritan Schoolmaster . . . cool in a time of great emotions, calmly setting the lesson for the day; the moral idealist . . . , the dogmatic prophet of democracy. . . ." The word *Puritan* suggests a moralist with no human warmth. Allen could have said *high-minded* and lessened the chill factor. And what does the word *schoolmaster* suggest that the neutral word *teacher* does not? Again, a strict, no-nonsense, unsmiling disciplinarian. The word *cool* reinforces this same feeling, as does *calmly.* The term *moral idealist* sounds at first totally complimentary—but is it? We associate idealists with good intentions, but a tinge of daydreaming unpracticality clings to the word. *Dogmatic* denotes closed-mindedness. And *prophet* suggests an aura of fanaticism, since the biblical prophets were always exhorting the fun-loving Old Testament sinners to repent of their evil ways or face the wrath of Jehovah. Allen has told us perhaps more through connotation in the sentence than he did through denotation. He uses connotative words to convey a picture of Wilson that he feels is accurate—the image of a cold, determined, perhaps misguided man with the best intentions.

Without the use of emotion-laden words, writing becomes lifeless. But you must be *aware* of connotations as you choose lively words, or you run the risk of producing unfortunate effects. Ignoring connotations can produce regrettable sentences, like this one:

Sandor moped around for a week before he killed himself.

The connotations of the phrase "moped around" are too frivolous for that statement (unless the writer has no sympathy whatsoever for Sandor). This sentence might be better:

Sandor was deeply depressed for a week before he killed himself.

Contraction   See *Apostrophe*, number 2.

Coordinating Conjunction   See *Comma Splice*, number 2.

Coordination   See *Subordination and Coordination.*

Correlative Conjunction   See *Agreement (Subject and Verb)*, number 4.

Dangling Modifier

$$\boxed{dm}$$

A *modifier* is a word, a phrase, or a clause that describes, qualifies, or in some way limits another word in the sentence.

1. Every modifier in a sentence needs a word to modify.

A.	*Dangling:*	Staring in disbelief, the car jumped the curb and crashed into a telephone booth.
	Improved:	While I stared in disbelief, the car jumped the curb and crashed into a telephone booth.
B.	*Dangling:*	When a girl of sixteen, we courted each other.
	Improved:	When I was sixteen, we courted each other.
	Improved:	When she was sixteen, we courted each other.
C.	*Dangling:*	When only seven years old, her father ran off with another woman.
	Improved:	When Marcella was only seven years old, her father ran off with another woman.

2. Be sure introductory elements have something to modify.

Unwise use of the passive voice often causes dangling modifiers. (In the last example here, *you* is understood as the subject of both *pin* and *cut.*)

Dangling: After carefully pinning on the pattern, the material may then be cut.

Improved: After carefully pinning on the pattern, you may then cut out the material.

Improved: First pin on the pattern; then cut the material.

In order to avoid dangling modifiers, think carefully about what you are writing. You can eliminate many of your modifier problems by writing consistently in the active voice: "I made a mistake," rather than "A mistake was made."

EXERCISE   **3-10**

Identify any dangling modifiers in the sentences below, and then revise to eliminate the problem.

1. After removing the reporters, the meeting resumed.
2. Driving through the lush, pine-scented forest, the air was suddenly fouled by the sulfurous belchings of a paper mill.
3. After bolting down lunch and racing madly to the station, the train left without us.
4. Looking back in history, Americans have often professed individualism while rewarding conformity.
5. The drive up there was quite scenic with its rolling hills and beautiful lakes.
6. I think love is when you get married and have children for the rest of your life.
7. Skiers like the wind blowing through their hair seeking adventure and excitement.
8. The poor child's face turned pure white and starts throwing up all over the place.
9. When writing on a formal level, dangling modifiers must be avoided.
10. After graduation, farming with a bank loan is my goal.

Dash

For quick advice, see the punctuation chart on page 68.

The dash—which requires your readers to pause—is more forceful than a comma. You can use dashes to gain emphasis, so long as you use them sparingly.

1. Use a dash to add emphasis to an idea at the end of a sentence.

Emphatic: Maybelle had only one chance—and a slim one at that.

Less emphatic: Maybelle had only one chance, and a slim one at that.

2. Use dashes instead of commas around an interrupter to emphasize the interrupting material.

To take away emphasis from an interrupter, use parentheses.

Emphatic: My cousin Caroline—the crazy one from Kankakee—is running for the legislature.

Less emphatic: My cousin Caroline, the crazy one from Kankakee, is running for the legislature.

Not emphatic: My cousin Caroline (the crazy one from Kankakee) is running for the legislature.

3. Use dashes around an interrupter if commas appear in the interrupting material.

All the dogs—Spot, Bowser, Fido, and even Old Blue—have gone camping with Cullen.

4. Use a dash following a series at the beginning of a sentence.

> Patience, sympathy, endurance, selflessness—these are what good mothers are made of.

If you want to be more formal, use a colon instead of the dash.

> *Note:* ***Do not confuse the dash with the hyphen.*** **On your typewriter, strike *two* hyphens to make a dash. To use a hyphen when you need a dash is a serious mistake: hyphens connect, dashes separate.**

Denotation See *Connotation and Denotation*

Determiner See page 27, Test 2.

Diction

mng?

d

Diction (meaning which words we choose and how we put them together) is vitally important since it affects the clarity, accuracy, and forcefulness of everything we write and say. (See also *Connotation and Denotation, Triteness, Wordiness.*)

1. Select exactly the right word.

> *Inaccurate:* I was ***disgusted*** because rain spoiled our picnic.
> *Accurate:* I was ***disappointed*** because rain spoiled our picnic.
> *Accurate:* I was ***disgusted*** by the mindless violence in the movie.

Use your dictionary to be sure the word you choose really means what you want it to mean. If you cannot think of the perfect word, consult your thesaurus for suggestions; then check the dictionary meaning of the term you select to be certain you have the right one. Even synonyms have different shades of meaning: you must keep thinking and looking until you find the precise word.

2. Do not—we repeat, *do not*—confuse words because they sound alike or are similar in meaning.

Wrong word: Today's society has been **pilfered** with a barrage of legalized drugs.

Improved: A barrage of legalized drugs has **proliferated** in today's society.

3. Use lively, concrete, specific terms.

Limp: We got into the car.
Improved: All four of us piled into Herman's Honda.

Limp: This dog came up, all excited.
Precise: "[A dog] came bounding among us with a loud volley of barks and leapt round us wagging its whole body, wild with glee at finding so many human beings together."

           —George Orwell, "A Hanging."

See also page 14.

4. Avoid bafflegab.

Bafflegab (or gobbledygook) is inflated, pretentious language that sounds impressive but obscures meaning.

Bafflegab: The production of toxic and noxious residue by hydrochloric acid obviates its efficacious application since it may prove incompatible with metallic permanence.

Translation: Don't use hydrochloric acid: it eats hell out of the pipes.

5. Avoid doublespeak.

Doublespeak is language that deliberately obscures the meaning with intent to deceive:

"protection reaction strike" (meaning **bombing**)
"to terminate with extreme prejudice" (to **assassinate**)
"that statement is inoperative" (it is **untrue**)

6. Be selective with euphemisms.

Euphemisms obscure meaning but in a benign way:

powder room (meaning **women's toilet**)
unmentionables (**underwear**)
passed away (**died**)
sanitation engineer (**garbage collector**)

Consider your audience. If you think they would be shocked by blunt language, then use a harmless euphemism.

7. Be careful with jargon and slang.

Jargon can mean the same thing as gobbledygook. But *jargon* also means the technical language used in a trade, profession, or special interest group: *printer's jargon, medical jargon, sports jargon.* If you are certain your readers will understand such specialized language, go ahead and use it. Otherwise, stick to plain English, and define any technical terms that you cannot avoid.

Slang can contribute a lively tone to *informal* writing, but you need to be sure your readers will understand current slang. Remember also that today's slang is tomorrow's cliché. Do not write vague expressions, like these:

Maybelle is simply far out.

Clyde's a real cool cat.

That movie just blew me away.

If you decide to use slang, do not apologize for it by putting it in quotation marks. Use it boldly. (See also page 6.)

8. Do not mix formal and colloquial language—unless you do so deliberately for effect.

You will give your readers a considerable jolt if you write a basically formal sentence and drop in a slang term:

One anticipates that the Boston Symphony will deliver its customary *dynamite* performance.

See also pages 191–192.

EXERCISE   3-11

All the sentences below misuse words in various ways. Point out what is wrong with each sentence, and then revise it using more effective diction.

1. *The Pawnbroker* is a heavy movie.
2. Time was when the past wasn't nearly so nostalgic.
3. This disturbed sibling does not observe sociologically compatible behavioral parameters.
4. "We will continue to fight in Vietnam until the violence stops."

        —President Lyndon B. Johnson.

5. The government apparently doesn't dig the potential disaster inherent in the problems of nuclear waste disposal.
6. The doctor asked to be appraised of any changes that might occur in the patient's condition, irregardless of the hour.
7. My dearly beloved Fido has departed this vale of tears.

8. We need to rethink this scenario in order to maximize resource utilization.
9. Several meanings can be implied from this poem.
10. Consumer elements are continuing to stress the fundamental necessity of a stabilization of the price structure at a lower level than exists at this point in time.

Digression See *Unity*.

Doublespeak See *Diction*, number 5.

Ellipsis Dots

1. **Use three spaced dots if your readers will be unable to tell that you have omitted words from a direct quotation.**

A. **Something left out at the beginning.**

> About advice, Lord Chesterfield wrote ". . . those who want it the most always like it the least."
>
> —Letter to his son, 1748.

B. **Something left out in the middle.**

> "The time has come . . . for us to examine ourselves," warns James Baldwin, "but we can only do this if we are willing to free ourselves from the myth of America and try to find out what is really happening here."
>
> —*Nobody Knows My Name.*

C. **Something left out at the end.**

> Thoreau declared that he received only one or two letters in his life "that were worth the postage" and observed summarily that "to a philosopher all *news,* as it is called, is gossip. . . ."
>
> —*Walden,* Chapter 2.

Note: **The extra dot is the period.**

2. **If you are quoting only a part of a sentence—and your readers can *tell*—do not use ellipsis dots.**

> Occasionally, like Eliot's Prufrock, we long to be "scuttling across the floors of silent seas."
> Judge William Sessions describes himself as a "West Texas tough guy" and subscribes to a law-and-order philosophy.

3. **Use either ellipsis dots or a dash to indicate an unfinished statement, especially in recording conversation.**

> "But, I don't know whether . . . ," Bernice began.
> "How could you . . . ?" Ferdinand faltered.

Elliptical Construction   See *Case of Pronouns,* number 4.

Emphasis

Work especially hard on the beginnings and ends of things—of sentences, of paragraphs, of essays—because those are the positions which require the most emphasis.

Any time you vary the normal pattern of your writing, you gain emphasis. Try the following variations:

1. **Periodic sentences.**
Save the word or words conveying the main idea until the end (just before the period):

> One thing they assuredly do not run at Bob Jones University is a democracy.
>
> —Larry L. King.

2. **Balanced sentences.**
Make all grammatical elements balance precisely:

> Wherever you go, I will go; and wherever you lodge, I will lodge; your people shall be my people, and your god my god; wherever you die, I will die, and there will I be buried.
>
> —Ruth, I:16–17.

See also pages 86–88.

3. *Ands* **to separate a series.**
Instead of commas, use *ands* to emphasize items in series:

> It is his privilege to help man endure by lifting his heart, by reminding him of the courage and honor and hope and pride and compassion and pity and sacrifice which have been the glory of his past.
>
> —William Faulkner.

4. **Dashes.**
Set off with dashes elements you want to emphasize.

A. **At the beginning:**

> Cardinals, blue jays, finches, doves—all come to frisk in the fountain.

B. **In the middle:**

> The trial allowed—indeed, required—a jury to pick between numerous flatly incompatible theories spun by credentialed experts.
>
> —George F. Will.

C. **At the end:**

> Dandy ideas these—or so it seemed at the beginning.
>
> —John Hurt Fischer.

See also pages 119–120.

5. **Deliberate repetition.**
Repeat key words deliberately for emphasis:

> Her working-class, middle-aged life was buffeted by an abusive husband, an abusive son, and a series of abusive supervisors at a succession of low-level jobs.
>
> —Hugh Drummond, M.D.

See also pages 162–163.

6. **Short sentences.**
A short-short sentence following sentences of normal length will get attention:

> If there is to be a new etiquette, it ought to be based on honest mutual respect, and responsiveness to each other's needs. Regardless of sex.
>
> —Lois Gould.

7. **A one-sentence paragraph.**
Punctuate a single sentence as a paragraph to make it extremely emphatic.

Euphemism See *Diction,* number 6.

Exclamation Point

! 1. **Do not use exclamation points merely to give punch to ordinary sentences. Write a good, emphatic sentence instead.**

> *Ineffective:* LeRoy's room was a terrible mess!
> *Improved:* We declared LeRoy's room a disaster area.

2. **Use exclamation points following genuine exclamations:**

> O kind missionary, O compassionate missionary, leave China! Come home and convert these Christians!
> —Mark Twain, "The United States of Lyncherdom."

> I'm mad as hell, and I'm not going to take it anymore!
> —Paddy Chayefsky, *Network.*

Note: **Avoid stacking up punctuation. Do not put a comma after an exclamation point or after a question mark.**

See also *Quotation Marks,* number 8.

Expletive

1. **An *expletive* can be an oath or exclamation, often profane.**
You will have no trouble thinking of the four-letter ones, so we will mention some socially acceptable ones: Thunderation! Tarnation! Drat! Oh, fudge! Use only when reproducing conversation.

2. **The words *it* and *there*, also expletives, serve as "filler" words to allow for variety in sentence patterns.**

> **It** is raining.
> **There** are two ways to solve the problem.

See also *Agreement* (*Subject and Verb*), number 7.

Figures of Speech

Figures of speech involve the imaginative use of language and can give your writing greater vividness and clarity, if used effectively.

1. **Metaphors and similes.**

These devices are imaginative comparisons characteristic of poetry but used frequently in prose.

> **A.** A **metaphor** is an **implied** comparison.
>   Clarence was a lion in the fight.
> **B.** A **simile** is a **stated** comparison (with **like** or **as**).
>   Clarence was like a lion in the fight.

The term *metaphor* now serves to describe both figures of speech. Here are some examples used in prose by professional writers:

> New York is a sucked orange.
> —R. W. Emerson.

> Like soft, watery lightning went the wandering snake at the crowd.
> —D. H. Lawrence.

> His voice was as intimate as the rustle of sheets.
> —Dorothy Parker.

The [courtroom] was as dismal and breathless as a tenement fire escape in August.

—Katherine Anne Porter.

See also *Analogy*.

2. Extended metaphors.

Skillful writers sometimes write imaginative comparisons that go on for several sentences, perhaps for a full paragraph, like this one describing the trials of editing bad prose:

And so, anticipating no literary treat, I plunged into the forest of words of my first manuscript. My weapons were a sturdy eraser and several batteries of sharpened pencils. My armor was a thesaurus. And if I should become lost, a near-by public library was a landmark, and the Encyclopedia of Social Sciences on its reference shelves was an ever-ready guide.

—Samuel T. Williamson.

3. Mixed metaphors.

Be careful of metaphors that do not compare accurately— that start off one way and end another way:

A. Our quarterback plowed through their defense and skyrocketed across the goal lines.
B. The FTC does nothing but sit on its hands and fiddle while Rome burns.

Remember: **Figures of speech should clarify the meaning through comparisons that increase understanding. Ambiguity fascinates the mind in poetry but tries the patience in expository prose. So, be creative; but when you revise, be sure that your metaphors clarify rather than confuse.**

4. **Personification.**

Personification means giving human characteristics to non-human things (objects or animals). Use with restraint.

> The missiles lurk in their silos, grimly waiting for the inevitable day when at last they will perform their duty.

5. **Avoid *trite* figures of speech.** See *Triteness*.

Formal Usage   See the discussion of levels of usage in Chapter 4, the "Glossary of Usage" (pages 191–192).

Fragment

$$frag$$

1. **A sentence fragment is only part of a sentence punctuated as a whole.**

Many professional writers use fragments for emphasis, or simply for convenience, as in the portions we have italicized and made boldface in the following examples:

> Man is the only animal that blushes. ***Or needs to.***
> —Mark Twain.

> I did not whisper excitedly about my Boyfriends. ***For the best of reasons.*** I did not have any.
> —Gwendolyn Brooks.

> This leaves me with only the dog and the wood duck and my own shortsighted blundering into other people's apartments and tulip beds, to deal with. ***Which is just as well.***
> —James Thurber.

> ***Easy to say, but hard to practice.***
> —F. L. Lucas.

We shall no doubt learn of a suitor for [Chrysler's] hand in a take-over move. ***Maybe Volkswagen, even though such a deal has been denied. Maybe one of a half-dozen cash-laden oil companies.***

—Paul Samuelson.

So Shelly asked her what was "real" and the student responded instantly. "Television." ***Because you could see it.***

—Harlan Ellison.

2. Avoid fragments in formal writing (term papers, business reports, scholarly essays).

Fragment:	Pollution poses a serious problem. ***Which we had better solve.***
Complete:	Pollution poses a serious problem—which we had better solve.
Complete:	Pollution poses a serious problem which we had better solve.

Note: **If you write fragments accidentally, remember that a simple sentence beginning with one of the following subordinating words will come out a fragment:**

after	before	so that	until	which
although	if	still	when	while
as, as if	only	though	whenever	
as far as	since	till	where	
because	so as	unless	whereas	

Fragment:	Although I warned him time after time.
Complete:	I warned him time after time.
Complete:	Although I warned him time after time, Clyde continued to curse and swear.

Note: **Words ending in *-ing* and *-ed* can cause fragments also. Although such words sound like verbs,** sometimes they're *verbals*—actually nouns or adjectives. Every complete sentence requires an honest-to-goodness verb.

Fragment: Singing and skipping along the beach.
Complete: Juan went singing and skipping along the beach.
Fragment: Abandoned by friends and family alike.
Complete: Alice was abandoned by friends and family alike.
Complete: Abandoned by friends and family alike, Alice at last recognized the evils of alcohol.

3. Use fragments in asking and answering questions, even in formal writing:

When should the reform begin? At once.

How? By throwing self-serving politicians out of office.

4. Use fragments for recording conversation, since people do not always speak in complete sentences:

"I suppose that during all [my sickly childhood] you were uneasy about me?"

"Yes, the whole time."

"Afraid I wouldn't live?"

After a reflective pause, ostensibly to think out the facts, "No—afraid you would."   —Mark Twain, *Autobiography.*

5. Be sure that two constructions connected with a semicolon are complete sentences.

Questionable: He looked a lot like Quasimodo; although I couldn't see him too well.
Improved: He looked a lot like Quasimodo, although I couldn't see him too well.
Improved: He looked a lot like Quasimodo; I couldn't see him too well, though.

EXERCISE 3-12

Some of the following constructions are not complete sentences. Correct the ones that you consider faulty. Defend the ones that you find effective.

1. Marion was late to his own wedding. To his eternal sorrow.
2. Broadcasting moment-by-moment, hour-by-hour, day-by-day reports.
3. What is the best policy? To do nothing—diplomatically.
4. Wealth, a taking advantage of another's resources by materialistic means.
5. A slow taking over, a slow control of the economy leading eventually into a usurpation of political principles.
6. The executive, who at the end of the day, can return to the comforts of home.
7. As an explorer with an intellectual curiosity, the scientific undoer of a riddle by empirical means.
8. One in which she was dictator, and because she was dictator, she held the reins.
9. A society's ignorance of a condition of human wants and needs.
10. Our highways, bridges, and water systems must be repaired. Regardless of the cost.

Function Words See pages 45–55.

Fused Sentence See *Run-On Sentence*.

Generalizations See *Coherence*, number 3.

Hyphen

div

-

Unlike exclamation points, hyphens are much in fashion today as a stylistic device.

1. Hyphenate descriptive phrases used as a whole to modify a noun.

George needs to get rid of his holier-than-thou attitude.

2. Hyphenate compound adjectives when they come before the noun.

ivy-covered walls	up-to-date entries
high-speed railroads	lighter-than-air balloon

3. Omit the hyphen if the descriptive phrase comes after the noun.

walls covered with ivy	entries that were up to date
railroads running at high speed	a balloon lighter than air

4. Hyphenate most compound words beginning with *self-* and *ex.*

self-employed	ex-wife
self-deluded	ex-slave
self-abuse	ex-President

5. Never use a hyphen in the following words.

yourself	himself	itself
themselves	herself	selfless
ourselves	myself	selfish
oneself (or one's self)		

6. **Consult your dictionary about other compound words.**
Some words change function depending on whether written as one word or two:

Verb: Where did I **slip up?**
Noun: I made a **slipup** somewhere.

7. **Use a hyphen to divide words at the end of a line.**
Divide only between syllables. Consult your dictionary if in doubt. Never put a hyphen at the beginning of a line.

8. **Use no hyphen between an adverb ending in -*ly* and an adjective:**

Stanley is a hopelessly dull date.
His conversation is endlessly self-centered.

Idioms

Idioms are expressions peculiar to the language for which there are no grammatical explanations. For instance, we say, "I disagree **with** that statement," but "I disapprove **of** that statement." Most of the time native speakers have no trouble with idiomatic prepositions, the ones which cause considerable grief for adults trying to learn the English language from scratch. But sometimes even native speakers choose the wrong preposition and write bothersome sentences like this one:

Unidiomatic: The young couple soon became bored **of** each other.

That should read,

Correct: The young couple soon became bored **with** each other.

If you sometimes write unidiomatic expressions, you should, during the editing process, find someone to read your paper who can tell you if your prepositions are correct.

Idioms Often Misused*

Wrong	Right
to my opinion	in my opinion
regardless to	regardless of
insight to	insight into
to dispense of	to dispense with
first step of success	first step toward success
opportunity of work	opportunity to work
to identify to	to identify with
job on the field	job in the field
aptitude toward	aptitude for
education depends of	education depends on
satisfied of	satisfied with
on the future	in the future

Infinitive See *Split Infinitive* and also page 33.

Informal Usage See the discussion of selecting usage levels on pages 191–192.

Interjection See *Exclamation Point* and also page 54.

Intransitive Verb See page 35.

Irregular Verb See *Tense*, number 6.

* Adapted from Mina Shaughnessy, *Errors and Expectations* (New York: Oxford UP): 192–93.

Italics See *Underlining.*

Jargon See *Diction,* number 7.

Levels of Usage See pages 191–192.

slk

Linking Verb

Linking verbs connect the subject of the sentence with the complement.

The most common linking (or copulative, as they used to be bluntly called) verbs are these: *to be, to feel, to appear, to seem, to look, to become, to smell, to sound, to taste.* See also *Adverb/Adjective Confusion,* number 4.

logic

Logic

Your purpose in writing is to convey your thoughts into the heads of your readers, but in order to be convincing, your thoughts must be logical. You should be aware of the most common pitfalls of slippery logic so that you can avoid them in your own thinking and writing, as well as detect them in the arguments of others.

1. **Avoid oversimplifying.**

Most of us have a tendency to like things reduced to orderly, easily grasped *either-or* answers. The only problem is that things are seldom that simple. Be wary of arguments that offer no middle way—the "either we continue to build nuclear weapons or the Russians will wipe us out" sort of reasoning.

2. Avoid stereotyping.

Stereotypes involve set notions about the way different types of people behave. Homosexuals, according to the stereotype, are all neurotic, promiscuous, immoral people bent only on sex and seduction. Such stereotypes seldom give a truthful picture of anyone in the group and could never accurately describe all the members.

3. Avoid faulty (sweeping or hasty) generalizations.

You will do well to question easy solutions to complex problems. A faulty generalization (broad statement) can result from stating opinion as fact:

> Rock music causes grave social problems by creating an attitude of irresponsibility in the listener.

The statement needs evidence to prove its claim, and such proof would be nearly impossible to find. Since you cannot avoid making general statements, be careful to avoid making them without sufficient evidence. At least, *qualify* your assertions.

> *Sweeping:* **All** Siamese cats are nervous.
> *Better:* **Many** Siamese cats are nervous.

Statements involving *all, none, everything, nobody,* and *always* are tough to prove. Instead, try *some, many, sometimes,* and *often.*

4. Watch for hidden premises.

Another sort of generalization that is likely to deceive involves a *hidden premise* (a basic idea underlying the main statement). This observation, upon first reading, may sound entirely plausible:

> If those anti-nuke demonstrators had left when the police told them
> to, there would have been no trouble, and no one would have been
> injured.

The hidden premise here assumes that all laws are just and
fairly administered; that all actions of the government are hon-
orable and in the best interest of all citizens. The statement
presumes, in short, that the demonstrators had no right or reason to be there and hence were wrong not to leave when told
to do so. Such a presumption overlooks the possibility that in a
free country the demonstrators might legitimately protest the
right of the police to silence their original protests.

5. Do not dodge the issue.

People use a number of handy fallacies in order to sidestep
a problem while appearing to pursue the point. One of the
most effective—and most underhanded—involves playing on
the emotional reactions, prejudices, fears, and ignorance of
your readers instead of directly addressing the issue.

> If we allow sex education in the public schools, the moral fiber of
> the nation will be endangered, human beings will become like
> animals, and the Communists will just walk right in and take over.

That sentence, which contains no evidence whatever to prove
that sex education is either good or bad, merely attempts to
make it sound scary.

In a variation of this technique (called *ad hominem*), people sometimes attack the person they are arguing with, rather
than the issue being argued. They call their opponents "ef-
fete, effeminate snobs" and hope nobody notices that they
have not actually said anything to the point.

Another favorite dodge is called *begging the question* or
circular argument. You offer as evidence arguments which
assume as true the very thing you are trying to prove. You say

that pornography is evil because pornography is evil, but you have to say it fancy, like this:

> If we want a society of people who devote their time to base and sensuous things, then pornography may be harmless. But if we want a society in which the noble side is encouraged and mankind itself is elevated, then I submit that pornography is surely harmful.
>
> —John Mitchell.

6. Keep an open mind.

Thinking is your best defense against logical fallacies. Think while you are reading or listening and think some more before you write. Be prepared to change your mind. Instead of hunting for facts to shore up your present opinions, let the facts you gather lead you to a conclusion. And do not insist on a nice, tidy, clear-cut conclusion. Sometimes there isn't one. Your conclusion may well be that both sides for various reasons have a point. Simply work to discover what you honestly believe to be the truth of the matter, and set that down, as clearly and convincingly as you can.

See also *Analogy, Coherence, Connotation and Denotation,* and *Unity.*

Misplaced Modifier

mm

Keep modifiers close to what they modify (describe, limit, or qualify).

Faulty: Once married, the church considers that a couple has signed up for a lifetime contract.

Improved: The church considers that a couple, once married, has signed up for a lifetime contract.

Faulty: I had been driving for forty years when I fell asleep at the wheel and had an accident.

Improved: Although I had driven safely for forty years, last night I fell asleep at the wheel and had an accident.

EXERCISE   3-13

In the following sentences move any misplaced modifiers so that the statements make better sense.

1. Also soft and cuddly, the main appeal of a kitten is its playfulness.
2. Registration assignments will not be accepted from students until the door attendant has punched them.
3. Although similar in detail, my purpose is to show how these two sea urchins differ.
4. Clem was robbed at gunpoint in the elevator where he lives.
5. At college I hope to start singing with a scholarship.
6. A crutch is a device to take the weight off an injured leg or foot by sticking it under the arm and leaning on it.
7. When I got there, I saw two men putting on ghost costumes just like the ones that robbed my house.
8. I found a marble that looked like candy walking home from church.
9. I do not see my Aunt Frieda much in Colorado.
10. Maribelle told her first falsehood in a panic by telephone.

Mixed Construction   See *Confused Sentence.*

Modifiers   See *Dangling Modifier.*
                  See *Misplaced Modifier.*
                  See *Squinting Modifier.*

Mood   See *Verbs,* page 32, and *Subjunctive Mood.*

Nominal   See *Nouns,* page 29.

Nonrestrictive Clause   See *Comma*, number 2.

No Punctuation Necessary

no punc

William Blake wrote that "The road of excess leads to the palace of wisdom," but all of us English teachers are sure that he was not referring to commas. If you are a comma fiend, you may be the victim of the ill-conceived and misleading rule that says commas belong wherever you would pause in speaking. That rule simply does not work: we pause far too often in speech, and different speakers pause in different places. Here are some situations that seem particularly tempting to comma abusers.

1. **When main sentence parts are long.**
   Some writers mistakenly separate the subject from the verb or the verb from the complement, like this:

   A. *Wrong:*   Tall people with large feet, are particularly good autoharp players.
   B. *Wrong:*   By the end of the year we all understood, that using too many commas would make us grow hair on our palms.

Neither of those sentences should have a comma in it. In sentence B, the clause serves as the direct object of the verb *understood* and thus should not be set off with a comma.

2. **When a restrictive clause occurs in the sentence.**
   Putting a comma on one end of an adjective clause and no punctuation at all on the other end is never correct. Nonrestrictive clauses always need punctuation on both ends (see *Comma*, number 1), and restrictive ones need no punctuation. Avoid errors like this one:

> *Wrong:* Ruthie's poem that compared a school to a prison, was the most moving one she read.

No comma is necessary in that sentence.

3. **When the word *and* appears in the sentence.**
Some people always put a comma before the word *and*, and they are probably right more than half the time. It's correct to put a comma before *and* when it joins a series or when it joins independent clauses. But when *and* does not do either of those things, a comma before it is usually inappropriate. This sentence, for instance, should have no comma:

> *Wrong:* Mark called the telephone company to complain about his bill, and got put on "hold" for an hour.

Noun See page 26.

Numbers

1. **Spell out numbers one hundred and under.**

2. **In general, write numbers over one hundred in figures.**

3. **Spell out round numbers requiring only a couple of words (two hundred tons, five thousand dollars).**
If a series of numbers occurs in a passage, and some of them are over one hundred, use figures for all of them.

4. **Always use figures for addresses (27 White's Place), for times (1:05 P.M.), for dates (October 12, 1950), and for decimals, code and serial numbers, percentages, measurements, and source references.**

Exception: **Never begin a sentence with a numeral; spell it out or rewrite the sentence.**

Object   See *Prepositions,* page 48; *Complement,* page 28; and Figure 2-1.

Overburdened Sentence

Do not try to cram more into one sentence than it can conveniently hold.

> The plot concerns a small boy, somewhat neglected by his mother, a recently divorced working woman who is evidently having a difficult time keeping her family, her emotions, and her household together, who discovers by mysterious means and befriends a small, adorable extraterrestrial creature.

That's just too much. It should be divided into two more graceful sentences.

> Two of the story's characters are a small boy and his somewhat negligent mother, a recently divorced working woman who is evidently having a difficult time keeping her family, her emotions, and her household together. By mysterious means, the boy discovers and befriends a small, adorable extraterrestrial creature.

Paragraph

The proofreader's mark ¶ means that your instructor thinks you should indent to begin a new paragraph at that point. When all your sentences are closely related, sometimes you forget to give your readers a break by dividing paragraphs.

Remember to indent when you shift topics or shift aspects of a topic. For instance, look at the break between the preceding paragraph and this one. Both of these paragraphs are on the same subject (paragraphing), but the topic shifts from *why* to begin a new paragraph to *when* to begin a new paragraph. Because of this shift, we indented.

When you notice that you have written a paragraph over eight sentences long, it may be time to look for places to break it into two separate paragraphs.

paral **Parallel Structure** See *Balanced Sentence*, page 86.

( ) **Parentheses**

For quick advice, see the punctuation chart in Table 3-1 at the beginning of this chapter.

1. **Use parentheses around parts of a sentence or paragraph that you would speak aloud as an aside.**

A slight digression or some incidental information that you do not particularly want to emphasize belongs in parentheses.

A. John Stuart Mill (1806–1873) promoted the idea of women's equality with men.

B. Although Clyde has lapses of memory (often he forgets what he went to the store to buy), he is the best auditor in the company.

2. **Sometimes you will choose parentheses to separate a part of a sentence that could be enclosed in commas.**

Commas separate material that is directly relevant to the main passage, and parentheses separate material that is indirectly related or less crucial. When you use dashes around a part of a sentence, they strongly stress that part, as neither commas nor parentheses do.

3. **Use parentheses around numerals when you number a list.**

Her professor did three things that bothered her: (1) he called her "honey," even though he didn't know her; (2) he graded the class on a curve, even though there were only ten students; (3) he complained that male students no longer wore suit coats and ties to class.

4. **Punctuation goes inside the parentheses if it punctuates just the words inside.**

Consumers can use their power by boycotting a product. (The word *boycott* is from Captain Charles C. Boycott, whose neighbors in Ireland ostracized him in 1880 for refusing to reduce the high rents he charged.)

5. **Punctuation goes outside the parentheses if it punctuates more than just the enclosed material.**

The comma does this in example 1B above. A numbered list, like that in number 3, is the *only* case in which you may put a comma, semicolon, colon, or dash before an opening parenthesis.

EXERCISE   **3-14**

Choose the best punctuation (parentheses, dashes, commas, or brackets) to put in place of the carats in the sentences below. Remember, dashes **stress,** parentheses **play down,** and commas **separate** for clarity.

1. The 1960 *World Book* encyclopedia claims that smoking marijuana ˄ *cannabis sativa* ˄ causes fits of violence.

2. I tasted his omelette and found ˅ how disgusting! ˅ that it was runny inside.
3. Stewart Alsop ˅ who my mother claims is a distant relation of ours ˅ was a well-known conservative journalist.
4. People often mistakenly think that Lenin ˅ our black and white cat ˅ was named after John Lennon of the Beatles.
5. Bateson includes in his reading list the "elongated biographical pieties ˅ about Carlyle ˅ of D. A. Wilson." (Bateson is reviewing D. A. Wilson's book, and you added the phrase "about Carlyle" to Bateson's words.)
6. Maria ran the entire obstacle course in record time ˅ three minutes!
7. Hubert ˅ the coordinator of our newsletter ˅ says he will crack up unless we get more typists.
8. If you are going to get married ˅ and most people eventually do ˅ you must not develop rigid daily habits.
9. Edgar Allen Poe ˅ 1809–1849 ˅ believed that beauty was the goal of poetry.
10. He thought ˅ in fact, he knew ˅ that if he continued his life of crime, he would one day find himself at the bottom of the river.

Participle   See *Verbs*, page 30.
See *Adjectives*, page 37.
See *Tense*.

Participle Endings

Do not omit the *-ed* from the ends of participles.

An adjective formed from a verb is called a participle. Examples are

a tired writer (from ***tire***)

an embarrassing moment (from ***embarrass***)

a delayed reaction (from ***delay***)

Many of the participles ending in *-ed* are said aloud without the *-ed* sound; thus, sometimes you forget to put the ending on in writing. Some examples of this error we have seen are

old fashion ice cream
air condition theater
vine ripen tomatoes
prejudice attitudes

Those phrases should read:

old-fashioned ice cream
air-conditioned theater
vine-ripened tomatoes
prejudiced attitudes

Passive Voice

pass

Passive voice contrasts with active voice as you can see in the following examples:

A. *Active:* My daughter solved the problem.
B. *Passive:* The problem was solved by my daughter.
C. *Passive:* The problem was solved.

In active voice, the agent of the action (the person who does the solving, in this case) is also the subject of the sentence. In passive voice, the agent of the action is not the subject of the sentence. In both example B and example C, even though the daughter did the solving, *problem* is the subject of the sentence, and in example C, the daughter is left out altogether and gets no credit for her ingenuity.

| . |

Period

Use a period at the end of a complete declarative sentence and after most abbreviations (see *Abbreviation*).

If a sentence ends with an abbreviation, let its period serve as the final period of the sentence, too: do not double up.

Personification   See *Figures of Speech.*

| p*h* |

Phrase

A phrase is a string of words that does not include a subject and verb combination. See *Phrases*, pages 55–59.

Point of View   See *Shifts in Tense and Person.*

Possessives   See *Apostrophe.*
              See *Case of Pronouns.*

Possessives with Gerunds

1. **A gerund is a verbal ending in *-ing* that serves as a noun in a sentence.**

  A. Squishing cake between your toes is a sensual pleasure.

Squishing is the subject of the sentence, and thus acts as a noun.

B. He got back at the telephone company by folding his computer billing card each month.

Folding is the object of a preposition, and thus acts as a noun.

2. **Use possessive nouns and pronouns before gerunds because gerunds act as nouns.**

You probably would not forget to use a possessive before a regular noun in a sentence like this:

A. I was embarrassed by John's insensitivity.

But you may forget to use the possessive before a gerund. The preferred usage is as follows:

B. I was embarrassed by John's popping out his glass eye to attract the waitress's attention.

Not "*John* popping out his glass eye."

C. I disapproved of his acting so indelicately.

Not "*him* acting so indelicately."

If you have other problems with possessives, see *Apostrophe.*

Predicate

The predicate of a sentence is the verb plus the complement (if there is one).

Predicate Adjective   See *Adjectives,* page 37.

Predicate Nominative

A predicate nominative is a noun or a nominal that follows the *to be* verb and renames the subject of the sentence.

faulty pred

Predication, Faulty

1. **This error comes from not rereading your sentences closely enough. A sentence with faulty predication is one whose predicate adjective or predicate noun does not match the subject in meaning.**

A. *Faulty:*   Your first big city is an event that changes your whole outlook if you grew up in a small town.
B. *Faulty:*   The importance of graceful hip movement is essential when doing the Bump.
C. *Faulty:*   Smoothness and precision are among the basic problems encountered by beginning dancers.

In sentence A, a city is not really an event; in B, the writer probably did not want to say something as banal as "importance is essential"; and in C, smoothness and precision are not problems.

To correct such errors, you can revise the subject, the predicate, or both to make them match up better. Here are possible revisions of our problem sentences:

A. *Improved:*   Your first visit to a big city is an experience that changes your whole outlook if you grew up in a small town.
B. *Improved:*   Graceful hip movement is essential when doing the Bump.
C. *Improved:*   Roughness and imprecision are among the weaknesses of beginning dancers.

2. **Your predication can be merely weak instead of utterly illogical. Important words should appear as the subject and predicate.**

> *Weak:* One important point of his speech was the part in which he stressed self-reliance.

The key subject and predicate words are *point . . . was . . . part*, which do not carry much meaning in the sentence. Here's an improvement:

> *Improved:* At one important point, his speech emphasized self-reliance.

Now the key subject and predicate words are *speech . . . emphasized . . . self-reliance*, which are more meaningful.

Preposition   See page 48.

Pronoun   See page 45.
See *Agreement (Pronoun and Antecedent)*.
See *Case of Pronouns*.
See *Reference of Pronouns*.

Proper Noun

A common noun names a class (like *dog, city*); a proper noun names a specific person, place, or thing (like *Rover, Chicago*).

Qualification

Avoid making absolute statements in writing:

Avoid: My gym instructor is never wrong.
Avoid: Cats are finicky.

Instead, qualify your remarks:

Better: My gym instructor is seldom wrong.
Better: Cats are often finicky.
Better: My cats are finicky.

---

quot

, ,

Quotation Marks

Quotation marks are among the most confusing marks of punctuation, perhaps because they serve so many different functions. We hope to clear up any confusion in your mind by first showing you the uses of quotation marks and then showing how to use other punctuation in combination with them. Here are the uses:

1. Put quotation marks around words that you copy just as they were written or spoken, whether they are complete or partial sentences.

A. "Gloria, please don't practice your quacky duck imitation while I'm trying to do my income tax," she said.
B. She said that Gloria's barnyard imitations made her "feel like moving to New York for some peace and quiet."

2. A quotation within a quotation should have single quotation marks around it.

I remarked, "I've disliked him ever since he said I was 'a typical product of the midwest,' whatever that means."

Do not panic if you read a book or article that reverses double and single quotation marks (that is, uses single around quotations and double around quotations within quotations). The British do it the opposite of the American way, so that book or article is probably British.

3. **If you paraphrase (i.e., change words from the way they were written or spoken), you are using indirect quotation and you need not use quotation marks.**

A. She said that Gloria's pig grunt was particularly disgusting.

Her actual words were, "Gloria's pig grunt is the worst of all."

B. He told me that he loathed levity.

He actually said, "I despise levity."

4. **When you write dialogue (conversation between two or more people), give each new speaker a new paragraph. But still put related nondialogue sentences in the same paragraph.**

After our visitor finally left, I was able to ask my question. "What did he mean by 'a typical product of the midwest'?" I said.

"Maybe he meant you were sweet and innocent," Mark suggested.

"Fat chance," I replied. "He probably meant I was corny." I doubt that he was that clever, though.

5. **Put quotation marks around titles of works that you think of as *part* of a book or magazine rather than a whole by itself: articles, stories, chapters, essays, short poems. *Do not*, however, *put quotation marks around titles of your own essays.***

Examples:

"Petrified Man," a short story by Eudora Welty
"We Real Cool," a poem by Gwendolyn Brooks
"My View of History," an essay by Arnold Toynbee

6. Underline the titles of works you think of as a *whole*: books, magazines, journals, newspapers, plays, and movies (*Walden*, *The New York Times*, *Casablanca*). Also underline the names of works of visual art (Dali's painting, *Civil War*).

Note: **Italics in print mean the same thing as underlining by hand or on a typewriter.**

7. Do not use underlining or quotation marks around the titles of series (Masterpiece Theatre) **or parts of books** (Preface, Appendix, Index).

8. Underline or put quotation marks around words used as words.

A. You used but and and too often in that sentence.
B. He thought "sophisticated" referred only to stylishness.

9. In general, do not put quotation marks around words that you suspect are too slangy.
It's tempting to do this:

A. *Weak:* Phys ed was really a "drag."
B. *Weak:* On the first day of class, my philosophy instructor showed that he was really "hot" on the subject.

But you should take the time to decide whether the informality suits your style or not. If it does, there's no need to set it off with quotation marks. If it does not, you should find a more fitting expression. In sentence A, since the writer used the slangy, abbreviated form of physical education, the informal word *drag* is suitable without any quotation marks. In B, the writer should probably substitute *enthusiastic about* for *"hot" on.*

Do not use quotation marks as a written sneer, either. Learn to express your feelings in a more exact way

10. Periods and commas always go inside quotation marks.

A. "Never eat at a restaurant named *Mom's*," my brother always said.
B. In James Joyce's story "Eveline," the main character is at once frightened and attracted by freedom.

Notice in examples 1A and 4 that we substitute a comma for the period at the end of a quoted sentence when the sentence is followed by tag words (like *he whined, she said, Gloria grunted*). When tag words interrupt a quoted sentence, the first part of the quotation as well as the tag words needs a comma after it:

C. "I must admit," Seymour said, "that Gloria sounds more like a rooster than anyone else I know."

11. Colons, semicolons, and dashes always go outside the quotation marks.

"If at first you don't succeed, try, try again"; "It takes all kinds"; "You can't get something for nothing": these shallow mottos were his entire philosophy of life.

12. Exclamation points and question marks go inside the quotation marks if they are part of the quotation and outside if they are not.

A. "That man called me 'Babycakes'!" Sandra screeched.
B. He said, "Hey there, Babycakes, whatcha doin' tonight?"
C. Isn't that what my father calls "an ungentlemanly advance"?

EXERCISE   3-15

Add single or double quotation marks or underlining to these items if needed.

1. Did you see the article Dietmania in *Newsweek?* she asked.
2. He called Gloria's performance an embarrassment to man and beast.
3. Until I heard Gloria, I thought that oink was the basic pig sound.
4. At first, Gloria said, I just did easy ones like ducks and lambs.
5. In March she mourned, I will never get the emu call right; however, by May she had learned it perfectly.
6. Deedee calls everything cute or nice.
7. Did you say a good life or a good wife? she asked.
8. After I read the story Death in the Woods, I reexamined my life.
9. The grass is always greener on the other side of the fence: I surely found this saying true.
10. Look! There's Patty! the bank customers yelped.

Redundance

red

    If you are not considering your word choice carefully, you can accidentally pile up two or more words that say the same thing, like these:

emotional feelings
round in shape
earthtone shades of color
fatally murdered

To avoid this redundance, just *emotions, round, earthtones,* and *murdered* would serve.

Redundant Prepositions

Avoid using a preposition at the end of any sentence involving *where.*

Colloquial:	Can you tell me where the action's at?
Standard:	Can you tell me where the action is?
Colloquial:	Where is our money going to?
Standard:	Where is our money going?

Reference of Pronouns

1. **Make sure pronouns have clear antecedents.**
   Pronouns are useful words that stand in for nouns so that we do not have to be forever repeating the same word (see page 45). Occasionally pronouns cause trouble, though, when readers cannot tell for sure *what* noun the pronoun stands for (or refers to). Say you write

A. Seymour gave Selma her pet parrot.

There's no problem: *her* clearly means Selma. But suppose you write instead

B. Seymour gave Clyde his pet parrot.

Instant ambiguity: *his* could mean either Seymour's or Clyde's. In order to avoid baffling your readers in this fashion, you must rephrase such constructions in a way that makes the pronoun reference clear.

C. Seymour gave his pet parrot to Clyde.

or

D. Clyde got his pet parrot from Seymour.

If you have difficulty with vague pronoun reference, start checking pronouns when you proofread. Be sure each pronoun refers clearly to only *one* noun. And be sure that noun is fairly close, preferably in the same sentence. You cannot expect your readers to track back two or three sentences to find the antecedent for a pronoun.

2. **Use *this* and *which* with care.**

Whenever you use the word *this*, try to follow it with a noun telling what *this* refers to. We're naturally lazy and take advantage of such a handy word which can be a pronoun and stand there all by itself meaning nothing in particular. Naturally, *this* will mean something to you when you write it, but you must be sure that the idea also gets onto the page. Too often *this* refers to an abstract idea or to a whole cluster of ideas in a paragraph, and your readers would require divine guidance to figure out exactly what you had in mind. So, if you write

A. The importance of this becomes clear when we understand the alternatives.

at least give your reader a clue: "this *principle*," "this *qualification*," "this *stalemate*" or even "this *problem*," if you cannot pinpoint the meaning any better than that. It takes extra time and energy, even though you may know exactly what you mean. But searching for a single word to express the idea sharpens your thinking and helps your readers understand you. If every *this* is followed by a noun, you are probably being clear.

Which causes similar problems. Often this handy pronoun refers to the entire clause preceding it. Sometimes the meaning is clear, sometimes not. Suppose you write

B. Jocasta has received only one job offer, which depresses her.

That sentence can be interpreted in two different ways:

C. Jocasta is depressed about receiving only one job offer, even though it *is* a fairly good job.

or

D. Jocasta has received only one job offer—a depressing one, at that.

Remember that such ambiguity is undesirable in expository prose. Check every *this* and *which* to be sure your readers will understand these words to mean exactly what you intended.

Look up *Agreement (Pronoun and Antecedent)* for a discussion of more pronoun problems.

EXERCISE   3-16

Revise the following sentences to eliminate unclear pronoun reference.

1. He prepared a delicious meal for Al and then criticized his cooking throughout dinner, which irritated him immensely.
2. Juan told Al that his soufflés never rose as high as his.
3. Al asked if Juan allowed a speck of egg yolk or a particle of grease to pollute the egg whites. This might keep the whites from fluffing up as much as they should.
4. Al also suggested making a foil collar for the soufflé pan, which encourages the soufflé to puff higher.

5. Juan told Al that he might as well just give up and try quiche instead.
6. The problems with elaborate cooking projects are so serious that Sherri dreads them.
7. Eating a simple meal in an outdoor setting, which I prefer, relaxes both host and guests.
8. This makes the evening enjoyable and free from anxiety.
9. She told her that her husband simply refused to eat casserole dishes.
10. The chefs were eager to discuss their problems with white sauce, but they were not very serious.

Regular Verb See *Verbs*, page 30.
See *Tense*.

rep | **Repetition**

Carefully designed repetition of terms can add emphasis and coherence to a passage, like this one by Dr. Hugh Drummond:

> I watched a woman slip into madness recently. Her working-class, middle-aged life was buffeted by an abusive husband, an abusive son, and a series of abusive supervisors at a succession of low-level jobs. She would come home day after day, year after year from her file-clerk tedium, exhausted by the subway commute and the stained city's air, only to begin caring for her indulged, soured men; with their impatient appetites and their bottom-rung entitlements, they waited for her like beasts in a lair.
>
> —"Power, Madness, and Poverty," *Mother Jones,* Jan. 1980.

The repetition reflects the tedious repetitiousness of the woman's life.

Careless repetition, though, lends emphasis to a word or phrase awkwardly and unnecessarily:

A. After the performance, we went to Karl's house to discuss whether it was an effective performance.

B. The length of his hair adds to the wild appearance of his hair.

Those sentences need revision because the repeated words have no reason to be emphasized.

A. After the performance, we went to Karl's house to discuss whether our production was effective.

B. The length of his hair adds to its wild appearance.

Restrictive Clauses See *Comma*, number 2.

Run-On Sentence (Fused Sentence)

Do not run two sentences together without a period between them.

A. Horace has a mangy dog without a brain in his head his name is Bowser.

Such a lapse is guaranteed to drive even the most patient readers to distraction. When you proofread, make sure that each sentence really *is* an acceptable sentence.

B. Horace has a mangy dog without a brain in his head. His name is Bowser.

Those sentences are standard English, but a good writer would revise further to avoid wordiness.

C. Horace has a mangy, brainless dog named Bowser.

EXERCISE 3-17

Put end punctuation where it belongs in the following items, and revise to avoid wordiness where necessary.

1. Playing blackjack is an absorbing hobby it might even absorb your bank account if you're not careful.

2. Blackjack is the only Las Vegas game in which the house does not have an overwhelming advantage in fact the players have an advantage if they use a system.

3. The best blackjack system involves remembering every card that has turned up the player keeps a running count of what cards are left in the deck and makes high or low bets accordingly.

4. The system is based on statistical tables compiled by computer expert Julian Braun of the IBM Corporation Braun does not play blackjack himself.

5. System players must be dedicated learning the system well takes 200 hours of memorization and practice.

6. Slot machines, on the other hand, are quite simple they do not require any practice.

7. However, the house has a stupendous advantage over the slot machine player the slot machine addicts cannot quite believe this.

8. Slot machine addicts are always hoping for the big jackpot these hopes are encouraged by the design of the machines.

9. Each machine boasts of its jackpot prize in large letters and pictures each one also makes loud noises whenever any payoff, however small, is won.

10. In spite of my wisdom I did start to play slots more often after January 1979 that is when I saw a man win a Cadillac on a machine at the El Cortez.

Semicolon

;

For quick advice see the punctuation chart in Table 3-1.

semi

1. The semicolon, which is similar to a period, means stop briefly; then go ahead.

Complete sentences connected by semicolons should be closely related.

    A. The story has three narrators; one of them is insane.
    B. When angry, count four; when very angry, swear.   —Mark Twain.

2. Use a semicolon (instead of only a comma) when sentences are joined with a conjunctive adverb rather than with a coordinating conjunction (*and, but, or, for, nor, yet, so*).

Here is a list of the most commonly used conjunctive adverbs:

accordingly	however	moreover	therefore
besides	indeed	nevertheless	thus
consequently	instead	nonetheless	too
furthermore	likewise	otherwise	
hence	meanwhile	then	

3. The type of connective you choose need not change the meaning, but it will change the punctuation.

The following sentences appear to require identical punctuation, but in standard usage the first requires a semicolon, the second only a comma.

    A. The demonstrators have a valid point; however, I can't condone their violence.
    B. The demonstrators have a valid point, but I can't condone their violence.

This rule may seem senseless, but there *is* a reason for the distinction. The conjunctive adverb is not a pure connective in the way the coordinating conjunction is. *However* in the first example can be picked up and moved to several other spots in the sentence as it suits your fancy. You could write:

> C. The demonstrators have a valid point; I can't, however, condone their violence.

or

> I can't condone their violence, however.

or even

> I, however, can't condone their violence.

You cannot take such liberties with the coordinating conjunctions without producing nonsentences like these:

> I can't, but, condone their violence.
> I can't condone their violence, but.
> I, but, can't condone their violence.

It's easy to tell the difference between the pure conjunctions and the conjunctive adverbs if you have memorized the seven coordinating conjunctions: *and, but, or, for, nor, yet, so.* Other words likely to deceive you into thinking they are coordinating conjunctions are actually conjunctive adverbs.

4. Do not use a semicolon to connect an independent clause with a dependent clause (a fragment).

> *Faulty:* He looked a lot like Robert Redford; although I couldn't see him too well.
> *Improved:* He looked a lot like Robert Redford, although I couldn't see him too well.

5. **The semicolon substitutes for the comma in separating items in series when any of the items listed *already contain commas*.**

For example:

A. Ann went to college and dropped out; lived with her parents for a year; worked as a veterinarian's assistant, a teacher's aide, and a clerk; and finally found her niche as an organic farmer.

Sometimes the series may follow a colon.

B. Henry made several New Year's resolutions: to eat sensible, well-balanced meals; to study harder, sleep longer, and swear less; and to drink no more rum, tequila, or gin.

EXERCISE   3-18

Add semicolons to the following items where appropriate.

1. He believed that spicy foods were good for the heart, therefore, he ate jalapeña peppers for breakfast each morning.
2. He was tall, handsome, and rich, everyone loved him.
3. She divided her life into four distinct eras: blissful childhood, 1940–1954, carefree student life, 1954–1964, motherhood, 1964–1974, and, finally, liberation, 1974 to the present.
4. He forgot to add oil, thus finding himself the victim of thrown rods and other incomprehensible malfunctions.
5. Seymour asked me to bring wine, preferably a rosé, baby Swiss cheese, and rolls, ideally fresh-baked whole wheat ones, little did he know I'd already packed peanut butter sandwiches, strawberry Koolaid, and cheese curls.
6. The picnic, however, was a smashing success.
7. We had to coax Seymour out of the fountain in front of City Hall, he was about to get arrested.
8. Our high spirits were due to good food, weather, and company, a

citywide air of celebration, fun, and song, and a holiday from work.

9. Although Seymour made a fool of himself, no one cared.
10. We ended the day with a swim at the gravel pit, then everyone went home.

Sentence Types

Every time you write a complete sentence, it falls into one of four categories: simple, compound, complex, and compound-complex. You may wonder what earthly good it does you to become acquainted with the four sentence types. For one thing, it gives you a pleasant sense of order to think of all those billions of sentences falling neatly into four groups. And more practically, the knowledge may help your style. Unless you are consciously striving for parallel sentences, you do not want a whole string of the same type: you want some variety in each paragraph.

1. A simple sentence consists of one independent clause and as many modifying words or phrases as you like.

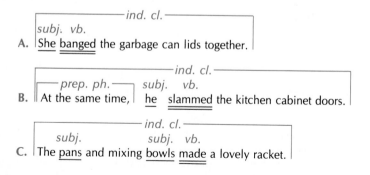

Example C has a compound subject, but is still a simple sentence. Simple sentences may also have compound predicates.

2. **A compound sentence consists of two or more independent clauses joined by a coordinating conjunction (*and, but, or, for, nor, yet, so*) or a semicolon.**

A compound sentence may have any number of modifying words and phrases too.

```
                                                         coord.
                          ─── ind. cl. ───               conj.
  subj. vb.                                                ↓
  He yanked the cookie sheets from the cabinet with glee, │ and

          ─── ind. cl. ───
  subj. vb.
  she rattled them enthusiastically.
```

3. **A complex sentence has one independent clause, one or more dependent clauses, and perhaps some modifying words or phrases.**

```
            ─── dep. cl. ───                      subj.    vb.
              subj.    vb.
  A. After the neighbors began to complain, │ │ the couple started

          ─── ind. cl. ───
                             vb.
     both their motorcycles and roared off.

                          ─── ind. cl. ───
  subj. vb.
  B. They went in search of an authentic air raid siren, a prize

          ─── dep. cl. ───
        subj.    vb.
  that they considered the ultimate in noisiness.
```

4. A compound-complex sentence, as you may have guessed, has two (or more) independent clauses plus one (or more) dependent clauses.

When <u>they</u> <u>were</u> finally <u>arrested</u> for disturbing the peace,
the pair <u>told</u> the judge that <u>they</u> <u>considered</u> noisemaking a new
art form, and the <u>judge</u>, banging his gavel gleefully, <u>said</u>
that <u>he'd</u> always <u>thought</u> so himself.

One more sentence type may have sprung to your alert mind by now: the sentence fragment. We have not forgotten it. Look up *Fragment*. Also see *Balanced Sentences* to learn about parallel structure.

shift

Shifts in Tense and Person

Sometimes your prose gets rolling along, and you shift into the wrong gear while you are moving, which results in an unpleasant grinding noise in your readers' heads. These shifts occur in tense and person.

1. You may write in either present or past tense, depending upon how you approach your material.

This sentence, for instance, is written in present tense:

A. Laurie cleans the dining room and stairway.

Past tense would be

B. Laurie cleaned the dining room and stairway.
C. Laurie was cleaning the dining room and stairway.

There is a good bit of variety within the two tenses, which we discuss under *Verbs* in Chapter 12 and under *Tense* in this chapter.

2. **Choose either present or past tense and stay with it unless you have a reason to change.**
Here's an example of faulty tense switch:

A. Laurie was quietly cleaning the dining room when in comes Sue with a bunch of her loud friends and puts on her B-52s record at full volume. Laurie had to go upstairs and sulk.

There's no call for the change from past to present tense. If Laurie *was cleaning*, then Sue *came* in and *put* on the B-52s. You can, of course, switch tenses to indicate a change occurring in time:

B. Laurie was cleaning the dining room, but now she is sulking.

Just be sure that you do not mix tenses without meaning to.

3. **When you are writing about literature, be especially careful about mixing past and present tense in your discussion of what happens in the book.**
It's traditional to describe literary happenings in the present tense (called the *historical present*):

Kingsley Amis's hero, Lucky Jim, **has** an imaginative humor that constantly **gets** him in trouble.

4. **Shifting *person* in a passage is a similar error.**
   Here's an example of a triple whammy:

   A. *Faulty:* As students we learn the ghastly effects of procrastination. You find out that you just cannot assimilate ten chapters of geography the night before a test. Most students know the grim thud in the gut that they feel when they stare at an exam and do not even understand the questions.

In that example the writer refers to the students in three different ways: *we* (first person plural), *you* (second person), and *they* (third person plural). To revise the passage, stick to one pronoun.

   B. *Revised:* As students, we learn the ghastly effects of procrastination. We find out that we just cannot assimilate ten chapters of geography the night before a test. We become familiar with the grim thud in the gut that we feel when we stare at an exam and do not even understand the questions.

EXERCISE 3-19

Correct the tense and person shifts in the following passages.

1. At the end of *Jane Eyre,* Jane is rewarded for her courage and virtue. She found happiness in an egalitarian marriage.
2. People often forget to file a change-of-address card at the post office when you move.
3. I saw that he was growing angry, so I jump up and leave the room.
4. My sister could not stand it when I wear her favorite jeans, but what can you do when all of yours are dirty?

5. Everyone who reads knows that government is corrupt. You can never be sure, though, that we know just how corrupt it is.
6. Sheila's new haircut is badly mangled, but I don't know what you can do about it.
7. Steve arrives, obnoxious as usual, and insulted the people at Lynn's party.
8. Richard wants to go see the play but claims that he didn't have time.
9. The philosophy students had a potluck last Friday, but then they ruin it by arguing about whether the food exists or not.
10. Dan's truck needed alignment, but he complains constantly about the cost.

Simile   See *Figures of Speech.*

Simple Sentence   See *Sentence Types.*

Slang   See *Diction,* number 7.

Spelling

See *Spelling Appendix,* page 380.

sp

If you get certain pairs of words confused, like *accept* and *except* or *affect* and *effect,* the "Glossary of Usage" beginning on page 191 will help you.

Split Infinitive

To many people, a split infinitive reads like a fingernail on the blackboard sounds. Such people would prefer that you keep the *to* and the verb (as in *to appreciate, to understand, to walk*) smack up against each other—not stick an adverb between them. But current usage finds most split infinitives perfectly acceptable, like:

                               adv.
  A. He tried ***to*** secretly ***cause*** fights between Chris and Ann.
                ↖ *inf.* ↗

Really is a common infinitive splitter, and it can usually be left out of the sentence entirely.

                                     adv.
  B. *Split:*   I began ***to*** really ***appreciate*** jug band music.
                        ↖ *inf.* ↗

      Improved: I began to appreciate jug band music.

Delete the infinitive-splitting adverb if it does not add appreciably to the meaning of the sentence.
    A widely split infinitive can be awkward.

  C. *Widely split:* He tried ***to*** purposely, secretly, and maliciously ***cause*** fights between Ann and Chris.
      Improved: Purposely, secretly, and maliciously, he tried ***to cause*** fights between Chris and Ann.

Squinting Modifier

               A squinting modifier is an ambiguous one; placed between two words (or phrases), it could conceivably refer to either one of them.

  Squinting: Marla thought ***secretly*** James ate too much.

Move the squinting modifier to a less confusing place in the sentence.

> *Clear:*   Marla ***secretly*** thought James ate too much.
> Marla thought James ***secretly*** ate too much.

Subject   See *Nouns,* page 26.
See *Agreement* (*Subject and Verb*).

Subjunctive Mood

See *Verbs,* page 32, for a discussion of *mood.*

mood

The verb forms you are most familiar with and use most often are in the *indicative* mood: I *cook,* you *eat,* he *washes* dishes, they *sweep* the floor. Indicative mood is used for statements of fact. For statements and wishes contrary to fact (or highly unlikely) or for suppositions, some people use *subjunctive* mood.

Indicative	Subjunctive			Indicative	Subjunctive
I am	I was	I be	I were	I take	I take
he is	he was	he be	he were	he takes	he take
you are	you were	you be	you were	you take	you take
they are	they were	they be	they were	they take	they take

Remember Patrick Henry's "If this *be* treason"? And the phrase "if need be"? Those are examples of subjunctive mood. It used to be commonplace to use the subjunctive mood of all verbs, like, "If he *take* to his bed, he will surely expire." But now the subjunctive mood of the *to be* verb is practically the only one anyone worries about.

Many people believe in polishing up the old subjunctive

mood and restoring it to everyday use. They want you to say, "If I *were* . . ." instead of "If I *was*. . . ." These folks can get quite nervous about your mood, so perhaps you should figure out whether they are in your reading audience. If they are, follow these rules:

1. Use subjunctive mood to express something contrary to fact, highly unlikely, doubtful, or speculative.

    A. If I were more refined, subjunctive mood would sound natural to me.
    B. Suppose he were confronted with an audience of subjunctive mood fanatics: he'd be in trouble if he were to use it incorrectly.
    C. He acts as though he were the smartest graduate of Podunk High, but he certainly doesn't know subjunctive mood.

2. Use subjunctive mood to express a strong necessity or a motion in a meeting.

    A. It is crucial that you be present at this week's meeting.
    B. I am going to move that all whale hunting be immediately banned.
    C. "To write well and worthily of American things one need even more than elsewhere to be a master."

                      —Henry James.

Subordination and Coordination

sub

1. You can enrich a sentence or series of sentences by subordinating some of the clauses—that is, by changing independent clauses to dependent ones or phrases.

    Plain simple and compound sentences may be the easiest ones to write, but they do not always get across the relationships between your ideas in the clearest way possible. And if you use simple sentences too often, you will have a third-grade writing style. Here are a couple of plain simple sentences:

> Lucy forgot how to spell *exaggerated*. She used the word *magnified* instead.

The idea in one of those sentences could be subordinated in these ways:

A. **By using subordinating conjunctions and adverbs** (*after, when, because, if, while, until, unless, etc.*)
> *Since Lucy forgot how to spell* exaggerated, she used the word *magnified* instead.

B. **By using an adjective clause**
> Lucy, *who forgot how to spell* exaggerated, used the word *magnified* instead.

C. **By using a participial phrase or an adjective**
> *Having forgotten how to spell* exaggerated, Lucy used the word *magnified* instead.

2. **Avoid stringing together simple sentences with coordinating conjunctions.**

Subordinate some of the ideas, using parallel structure (see also *Balanced Sentences*).

Ineffective: Phoebe got a hot tip on the phone, and she grabbed her tape recorder and hurried to the corner and an angry mob was gathered there, and she ran to a phone booth and called the paper's photographer and said, "Dave, get down here quick!"

Improved: After getting a hot tip on the phone, Phoebe grabbed her tape recorder and hurried to the corner where an angry mob was gathered. She ran to a phone booth, dialed the paper's photographer, and said, "Dave, get down here quick!"

3. **Choose the subordinating element that best shows how the ideas are connected, and be sure the main idea ends up in the *independent* clause, unless you are writing satire.**

Faulty: Anna met Alexis in the lobby of the casino, while he complimented her on her gown.

Improved: Alexis complimented Anna on her gown when they met in the lobby of the casino.

EXERCISE   3-20

The following sentences are examples of excessive coordination. Revise each sentence, using subordination.

1. Moose is my cat, and he has stripy fur and is inordinately lazy, but he is busy now and is washing himself.
2. Clarence has a new motorcycle, and it's a huge Harley-Davidson, and he went to a wild party on it and drank six beers, and then crashed into a tree at sixty miles per hour.
3. Jocasta was lonely, so she joined the YWCA, signed up for disco dancing lessons and has been practicing her bored expression and has got her hip movement perfect and is now the life of the party.
4. Our fire fighters went on strike and are now in jail because they want a written contract and better working conditions and also they want their lieutenants in the union, but the town council opposes the fire fighters' demands, so the situation is at a stalemate.
5. Joyce Carol Oates writes superb short stories and is interested in women and in their fear of loneliness and she shows that women perpetually fear rape and violence and abandonment and she seems to suggest that women feel this way because they have few options and thus seek connections with men to give meaning to their lives.
6. Our trip to Bloomington was perfect and we had iced tea and spinach salads and stayed up late but we felt great the next day anyway.

7. Mark is out running errands and he plans to go to the bank and then he will stop and talk to his boss and then he needs to pick up some papers from my office.

8. I always remember my mother's birthday but I have a hard time figuring out what to get her and sometimes I'm afraid I got her the same thing I got her last year.

9. Laurie plays lead guitar in a rock and roll band and all the band members are female and they choose old songs that are from the male point of view and rewrite the lyrics to reflect the female point of view.

10. Marsha has a job at a gift shop and it is much more demanding than it sounds and she has to take inventory and arrange displays and do the bookwork and work as a cashier also.

Tense

t

Tense indicates time relationships. When you start trying to explain how it all works, you realize how amazing it is that most people do it right. Here are the basic tenses of English:

Present:	I walk
Past:	I walked
Future:	I will walk
Present perfect:	I have walked
Past perfect:	I had walked
Future perfect:	I will have walked

1. When you are writing about an event in present tense, it is natural to use past tense for past events and future for future events.

I think that Hornsby wanted Clara to quit her job yesterday because he will not need as many clerks after the Christmas rush is over.

2. **When you are writing about an event in past tense, you must use past perfect for events earlier in the past.**

> Hornsby regretted that he had hired Clara for a permanent, full-time job.

3. **The three perfect tenses (present perfect, past perfect, and future perfect) always show completed action.**

> A. I have ridden the bus to campus for the past month.
> B. I had expected my Subaru to be fixed by last Monday.
> C. By the time I get my car back, I will have paid $215.39 just to get that windshield wiper fixed.

4. **Sometimes the tense of a statement gets tricky when the surroundings of the statements are in past or future tense, but the statement itself is presently true or applicable.**

> A. Clara realized last week that Hornsby is a greedy, manipulative egomaniac.

Hornsby is still a greedy, manipulative egomaniac, so the present tense is appropriate even though Clara figured him out a week ago.

> B. Jacob said that reading fiction is so pleasant it feels sinful.

Jacob said this in the past, but his statement about fiction still applies today, so the present tense is fine.

5. **Every English verb has three principal parts that you need to know in order to form the tenses.**
   Usually, the principal parts are just the present infinitive plus *-d*, *-ed*, or *-t:*

Present	Past	Past participle
walk	walked	(have, had) walked
dance	danced	(have, had) danced
spend	spent	(have, had) spent

6. **Some verbs are *irregular;* that is, they form their past tense or past participle in odd ways.**

You just have to memorize the principal parts of these verbs. Here are twenty of the most common irregular verbs:

Present	Past	Past participle
am	was	been
begin	began	begun
break	broke	broken
burst	burst	burst (*not* busted)
choose	chose	chosen
come	came	come
do	did	done
drink	drank	drunk
forget	forgot	forgotten (*or* forgot)
go	went	gone
get	got	got (*or* gotten)
have	had	had
lay	laid	laid (meaning "placed")
lead	led	led
lie	lay	lain (meaning "reclined")
ride	rode	ridden
rise	rose	risen
run	ran	run
see	saw	seen
swim	swam	swum
take	took	taken
wake	waked (*or* woke)	waked (*or* woke)

Also see *Verbs,* page 30.

Thesis Statement

A successful essay needs a *thesis*, or controlling idea, either expressed in a single sentence in the introduction or implied, as in narrative or descriptive writing.

1. **Narrow the topic.**
If you're assigned a 500-word paper on "Solving the Energy Shortage," you need to find a suitable thesis idea that you can handle within the word limit. You might, for instance, focus on the need to develop alternative energy sources. But that still is too broad a topic to cover in 500 words. You could then narrow your idea to one neglected source, like solar energy. But you will need an approach—a *focus*—for your paper.

2. **Give the direction of your thinking.**
Your thesis should state more than just your general topic. Do not settle for just "solar energy" or even "the need for solar energy." Write a complete sentence—with a *verb* as well as a subject—to indicate what you plan to say about the subject. You might propose the need for solar energy like this: "Our economy needs to convert to solar power because it remains our only nonpolluting source of energy."

3. **Make all ideas relate to your thesis.**
Once you've decided on a clear, concise thesis statement, make sure that every major and minor point in the paper relates directly to that controlling idea so that your essay will be unified.

This and Which

These words are often used too loosely. See *Reference of Pronouns,* number 2.

Title Tactics

Your title should tell the readers, so far as possible, what the paper is about.

1. **Do not use a complete sentence but give more than a hint about your topic.**

   Useless: The Teacher and Research
   Better: The Teacher and Research in Education
   Good: Practical Research Ideas for High School Teachers

2. **Experiment with a colon.**
   Sometimes a colon can make an uninspired title more impressive.

   Grass Roots Organization: A Key to Political Success
   Legal Liability: What Everyone Needs to Know About Mercy Killing

3. **Do not put quotation marks around your own title.**
   See also *Quotation Marks,* numbers 5, 6, and 7, for advice on punctuating other people's titles.

Topic Sentence

The topic sentence expresses the central idea of a paragraph. Most of your paragraphs should have one. See page 13.

Transitions

trans

1. Transitional words are verbal signals that help your readers follow your thought.

Some of the most useful ones function this way:

A. **To move to the next point:**   also, besides, too, furthermore, moreover, next, in the first place, second, third, again, in addition, further, likewise, finally, accordingly, at the same time, first, to begin with.

B. **To add an example:**   for instance, for example, in the same manner, such as, that is, in the following manner, namely, in this case, as an illustration.

C. **To emphasize a point:**   in fact, without question, especially, without doubt, primarily, chiefly, actually, otherwise, after all, as a matter of fact.

D. **To contrast a point:**   yet, although, after all, but, still, on the other hand, on the contrary, nevertheless, contrary to, however, nonetheless, conversely, granted that, in contrast, in another way.

E. **To conclude a point:**   thus, therefore, in short, consequently, so, accordingly, then, as a result, hence, in sum, in conclusion, in other words.

2. Use special transitional techniques when moving from one point to the next.

A. Occasionally you can pose a question for yourself and answer it, like this:

> How does vitamin E work to repair body tissues? Nobody knows for sure, but . . .

B. A more useful method is the ***echo transition*** in which you touch on the idea from the previous paragraph as you introduce the idea for your next one, like this:

He also ***gave up coffee, cigarettes, and alcohol.***

Despite ***this stringent health program,*** Sylvester continued to be depressed until . . .

3. **Within paragraphs provide transitions by repeating nouns and using pronouns to refer back to them, thus linking your sentences together.**

Dan loves remodeling projects, especially if they are big and complex.

In fact, the bigger and more complex they are, the better he likes them.

Transitive Verb   See *Verbs*, page 35.

Triteness

trite

A *cliché* is a worn-out series of words which usually expresses a simple-minded or trite idea: "It takes all kinds to make a world." But you can express superficial ideas without using clichés too. Here is an example of a sentence your reader might think trite:

Motherhood is a joyful experience that no woman should miss.

The writer has not thought very deeply about the idea. Is motherhood joyful for a poor woman with nine children? Are women's personalities so alike that such a generalization could be true?

We all find ourselves mindlessly writing down unexamined ideas once in a while. A thoughtful rereading of whatever you write can help you avoid making this weakness public.

Underdeveloped Paragraphs

¶dev

A friend of ours says that throughout college she got her papers back marked with "Underdeveloped ¶" in the margins. To correct this problem, she would carefully restate the topic four or five different ways in each paragraph, and she would still get "Underdeveloped ¶" marked in her margins.

Our friend finally realized, too late, what *underdevelopment* meant. She resents the fact that her teachers never wrote in her margins, "Add an example or illustration here," or, "Give some specific details," or, "Describe your reasoning step by step." She would have understood *that*.

When you find one of your skimpy paragraphs marked *undernourished* or *lacks development*, you will know what it means: add examples, provide specific details, describe your reasoning, or do all three.

Underlining

und

ital

Underlining by hand or with a typewriter is the same as italics in print. It is used three ways:

1. **To indicate titles of long or self-contained works.**
   See *Quotation Marks* for a list of what titles to underline and what titles to enclose in quotation marks.

2. **To print out words used as words.**

   A. <u>Manipulative behavior</u> is my therapist's favorite phrase.
   B. You have used twelve <u>in other words</u>'s in this paragraph.

3. **To indicate foreign words.**
   In informal writing, you do not have to underline foreign

words that are widely used, like *et cetera* or *tortilla* or *tango*.

But underline foreign words when they are less familiar or when you are writing formally.

> After graduation, Jocasta seemed to lose her <u>joie de vivre</u>.

Unity

un

Unity is something we never require of casual conversation: it's fine if you wander a little off the track and tell about the Bluebird Saloon in Denver in the middle of a discussion about Humphey Bogart films.

But in an expository essay, unity is important: you must not go on about the Bluebird in the middle of an essay about Bogart films, even though you had a beer there after seeing *The Maltese Falcon* at a nearby theater. Such a departure from the main subject is called a *digression.* A paragraph or essay has unity if it sticks to the main point. It lacks unity if it wanders across the street for a drink.

See also *Coherence.*

Usage See *Levels of Usage,* pages 191–192.
See *Diction,* number 8.

Variety See *Sentence Types.*

Verb See *Verbs,* pages 30–36.
See *Agreement* (*Subject and Verb*).
See *Linking Verb.*
See *Tense.*

Verbal   See *Nouns,* page 29.

Word Division   See *Hyphen.*

Wordiness

w

   A *wordy* sentence has words and phrases which add nothing to its meaning; in fact, extra verbiage can actually blur the meaning and spoil the style of a sentence. Here, for instance, is a wordy rewriting of the last sentence:

> A sentence that is wordy usually consists in part of words and phrases which do not add anything in the area of meaning; in fact, the meaning of a sentence, in addition to its style, can be blurred or otherwise spoiled due to the fact that it is wordy.

To cure your writing of wordiness, practice sentence-by-sentence revision, hacking and slashing zealously. Passive voice makes a sentence wordy (see *Passive Voice*). So does using canned phrases like *due to the fact that* instead of *because* and *in addition to* instead of *and.*

COMPREHENSIVE EXERCISE   3-21

Correct or improve each of the following sentences.

1. Care should be taken by new students not to alienate their roommates.
2. Every semester, Sandra makes two resolutions, first, not to spend all her money on tropical fish, and second, not to put off schoolwork until the last minute.

3. Hubert went to school five days early, and found himself alone on campus.
4. Luckily, he had remembered to actually bring his copy of *Paradise Lost* in case he had leisure reading time.
5. Hubert did feel badly because his roommate was not there to share the fun.
6. Sandra on the other hand did not arrive until a week after registration began.
7. She had only 3 paperback books with her.
8. She surprised her teachers by acting as though she was right on time.
9. Each of the books Sandra brought were special to her.
10. The books were Libra: Your Horoscope, Adventures of Huckleberry Finn, and Webster's New World Dictionary.
11. Although she didn't really believe in astrology Sandra found that reading over the list of Libra's good qualities cheered her up in times of depression.
12. *Huckleberry Finn* also cheered her up, supported her philosophy of life, and she never got bored no matter how many times she read it.
13. These characteristics of the novel were important to Sandra, for it meant that she never lacked a good book to read.
14. She sometimes forgot how to spell long words, therefore the dictionary was essential.
15. The dictionary was frequently used when she wrote papers.
16. It also helped her become drowsy when she'd drank too much coffee.
17. Huberts ability to spell was much better than most peoples.
18. His ability to dance, though, was lower than an elephant.
19. Sandra admired Hubert coming up with the correct spelling of *embarrass* every single time.
20. In her opinion, she had to admit that in the field of dancing, Hubert's Hustle was hopeless.
21. Sandra learned the Hustle at the New Age discotheque.
22. The surprising thing about some of Hubert's dance attempts, that include stumbles, jerks, and sometimes falls, do look quite fashionable sometimes.

23. Spelling, Hubert explained to Sandra, is a problem that can be cured only through memorization.
24. Dancing, Sandra explained to Hubert, becomes easy as pie with practice.
25. Hubert was eager to improve his dancing. Sandra wanted to become a better speller. They agreed to give each other lessons.
26. Hubert suggested, We could create a dance called the disco dictionary.
27. It has already been created replied Sandra. I read about it in an article called Discomania in the New York Review of Books.
28. Walking into Sandra's room, Hubert's eye was caught by all the empty bookshelves.
29. He thought her lack of books was very strange he decided not to mention it, though.
30. She might still have her books packed up, he thought. Although it was the fifteenth week of the semester.
31. Sandra was not embarrassed by her empty bookshelves, in fact, she thought people often filled their shelves up just to impress others.
32. After supper on Tuesday, Sandra asked Hubert if he would like to go to a lecture on how the *Oxford English Dictionary* was compiled in two hours.
33. She said that if students went to all the lectures that came up, you would be busy every night of the week.
34. Hubert believed that people whose interests changed with every passing breeze were building on a foundation of jelly.
35. Sandra decided to go to the lecture while Hubert practices his Bump in front of the mirror.

Chapter Four
Glossary of Usage

In this section we distinguish between a number of words that people often confuse, like *sit* and *set, effect* and *affect.* We also describe the current usage of some terms that are questionable as standard English, like the word *irregardless* and the use of *quotes* as a noun. In making decisions on usage, we have been guided by Robert C. Pooley, *The Teaching of English Usage;* Roy H. Copperud, *American Usage: The Consensus;* Theodore Bernstein, *Dos and Don'ts and Maybes of English Usage;* several current collegiate dictionaries; a stack of widely used composition handbooks; and sometimes our own generous hearts.

LEVELS OF USAGE

Usage simply means the way the language is used. But different people use the language in different ways. And even the same people use the language differently on different occasions. You probably speak more carefully in the classroom or on the job than you do when relaxing among friends. Good usage, then, is a matter of using language *appropriate* to the purpose and the occasion. In this chapter we give you clues about which expressions are appropriate for various occasions. Although we have already discussed *levels of usage* in some detail in Chapter 1, we will review them again here briefly:

Standard: Safe for any level of usage—formal, informal, or collo-quial. Be sure **all** terms are standard if you are writing on the formal level.

Formal: Much of your college writing and considerable busi-ness writing must be done on a formal level. This means only standard English is appropriate. Do not use slang or contractions—no **can'ts** or **don'ts.** Completely formal writing requires one to write in the third person (as we just did in this sentence).

      Formal: One can observe . . . ; this writer believes . . .

      Informal: We can observe . . . ; you can see . . .

Informal: You get considerable leeway in informal writing. Some slang is acceptable, depending on the tolerance of your audience, and you may be able to use a few contractions. This textbook is written on an informal level.

Colloquial: Since *colloquial* means the language of everyday speech of educated people, both contractions and slang are all right. But there is not much call for collo-quial writing in your college courses, and it would be devastatingly inappropriate in most business writing. Use with proper caution.

Nonstandard: Most nonstandard phrasing (like **it don't**) will get you into big trouble in writing. Unfortunately, dialectical expressions are also considered nonstandard. Some dictionaries even label nonstandard constructions as **illiterate,** which seems harsh to us, but you should be advised that many people are unalterably prejudiced against nonstandard English. **Avoid it in writing.**

If you are in doubt about any terms that do not appear in this glossary, consult your trusty collegiate dictionary—but be sure it is of recent vintage. Even the best of dictionaries will be out of date on usage within ten years.

a/an

Use *a* before words beginning with consonant sounds; use *an* before words beginning with vowel sounds (*a, e, i, o, u*).

a martini	an Irish coffee
a tree toad	an armadillo
a hostile motorist	an hour exam (the *h* is silent)
a hopeful speech	an honest decision (the *h* is silent)
a one-car accident (*o* sounds like *w*)	an only child
a history text	an historical event (who knows why?)

accept/except

Accept, a verb, means "to receive or to agree with."

We ***accept*** your excuse with reluctance.

Except as a preposition means "but or excluding."

Everyone's coming ***except*** Dinsdale.

Except as a verb is not used much but means "to leave out."

The Dean agreed to ***except*** the foreign language requirement since I have lived in France.

advice/advise

When you *advise* someone, you are giving *advice*.

vb.
We ***advise*** you to stop smoking.

n.
Mavis refuses to follow our good ***advice***.

affect/effect

The verb *affect* means "to influence." The noun *effect* means "the result of some influence."

    n.   *vb.*
The **effect** on my lungs from smoking should **affect** my decision to quit.

              vb.
Smoking adversely **affects** our health.

                                      n.
LeRoy cultivates a seedy appearance for **effect.**

Just to confuse things further, *effect* can also be a verb meaning "to bring about." And *affect* can be a verb meaning "to cultivate an effect" or a noun meaning "emotional response."

                vb.
We need to **effect** (bring about) some changes in the system.

         vb.
Clyde **affects** (cultivates) a seedy appearance.

                                          n.
Psychologists say that inappropriate **affect** (emotional response) is a feature of schizophrenia.

These last three meanings are seldom confused with the more widely used words above. Concentrate on getting those first common meanings straight.

ain't

Still colloquial usage. Do not use it unless you are writing dialogue or trying to get a laugh.

all right/alright

Usage is divided on this term, but to be safe, stick with *all right*. You could argue that since we have *all ready/already* and *all together/altogether,* we should be allowed *all right/ alright.* But many will disagree:

> **Alright** is definitely not **all right** with everybody yet.

allude/refer

To *allude* means "to *refer* indirectly or briefly."

> Mark **alluded** to some previous shady dealings on the mayor's part but concentrated his attack on the present scandal.

Refer is more direct.

> Mark then **referred** to the mayor's illegal Swiss bank account.

allusion/illusion

An *allusion* is an indirect reference.

> This line of poetry contains an **allusion** to Dante's *Inferno*.

An *illusion* is a deception or fantasy.

> Seymour clung to the **illusion** that he looked like Robert Redford.

almost/most

Do not write *most all;* standard usage still requires *almost all.*

Jocasta drank **almost** all the Kool-Aid.
Melvin sloshed down **most** of the iced tea.

a lot/alot

Even though *alike* is one word, *a lot* remains two.

Misspellings can cause you **a lot** of trouble.

already/all ready

Already means "before, previously, or so soon."

Jennifer has **already** downed three martinis.

All ready means prepared.

Seymour is **all ready** to deliver his temperance lecture.

altogether/all together

Altogether means "entirely, thoroughly."

Clarence's analysis is **altogether** absurd.

All together means "as a group."

Let's sing it **all together** from the top.

a.m./p.m. See *Abbreviation*, number 1C, in the "Revising Index," Chapter 3 (page 69).

ambiguous/ambivalent

If something is *ambiguous*, it can be interpreted in several different ways.

> When Clyde mentioned the word "faithful," Marcella gave Jeannie a significant, but *ambiguous,* glance.

Ambiguous can also mean "uncertain or doubtful."

> The test results proved *ambiguous.*

But if you feel *ambivalent* about something, you are of two minds, having conflicting thoughts or feelings.

> Juanita has felt *ambivalent* toward Maurice ever since he joined the Hell's Angels.

among/between

Use *among* when referring in general terms to more than two.

> Maureen found it difficult to choose from *among* so many delectable goodies.

Use *between* when referring to only two.

> She finally narrowed it down to a choice *between* the raspberry tart and the lemon meringue pie.

You can also use *between* when naming several persons or things individually.

> Elspeth vacillates *between* the key lime pie, the Bavarian cream, and the baked Alaska.

amount/number

In formal writing be sure to use *amount* to refer to things in a mass or in bulk; use *number* to refer to things that can be counted.

> Andrew bought a goodly ***amount*** of peanut butter from which Dave made a considerable ***number*** of cookies for the bake sale.

analyzation

Do not use it. The word is *analysis,* and tacking on an extra syllable will not make it any grander.

> Luis offered a brilliant ***analysis*** of entropy in *Winnie the Pooh.*

and

Be careful not to write *an* when you mean *and.*

> *Careless:* I'm going to go out ***an*** get a pizza.
> *Correct:* I'm going to go out ***and*** get a pizza.

And do not get lazy and use the symbol &. Write the word out, except when taking notes.

any more/anymore

Some authorities consider only the first expression acceptable. But recent dictionaries cite *anymore* (one word) as standard English. Use *anymore* in writing only with the negative:

Correct: Elvis is not with us *anymore.*
Nonstandard: *Anymore* all you hear are his records.

anyways/anywheres

Nonstandard. Use *anyway* and *anywhere.*

apprise/appraise

To *apprise* means to "inform or serve notice."

Eloise said the officer neglected to *apprise* her of her constitutional rights.

To *appraise* means to "evaluate or judge."

Egbert *appraised* the situation carefully and caught the next plane for Venezuela.

as

Do not use *as* to mean *because.*

Informal: Egbert returned from Venezuela, *as* the charges were dropped.
Improved: Egbert returned from Venezuela *because* the charges were dropped.

as/like

Hardly anyone takes serious umbrage over the confusion of *as* and *like* anymore, but in formal writing you might well observe the distinction. *As* is a conjunction; hence it introduces clauses.

This pie tastes good *as* lemon pie should.

Like is a preposition; thus it introduces phrases.

This pie tastes *like* artificial lemon.

as to

Many people feel that this phrase does nothing but clutter your sentence; they consider it a borrowing from the worst and wordiest of legalese. You can probably substitute the single word *about*.

Awkward: Melvin explained the rules *as to* registration.
Improved: Melvin explained the rules *about* registration.

author

Some people still cringe at its use as a verb, but this usage is gaining wide acceptance.

Colloquial: Ann *authors* our monthly newsletter.
Improved: Ann *writes* our monthly newsletter.

awhile/a while

Written as one word, *awhile* is an adverb.

Spot frolicked *awhile* with Bowser.

A *while* is an article plus a noun.

> After *a while* Spot got bored and chased Bowser home.

bad/badly   See *Adverb/Adjective Confusion*, page 70.

being as/being that

Do not use either one. Write *because* or *since*.

beside/besides

Do not use *beside* (at the side of) if you mean *besides* (in addition to).

> He leadeth me *beside* the still waters.
> Bumper has a math exam tomorrow *besides* his physics test.

better/best

Use *better* when comparing two people or things.

> Mickey is a *better* dancer than Melvin.

Use *best* when comparing more than two.

> Mickey is the *best* dancer in the place.

This rule holds true for all comparative adjectives: *prettier/ prettiest, littler/littlest, happier/happiest, sadder/saddest, bigger/biggest,* etc.

between/among   See *among/between*.

busted

Do not write busted in formal writing if you mean *broke*.

Colloquial: Chris ***busted*** his leg skiing.
Standard: Chris ***broke*** his leg skiing.
Colloquial: Lulu's balloon got ***busted***.
Standard: Lulu's balloon ***burst***.

There are a number of slang meanings for *busted;* do not use these in formal writing.

Slang: Norman got ***busted*** at the demonstration.
        Sergeant Snafu got ***busted*** to private.
        Sedgewick is flat ***busted***. (no money)
        Maribelle is flat-***busted***. (no bosom)

can/may

Few people even recognize the distinction between these two words anymore, but in formal usage *can* means "to have the ability."

Percy ***can*** sleep for twelve hours straight.

May is used to suggest a possibility or to request (or grant) permission.

Percy ***may*** be awake by now.
May I wake him, if he's not?
Yes, you ***may***.

can't help but/cannot help but

Technically, this expression is a double negative; hence some people object to it in formal writing.

> *Informal:* I **can't help but** question Melvin's intentions.
> *Formal:* I **cannot help** questioning Melvin's intentions.

center on/center around

Some people think that as a matter of logic, you cannot *center around* anything. To be safe, use *center on* in writing.

> *Illogical:* Our difficulty **centers around** Ruth's refusal to sleep in the bathtub.
> *Improved:* Our difficulty **centers on** Ruth's refusal to sleep in the bathtub.

choose/chose

Choose (rhymes with *ooze*) means a decision is being made right now.

> I find it hard to **choose** from a long menu.

Chose (rhymes with *toes*) means a choice has already been made.

> I finally **chose** the eggplant surprise.

compare/contrast

These words overlap in meaning. When you *contrast* two things, you are making a comparison. But as most instructors use the terms on examinations or in writing assignments, *compare* generally means to focus on similarities; *contrast* means to focus on differences.

> **Compare** the music of the Beatles and the Rolling Stones.
> **Contrast** the music of Lawrence Welk and the Sex Pistols.

complected

Nonstandard. Use *complexioned*.

> Marilyn always longed to be sultry and dark **complexioned**.

complement/compliment

A *complement* is something that completes.

> Her purple scarf **complemented** her lavender sweater.

A *compliment* is a word of praise.

> She got many **compliments** on her purple scarf.

continual/continuous

Careful writers will make a distinction. *Continual* means "repeatedly."

> Carlos was **continually** late to class.

Continuous means "without interruption."

> We suffered **continuous** freezing weather for almost three months.

could of/should of/would of

Nonstandard. Use *could have, should have, would have* in writing.

> I **should have** (not **should of**) stopped at the grocery store.

deduce/infer/imply

Deduce and *infer* mean essentially the same thing—to reach a conclusion through reasoning.

> Theodore **deduced** (or **inferred**) that Juanita was angry with him when she poured a pitcher of water over his head.

Do not confuse these words with *imply,* which means "to state indirectly or hint."

> Juanita had **implied** several times earlier in the evening that she was displeased.

differ from/differ with

To *differ from* means "to be different."

> Victoria and Steve **differ from** each other in their choice of records.

To *differ with* means "to disagree."

> Victoria and Steve **differ with** each other on the issue of free speech.

different from/different than

To be safe, stick with *different from* in formal writing.

Turtles are **different from** terrapins in several ways.

You can save words, though, by introducing a clause with *different than;* this usage is now widely accepted.

Wordy: Your hair looks **different from** the way I remembered.
Improved: Your hair looks **different than** I remembered.

disinterested/uninterested

The distinction between these words is extremely important. Do not confuse them. *Disinterested* means "impartial."

We need a totally **disinterested** person to judge the debate.

Uninterested means "not interested."

Albert is totally **uninterested** in the moral tension of Renaissance drama.

dominant/dominate

Dominant is an adjective or a noun.

George has **dominant** parents.
Brown eyes are genetically **dominant.**

Dominate is always a verb.

George's parents **dominate** him.

effect/affect See *affect/effect*.

enthuse

Now acceptable in speech, but since the term still offends many people, avoid it in writing. Stick with *enthusiastic*.

> *Colloquial:* Gary **enthuses** endlessly about the benefits of jogging.
> *Standard:* Gary is **enthusiastic** about the benefits of jogging.

etc.

Do not use this abbreviation (meaning "and so on") unless you have a list in which the other examples are obvious (like large cities: Paris, London, Rome, etc.). Do not ever write *and etc.*, because *etc.* means "*and* so forth"; thus you are saying it twice.

everyday/every day

Use *everyday* as an adjective to modify a noun or pronoun:

> Josh is wearing his **everyday** clothes.

Use *every day* to mean *daily:*

> It rains here almost **every day.**

except/accept See *accept/except*.

farther/further

Either word is acceptable to mean distance.

> I can't walk a step ***farther,*** yet we have two miles ***further*** to go.

To indicate something additional, use *further*.

> The judge would hear no ***further*** arguments.

fewer/less

The distinction between these words is disappearing, but if you value precision, use *fewer* to refer to things that can be counted.

> Marvin catches ***fewer*** colds than Marlene.

Use *less* to refer to qualities or things that cannot be counted.

> Stanley has ***less*** patience than Travis.
> We have had ***less*** rain than usual this fall.

figuratively/literally   See *literally/figuratively*.

former/latter

Unless you are a skillful writer, do not use these terms. Too often readers must look back in order to remember which was the former (the first mentioned) and which the latter (the second mentioned). For greater clarity, repeat the nouns.

got/gotten

Both words are acceptable as past participles of the verb *to get.*

> Brandon ***has got*** an interesting new job.
> Brandon ***has gotten*** an interesting new job.

hanged/hung   See *hung/hanged.*

he or she/his or her

In order to include women in the language, many socially conscious people deliberately use *he or she* (instead of simply *he*) or *his or her* (instead of simply *his,* as grammarians have decreed correct for over a century now.)[1] Equally as many people, though, still consider the double pronoun awkward, as indeed it can be if used ineptly, like this:

> *Awkward:*   The student must have his or her schedule signed by an adviser before he or she proceeds to pick up his or her class cards.

But that sentence can be easily revised to eliminate the excess pronouns.

---

[1] For an enlightening historical study explaining how the male bias in our language became so pronounced, see Julia P. Stanley, "Sexist Grammar," *College English,* 39 (March 1978): 800–811. Stanley contends that "The usage of *man, mankind,* and *he* in the early grammars of English was not generic in any sense of that term, however one might wish to construe it" (p. 801), and supplies the evidence to prove her point.

Improved: The student must have his or her schedule signed by an
adviser before picking up class cards.

Better yet, that sentence can be recast in the plural to eliminate the problem altogether.

Improved: Students must have their schedules signed by an adviser
before picking up class cards.

Notice that the *idea* in the previous example was plural all
along, even though the first two versions were written in the
singular. We are taught early on to write in the singular even
when we mean the plural. We write sentences like this:

A child should memorize **his** multiplication tables.

Really we mean *all* children should memorize *their* multiplication tables. We need to kick that singular habit and cultivate
the plural, since our language has perfectly good nonsexist
pronouns in the plural—*they, their, them.*

If you cannot avoid using the singular—and sometimes
you can't—try to eliminate unnecessary pronouns.

Avoid: The winner should pick up **his** prize in person.
Better: The winner should pick up the prize in person.

If you cannot eliminate the pronoun, an occasional *his or
her*—or *her or his*—is quite acceptable in current usage.
See also *man/person.*

hisself

Nonstandard. Do not use it unless writing dialect.

hopefully

Almost everybody now accepts *hopefully* as a sentence modifier.

> **Hopefully** we can get the contract signed today.

But if you are writing for an older audience, you will do well to use *hopefully* only as an adverb meaning "in a hopeful manner":

> I signed the contract **hopefully,** thinking my life would improve.
>
> We **hope** to get the contract signed today.

hung/hanged

If you are talking about hanging pictures or hanging out, the verb *hang* has these principal parts: *hang, hung, hung, hanging*. But if you are referring to people hanging by the neck, the verb goes *hang, hanged, hanged, hanging*.

> Some people felt that Melvin should have been **hanged,** drawn, and quartered for forgetting to put gas in the car.

illusion   See *allusion/illusion*.

imply/infer   See *deduce/infer/imply*.

in/into/in to

To be precise, use *in* to show location; use *into* to indicate motion.

I was **in** the back seat when our car crashed **into** the train.

Often we use *in* not as a preposition (see previous example) but as an adverb functioning almost as part of a verb: *to go in, to sleep in, to give in.* With these fused verb-adverb constructions, keep *to* as a separate word.

>   *adv.*
> Do not give **in** to pressure.
>   *prep.*
> Do not play **into** their hands.

irregardless

Most people still steadfastly refuse to accept *irregardless* as standard English. Do not use it; say *regardless* or *nonetheless.*

is when/is where

Do not use *is when.*

> *Avoid:*   In tragedy, catharsis **is when** the audience feels purged of pity and fear.
> *Improved:* In tragedy, catharsis involves purging pity and fear from the audience.

Use *is where* only when you mean a place:

> That **is where** I lost my keys.

> *Avoid:*   An accident **is where** someone gets careless.
> *Improved:* Accidents **occur when** people get careless.

its/it's

Do not confuse these two terms. Memorize the two definitions if you have trouble with them, and when you proofread, check to be sure you have not confused them accidentally. *Its* is a possessive pronoun.

> The dog chomped **its** own tail.

It's is a contraction of *it is* or *it has*.

> **It's** not an exceptionally smart dog.

If you never can keep the two straight, quit using the contraction. If you always write *it is*, then all you have to remember is this: no apostrophe in *its*.

kind of/sort of

Colloquial when used to mean *rather* or *somewhat*.

> *Colloquial:* Melvin is **sort of** snarly today.
> *Standard:* Melvin is **somewhat** touchy today.

The phrases can be used in standard English, but not as adverbs.

> *Standard:* What **kind of** junk food does Myrtle like?

Be careful, though, to avoid wordiness.

> *Wordy:* Myrtle prefers a less salty **sort of** snack.
> *Improved:* Myrtle prefers a less salty snack.

Never use *kind of a* or *sort of a* in writing.

> *Avoid:* Grandpa is **kind of** a grouch today.
> *Improved:* Gramps is grouchy today.

latter/former See *former/latter*.

lay/lie

To lay means to put or place; *to lie* means to recline. Be sure you know the principal parts; then decide which verb you need: to place—*lay, laid, laid, laying;* to recline—*lie, lay, lain, lying.* Remember that *lay* requires a direct object: you always *lay* something. But you never *lie* anything: you just *lie down,* or *lie quietly,* or *lie under a tree,* or *lie on a couch.* Notice the difference:

> *No object:* Selma **lies** in the hammock.
> *Direct object:* Selma **lays** her weary body in the hammock.

If you absolutely cannot keep these verbs straight in your mind, choose another word.

> Selma **lounges** in the hammock.
> Selma **plops** her weary body in the hammock.

The verb *lie* meaning "to tell a falsehood" causes no problems since its principal parts are *lie, lied, lied, lying.* Hardly anyone past the age of five would say "Selma *lied* down in the hammock." Similarly, the slang meaning of *lay* never confuses people. Nobody ever asks, "Did you get *lain* last night?"

lead/led

Pronunciation causes the confusion here. *Lead* (rhymes with *bed*) means a heavy, grayish metal.

> Our airy hopes sank like ***lead.***

Lead (rhymes with *seed*) is present tense of the verb meaning to guide.

> He ***leads*** me beside the still waters.

Led (rhymes with *bed*) is the past tense of the verb *lead.*

> LeRoy ***led*** the march last year, but he vows he will not ***lead*** it again.

leave/let

Standard usage allows either "*Leave* me alone" (meaning "go away") or "*Let* me alone" (meaning "stop bothering me"). But since *let* really means *to allow,* "*Leave* me give you some advice" is definitely nonstandard. Use "*Let* me give you some advice before you *leave.*"

lend/loan

You may now correctly ask a loved one either to *lend* you some socks or to *loan* you some socks. Only a traditionalist would be likely to object today to *loan* as a verb.

less/fewer   See *fewer/less.*

lie/lay   See *lay/lie.*

like/as   See *as/like*.

likely/liable

Although these words are virtually interchangeable today, the careful writer will use *likely* to mean "quite possibly" and *liable* to suggest responsibility.

Your roommate is ***likely*** to be upset since she is ***liable*** for damages.

literally/figuratively

Some people use the word *literally* to mean *figuratively*. They say,

The sun was so hot today we ***literally*** roasted.

They mean that *figuratively* they roasted and should say,

The sun was so hot today we ***almost*** roasted.

lose/loose

This is another problem in pronunciation and spelling. *Lose* (rhymes with *ooze*) means to fail to keep something.

    vb.   *vb.*
If we ***lose*** our right to protest, we will ultimately ***lose*** our freedom.

Loose (rhymes with *goose*) means "not tight."

                    adj.
The noose is too ***loose*** on your lasso.

man/person

The generic *man* (as the term is called) is supposed to include both sexes—all human beings. But unfortunately the same word, *man*, also means simply a male human being; thus the term is ambiguous. Sometimes it includes both sexes; sometimes it does not—and sometimes nobody can tell whether it does or does not. Also, *man* is another word, like the generic *he*, that eclipses the female. To avoid this subtle sexism, use *person* or *people* when you mean a person or people, not just males.

> *Sexist:* We want to hire the best **man** we can get for the job.
> *Fair:* We want to hire the best **person** we can get for the job.

A number of compound words using the word *man* can be avoided with little difficulty.

Avoid	Prefer
chairman	chairperson, chair, moderator
congressman	representative, senator
councilman	council member
fireman	fire fighter
foreman	supervisor
mailman	mail carrier
mankind	humanity
manpower	work force
manmade	artificial, manufactured
policeman	police officer
salesman	salesperson

The tough one to replace is *manhole*. But did you ever stop to think that it could just as well be called a *streethole* or a *sewer cover?*

See also *he or she/his or her.*

may/can   See *can/may*.

most/almost   See *almost/most*.

Ms.

Accepted by most and preferred by many, the term *Ms.* (rhymes with *fizz*) allows us to address women without indicating (or even knowing) their marital status, as the term *Mr.* has always done for men.

myself

Properly used, *myself* is either an intensive (I am going to fix the faucet *myself*) or a reflexive pronoun (I cut *myself* shaving). Do not use *myself* as a subject or an object in writing.

> *Colloquial:*   Jocasta and **myself** are going to be partners.
> *Preferred:*   Jocasta and **I** are going to be partners.
> *Colloquial:*   Will you play tennis with Jocasta and **myself?**
> *Preferred:*   Will you play tennis with Jocasta and **me?**

number/amount   See *amount/number*.

orientated/oriented

The word *orientated* means "facing the east." Do not use this term if you mean *oriented*.

> That college **is oriented** in the liberal tradition.

Orientation is the correct form of the noun:

Freshman ***orientation*** begins in August.

prejudice/prejudiced

Although we seldom pronounce the *-ed*, do not leave it off in writing.

Prejudice remains engrained in our society.
Our society remains ***prejudiced*** against minorities.
Almost everyone is ***prejudiced*** against something.
Almost everyone harbors some sort of ***prejudice.***

prescribe/proscribe

Because these words have almost opposite meanings, you will badly confuse your readers if you use the wrong one. *Prescribe* means to recommend or to establish rules, while *proscribe* means to prohibit or denounce.

The legislature ***proscribes*** the use of certain drugs unless ***prescribed*** by a physician.

principal/principle

Although we have numerous meanings for *principal,* the word *principle* means a rule: a person of high moral *principle,* a primary *principle* of physics. You can remember the *-le* spelling by association with the *-le* ending on *rule.* All other uses will end with *-al*: a high school *principal,* the *principal* on a loan, a *principal* cause or effect, the *principal* (main character) in a film or play.

probable/probably

The adjective *probable* (sounds at the end like *capable*) and the adverb *probably* (ends with a long *e* sound, like *capably*) both mean likely.

> The **probable** involvement of the CIA in the revolution **probably** caused the rebels to lose.

proved/proven

Either form is acceptable as the past participle of the verb *to prove.*

> Carlyle's innocence **was proved** in court.
> Carlyle's innocence **was proven** in court.

quite/quiet

Be careful not to confuse these words. *Quite,* an adverb, means *entirely, truly; quiet* means the opposite of *loud.*

> Carol was **quite** ready to yell, "**Quiet,** please!"

quotes

As a verb, *quotes* is standard English.

> Louella **quotes** Shakespeare even in bed.

But as a shortening of *quotation* or *quotation marks,* the term *quotes* is still considered colloquial.

> *Avoid:* You no longer need to put **quotes** around slang.

raise/rear

You never *rear* chickens; you just *raise* them. But nowadays you can either *rear* or *raise* children.

real/really

Do not use *real* as an adverb in writing.

> *Colloquial:*   Charlie saw a ***real*** interesting movie.
> *Standard:*   Charlie saw a ***really*** interesting movie.

But *really* (like *very* and *basically* and *currently*) is a limp, overworked word. Either leave it out or find a more emphatic word.

> *Improved:*   Charlie saw an interesting movie.
> Charlie saw an extremely interesting movie.

reason is because

Because many readers expect a noun or adjective as complement of the *to be* verb (*am, is, was, were,* etc.), you should write "The reason is that . . . ," or rephrase your sentence.

> *Avoid:*   The reason we are swamped with trash is because I forgot to put the garbage out.
> *Better:*   The reason we are swamped with trash is that I forgot to put the garbage out.
> *Better:*   We are swamped with trash because I forgot to put the garbage out.

refer   See *allude/refer.*

rise/raise

You never *rise* anything, but you always *raise* something. Prices *rise*, spirits *rise*, curtains *rise*, but you *raise* cain, or *raise* corn, or *raise* prices.

> Taxes are **rising** because Congress has **raised** the defense budget again.

If you cannot keep these verbs straight, avoid them.

> Taxes are going up.
> Congress keeps increasing taxes.

shall/will

A few years back, "I *shall*" expressed simple future tense, while "I *will*" was considered emphatic. Current usage has erased this distinction. Most people use *will* consistently and rely on other means of gaining emphasis.

she or he   See *he or she/his or her.*

should of   See *could of/should of/would of.*

sit/set

The principal parts of these two verbs are as follows:

sit	sat	sat	sitting
set	set	set	setting

You seldom *sit* anything and you always *set* something (with these exceptions, which are never confused: the sun *sets,* jello and concrete *set,* hens *set*). We *sit* down or we *sit* a spell; we *set* a glass down or we *set* a time or we *set* the table.

One notable exception: the verb *sit* can mean "to cause to be seated." Thus, it is quite correct to write:

The teacher *sat* Buffy down and gave her a lecture.

sort of/kind of   See *kind of/sort of.*

split infinitives

Split infinitives are now acceptable in standard English, but try not to rend them asunder. A single adverb between *to* and the verb (*to* hastily *plan* a party) will not offend most readers, but purists still find any split infinitive objectionable. Know thy audience. (For a longer discussion, see *Split Infinitive* in the "Revising Index," Chapter 3.)

supposed to/used to

Since we never hear the *-d* sound in these phrases when we talk, the *-d* is easy to forget in writing. Whenever you write either term, be sure to add the *-d.*

than/then   See *then/than.*

their/there/they're

Do not confuse these words. *Their* is a possessive adjective or pronoun.

> **Their** dog is friendly. That dog is **theirs.**

There is an adverb or an expletive.

> **There** she goes. **There** is no problem.

They're is a contraction of *they are*.

> **They're** gone.

If you have trouble spelling *their*, remember that all three (*they're/there/their*) start with *the*.

theirselves

Do not use it unless writing dialect. The accepted term is *themselves*.

then/than

These words have quite different meanings. *Then* usually suggests a time.

> First we need to pick up the ice; **then** we can get the ice cream salt.

Than usually suggests a comparison.

> No one talks faster **than** Michael.
> Claudia would rather talk **than** eat.

thusly

Do not use it: always write simply *thus*.

---

to/too/two

To is usually a preposition, sometimes an adverb, and also introduces an infinitive.

> **to** the depths, push the door **to, to** swing

Too is an adverb.

> **Too** much noise.
> Selma is going **too.**

Two is the number.

> **two** paychecks, **two** miles

try and/try to

Although we frequently say, "I'm going to *try and* get this job done," the usage is still colloquial. In writing stick with *try to*.

> I am going to **try to** get this job done.

two See *to/too/two*.

uninterested/disinterested See *disinterested/uninterested*.

used to/supposed to   See *supposed to/used to.*

very

Avoid this colorless, exhausted word. Find one more exact and expressive (extremely, considerably, fully, entirely, completely, utterly) or else leave it out. See also *real/really.*

weather/whether

Do not confuse these words. *Weather* is what goes on outside; *whether* introduces an alternative.

> We cannot decide **whether** the **weather** will be suitable for a picnic.

who/which/that

Use *who* to refer to people (or animals you are personifying).

> The person **who** lost three keys . . .
> Lenin, **who** is Susie's cat, . . .

Use *which* to refer to animals or nonliving things.

> The earth **which** blooms in spring . . .
> The cat **which** lives at Susie's . . .

Use *that* to refer to either people or things.

> The person **that** lost these keys . . .
> The earth **that** blooms in spring . . .
> The cat **that** lives at Susie's . . .

If you are in doubt about whether to use *who* or *whom*, see *Case of Pronouns*, number 5, in the "Revising Index," Chapter 3.

will/shall   See *shall/will*.

would of   See *could of/should of/would of*

you (indefinite)

In informal writing, you may always address your readers as *you* (as we have done in this sentence). Somewhat questionable, though, is the use of *you* to mean just anyone (the *indefinite you*):

In France if **you** buy a loaf of bread, **you** get it without a wrapper.

If writing on a formal level, you should use the third person singular *one*.

In France if **one** buys a loaf of bread, **one** gets it without a wrapper.

your/you're

Your is a possessive adjective or pronoun.

This is **your** book; this book is **yours**.

You're is a contraction of *you are*.

Let me know when **you're** leaving.

COMPREHENSIVE EXERCISES 4-1

A. **Words frequently confused**

The following sentences contain words that sound alike but mean different things, like *quite/quiet*, *its/it's*, and *sit/set*. In each sentence, choose the appropriate term from the words in parentheses.

1. I have been (lead, led) astray again.
2. Tristan is plumper (then, than) a teddy bear.
3. (Its, It's) not the money; (its, it's) the (principal, principle) of the thing.
4. Those most in need of (advice, advise) seldom welcome it.
5. Horace cannot study if his room is (to, too) (quiet, quite).
6. The automobile is a (principal, principle) offender in contributing to air pollution.
7. Our spirits (rose, raised) with the sun.
8. They had a frisky time when (there, their) goose got (lose, loose).
9. Let's (lie, lay) down and talk this over.
10. That (continual, continuous) drip from the faucet is driving me to drink.
11. You ought to (appraise, apprise) the situation carefully before you decide (weather, whether) to file a complaint.
12. (You're, Your) decision could (affect, effect) your career.
13. If you (choose, chose) to file, you should not harbor the (illusion, allusion) that all (you're, your) problems will be solved.
14. Why don't we (sit, set) this one out?
15. (Your, you're) going to be sent to Lower Slobovia if you (accept, except) this job.
16. Virgil tends to (dominant, dominate) the conversation with his (continual, continuous) complaints about the IRS.
17. I could (infer, imply) from his complaints that he owes back taxes.
18. If the (weather, whether) improves, (then, than) we will plant the garden.
19. Any news program will usually (appraise, apprise) you of a late frost.
20. Snow peas will not be (affected, effected) by a light frost.
21. I (advice, advise) you to pick them young.

22. The dean has (lain, laid) down firm rules concerning class attendance.
23. I (chose, choose) strawberry last time, and it was all right, (accept, except) there weren't any strawberries in it.
24. Sherman was (quiet, quite) outraged by Marvin's (illusion, allusion) to his bald spot.
25. How did that dog (lose, loose) (its, it's) tail?
26. Many people mistakenly think (their, they're) being witty when they (dominant, dominate) the conversation.
27. Please (set, sit) that plant over (their, there) near the window.
28. Whenever I (lie, lay) down for a nap, the children outside (rise, raise) cain.
29. Stanley is a person of firm, moral (principle, principal) who should (rise, raise) to national prominence.
30. He (implied, inferred) that using artificial chocolate (affects, effects) the taste of the cookies.
31. Which would you rather (loose, lose)—your mind or your heart?
32. In his paper, Clovis (inferred, implied) that Milton is a crashing bore, but *Paradise Lost* (affects, effects) me deeply.
33. A large (amount, number) of students love English courses.
34. There are few differences (among, between) trashy romantic novels.
35. The (principle, principal) cause of indigestion is overeating.

B. Assorted matters of usage

Most of the sentences below contain examples of questionable usage. Revise those sentences that need changing in order to be acceptable as standard English. Some contain multiple mistakes.

1. My roommate and myself moved in an apartment.
2. We need to quickly, thoroughly, and painstakingly perform the analyzation of that substance again.
3. Did Everett author that report all by hisself?
4. Having been raised on a farm, Henrietta is disinterested in urban entertainments.
5. George baked a considerable amount of cookies.
6. You could of busted the lawn mover on that huge rock.

7. For once, try and do what you're suppose to.
8. Hopefully, we are already to go now.
9. I am going to put quotes around this slang, irregardless of what the book says.
10. Most everyone which is liable to come has all ready got here.
11. A banquet is where you eat alot of food and can't help but be bored by the speeches.
12. If we go altogether, we should be alright.
13. A person may buy his or her ticket from his or her union representative.
14. You would of had less problems if you would of centered around the main issue better.
15. The real reason I am not coming is because I am not interested anyways.
16. My ideas are all together different than those of the speaker.
17. If you live in Rome, you should do like the Romans do.
18. Clarence and Claudia got theirselves involved in a accident all ready on their new motorcycle.
19. Clarence use to enthuse about the virtues of being safety-conscious.
20. Now his safety record ain't any different from anybody else's.
21. Can I loan you my motorcycle?
22. If you turn the key, thusly, the engine shall start.
23. Where is the monkey wrench at?
24. Being as you are between a rock and a hard place, you do not have much choice anymore, do you?
25. In areas where muggers, rapists, etc., abound, a large dog really is man's best friend.
26. You tore my heart out and stomped on it: now what am I suppose to do?
27. The main reason we overeat is because food is so delicious.
28. If I had known you were coming, I would of left.
29. Sally and Samantha both wrote poems about air pollution; Sally's was best.
30. Charmain use to scrub the bathtub every day.

Part Two

Special
Skills

Chapter Five
Reading and Writing in College Classes

The reading that transmits ideas into your head is just as important as the writing process. You get plenty of ideas from conversation, television, radio, and your instructors' lectures, but the printed word offers you much more range and variety—and time to think. Paul Harvey's words are gone, off into space, after you hear them on the radio, but a written editorial stays right there for you to reread, question, and rethink.

Your college classes require much reading, and some people continue reading regularly after college to satisfy curiosity or to form educated opinions. In this chapter, we will recommend methods of improving your reading and for managing the chores every college student needs to do—studying, taking notes, and taking tests.

IMPROVING YOUR READING

If you are not a good reader, you will be hampered throughout your college career. We have some suggestions (furnished by our invaluable colleague Janet Youga) to help you get more out of what you read. The most important piece of advice is to look over the reading material carefully before you actually read it. Or, as Ms. Youga puts it, "Map out your trip before you leave." Let us explain how.

Reading a Textbook: Survey, Read, Write

1. Get to know your book. Textbooks often provide chapter summaries at the end or study questions that help to focus your attention on the main points. Find these before you start so that you will be able to concentrate on learning what you need to know when you have finished the reading.
2. Use the table of contents and the section headings to get an overview of the material. Those section headings (and subheads) are designed to direct you to the key ideas in each chapter.
3. Write a preliminary outline of the chapter, using the headings and subheadings as a guide.
4. Read the chapter and fill in your outline *in your own words* as you go. If you simply copy sentences from the text, you may be fooling yourself into thinking you understand passages that would baffle you if you had to supply the information out of your own head.
5. Use these outlines to study for tests and examinations.

Reading a Nontextbook

During your college career you will have to do a certain amount of "outside reading," as instructors call it. You will be assigned to read books that lack the reading aids provided in textbooks. Thus your strategy will need to be a bit different.

1. Read the preface or introduction to discover the thesis or main idea of the book—or at least its purpose.
2. Read the first line of each paragraph in the first chapter. You are just trying to discover the general content and structure in this step.
3. Write a rough outline from this prereading.
4. Read the chapter, filling in the outline *in your own words* as you go.
5. Keep these outlines to use in studying for tests or in writing reports.

EXPANDING YOUR STUDY SKILLS

In *How to Study* (2nd ed., New York: McGraw, 1969), Clifford T. Morgan and James Deese analyze the most common difficulties students have when they try to study. These experts suggest that a study schedule can solve many such problems. Here is a summary of their advice.

Scheduling Your Study Time

As a typical student, you have probably run into the following troubles:

1. Even though you try, you do not study as much as you know you should.
2. You are disorganized and waste time when you finally sit down to study. You plan to do too much in too short a time.
3. It's hard for you to start studying; things keep interfering with getting down to work.

All three problems come from slipshod use of your time. You can sweat and stew for hours over a task that would take you fifty minutes if you were well organized. A schedule for studying can help you make the best possible use of your time.

To help you develop a plan of your own, we have designed a sample schedule for a person who takes five college courses and works nineteen hours a week (Figure 5-1). Most of the study time is in one-hour blocks. Psychological research has shown that people work well when they work steadily for a period of time and then rest or change tasks. For studying, the best period of time is forty or fifty minutes of work followed by ten minutes of rest. A clear schedule takes the optimum work-and-rest cycle into account and thus makes your studying more efficient.

	Monday	Tuesday	Wednesday	Thursday	Friday	Saturday	Sunday
8:00–9:00		Economics class		Economics class			
9:00–10:00	Literature class	Study economics	Literature class	Study economics	Literature class	Study economics	
10:00–11:00	Biology class	Study biology	Biology class	Study biology	Biology class		
11:00–12:00	Study biology		Study biology		↓		
12:00–1:00							
1:00–2:00	Study Spanish	Study Spanish	Study Spanish	Study Spanish	Study Spanish	Work	Work
2:00–3:00	Spanish class	Spanish class	Spanish class	Spanish class	Spanish class		
3:00–4:00							
4:00–5:00	Work	Health class		Health class			
5:00–6:00		Study health		Study health			
6:00–7:00						↓	↓
7:00–8:00		Study literature		Study literature			Study literature
8:00–9:00	↓						

Figure 5-1 (opposite) Sample study schedule. This student works part time and carries five classes a semester. The gaps in the chart are for catch-up study, library time, or fooling around. When you make up your own schedule, be sure to make it consistent with your own preferences and habits. For instance, if you study well late at night, your chart will not be so empty at the bottom. Realize that you need room for flexibility, as you won't be able to follow your plan exactly week after week.

The study hours on the schedule are marked for specific subjects. That way, you will not waste time figuring out what to do, and you can plan in advance to have on hand all the study materials you need. You have probably experienced the frustration of finally settling down at the library to study only to find that you left an important notebook at home. Scheduling regular hours to study specific subjects will also help you avoid the vicious cycle of falling behind in one class as you cram for another.

Notice three more advantages of the sample schedule:

1. It gives less time to easy subjects and more to difficult ones. We have scheduled four hours of study for biology, but only two for the snap course health.
2. It spreads out your studying. Research shows that you learn and remember better if you distribute eight hours of study over a week's time than if you study eight hours in a row.
3. It attempts to place studying at the best time possible for each course. In general, studying a subject close to its class period helps. For a lecture course, the best time to study is after class; for a recitation course, the best time to study is before class. Thus, we have scheduled time to study Spanish right before class and time to study health and economics, both lecture courses, directly after the class periods. The literature and biology classes are mixed lecture and recitation courses.

These suggestions may have helped you face the grim facts about studying: you have to do it, and it takes time. Once you get used to those ideas, it is possible to find satisfaction in developing your study techniques to peak efficiency.

Analyze Your Study Habits

Research supports the idea that each of us has energy and alertness cycles of our own. Some find it exhilarating to hop out of bed at 7 A.M. to write an argumentative essay; others could not effectively sign their own names at that hour but are at their persuasive peak at six in the afternoon.

The factors involved in these peaks and valleys are too numerous to figure out scientifically, but if you pay attention to your own successes and failures, you may learn valuable lessons. Try this system: whenever you have a particularly good or bad study session, take note of the following four variables.

1. **Time of day.** A study of California college students identified two peak learning periods occurring between 8 A.M. and 5 P.M. The students worked best between 9 and 11 in the morning and 3 and 4 in the afternoon. They were at their worst, as many of us notice in ourselves, right after lunch. You may or may not fit this pattern, but you probably have one of your own. Record the times of your best and worst study sessions, and see if you can adjust your schedule accordingly.

2. **Your stomach.** Many people feel alert and zesty when they are a bit hungry. Others either suffer mentally-dulling physiological effects of hunger or else cannot concentrate on anything but a snack. If hunger does not make you feel perky, a high-protein morsel (peanuts, cheese, yogurt) may help.

3. **Your worries.** Letting worries interfere with your efforts is probably one of the most common syndromes. (Some people, though, are quite able to "throw themselves into their work" to escape their problems.) If worries get in your way, try fifteen minutes of meditation, music, or exercise; a brief talk with a friend; or even a page or

two of free writing about your problem. Eventually you have to get down to work, no matter what is bugging you, but sometimes half an hour of self-therapy will save you hours of inattentive studying.

4. **Your setting.**   Do your good study sessions happen at a clean, bare desk or among a sea of stimulating clutter? Sitting in the library or lying on the parlor carpet? What kind of music, if any, plays in the background? Do you prefer the tomblike atmosphere of 4 A.M. or the company of your fellow students turning pages and rattling type-writers? The differences among people are immense. Being sensitive to your own quirks will help you to design a study system that will work, as well as one that will help you avoid situations in which learning is depressingly hopeless for you.

Note-Taking

Two kinds of note-taking are usually called for in college: note-taking from lectures and note-taking from texts. Taking clear, well-organized notes can save you time when you study for tests, because writing plants the ideas more firmly in your mind, and if the material is tiresome, moving your pen can help you stay awake.

Our clever note-keeping system is designed for those read-the-book, listen-to-the-lecture, take-the-test courses that are so plentiful in your first years of college. We assume that you use a spiral or three-ring notebook and have a separate section for each of your subjects. This system integrates what you learn from books and what you learn from lectures by placing your notes on them conveniently next to each other: use the left-hand side for textbook notes and the right-hand side for lecture notes, as shown in Figure 5-2.

If you read the textbook assignment before the related lecture, you will have the backs of several pages filled with notes when you go to class. Take your lecture notes on the pages facing each of those pages, right across from the information

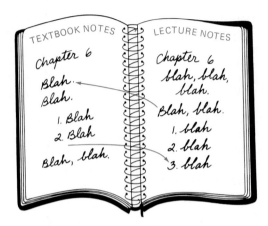

Figure 5-2 Note-taking system.

you got from the book. If you read the text after hearing the lecture, do it the other way around. You can even draw little arrows to point out relationships between the two sets (when, for instance, your teacher brings up a different and better example of some general principle that the book discusses).

Many students, especially in humanities and social sciences courses, find it helpful to underline important passages and write notes in the margins of the textbooks themselves. Since most college students own their books, the prohibition against marking in a text no longer applies.

Lecture Notes. Good lecturers start the class by previewing the topic or main points to be covered that day, and you can write these important items (and the date) at the top of the page. Your syllabus will often tell you what the topic of the day is.

Next you have to figure out the outline of the lecture—the main points and the details connected with them. Some lecturers list their main points on the blackboard, which makes it easy. Between main points, some of them pause, riffle their lecture notes, change their tone of voice, or use transitions like "The next solution has three drawbacks," in which case you can get ready to note the solution and list three items under it.

Do not, of course, try to take down every word. Record only key words, and use abbreviations and symbols to save time (so long as you can be sure to remember their meaning later), like this note from an accounting lecture:

Diff. in cost & selling price = *gross margin* or *profit gross*. Used to pay operating exp. Prod. cost = exp. matched w/sales rev.

As you read this note back to yourself, you reconstruct it in your mind this way:

The difference between the cost and the selling price is the *gross margin,* or *profit gross*. This money is used to pay the operating expenses. The cost of the product is the expense that is matched with sales revenue.

You are in much better shape if you have read and taken notes on the relevant textbook assignment before the lecture. Then you will not furiously struggle to get down details from the lecture which also appear in the book. Writing down the main points more than once, though, will probably help you remember them.

You will eventually develop your own style of note-taking, one you feel comfortable with. Perhaps you will start jotting things in the margins of your notebook—your personal responses to the lecture or questions to ask at the end. Such a system will save confusion later when you may have forgotten which ideas were yours and which were the professor's.

If you do not have good lecturers, you may have to scribble down everything (except stuff like their son's piano recitals and their crummy jokes) and try to organize it later. In this case, it's good to have a three-ring notebook instead of a spiral, because it's easier to discard and replace pages.

Textbook Notes.   Taking notes from textbooks is much more comfortable. Writers usually provide headings and subheadings that tell you what the important concepts are. Many experts on study skills suggest that you look over a chapter's headings, subheadings, and emphasized type. Then jot down some questions that you suspect the chapter will answer. As you read the chapter, note the answers to the questions.

Here are the headings from a section of Elizabeth McMahan's *A Crash Course in Composition,* 2nd ed. (New York: McGraw, 1977):

Main heading:	A QUICK LOOK AT LOGIC
Subhead:	Avoid Oversimplifying
Italic type:	*either/or, false dichotomy*
Subhead:	Sweeping Generalizations

Here are some questions you might write before reading the text:

1. What does she mean by *logic?*
2. How quick is this going to be?
3. What is oversimplifying?
4. How are *either/or* and *false dichotomy* related to oversimplification?
5. What is one example of oversimplifying?
6. Where is the best place to sweep a generalization?
7. How do you know when a generalization is sweeping?

Some of these questions will turn out to be irrelevant (as well as irreverent), but they will give you a start on your thinking and note-taking.

If the book or article you are studying does not provide helpful headings, remember that a paragraph usually has a stated or implied topic sentence. Trying to find and note down these topics can be a healthy exercise. You will end up with a skeleton of the chapter or article, and as a result be able to see clearly how it's put together, what the logic underlying it is (just like looking at a human skeleton).

No bones about it, note-taking can really help you focus on the major, minor, and supporting points of a lecture or reading selection. Highlighting or underlining in your text will not do you as much good, as it does not require such a high level of involvement (psychologically or physically). If you will develop your note-taking skill, you will find that you can cut your studying time for an exam in half. Meanwhile, you will double the length of time that you recall what you learned (and that's what getting a college education is supposed to be about).

EXERCISE   5-1

1. Take lengthy notes on a single lecture by each of three teachers. Try to organize each set of notes into an outline of major and minor points. Which lecture was easiest to organize? Which was most difficult? Why?

2. Here are the headings from Chapter 6 of X. J. Kennedy's *An Introduction to Poetry*, 2nd ed. (Boston: Little, Brown, 1971). Make up study questions from them.

Chapter title:	Figures of Speech
Heading:	Why Speak Figuratively?
Heading:	Metaphor and Simile
Emphasized type:	*implied metaphor*
Heading:	Other Figures
Emphasized type:	*personification, apostrophe, understatement, overstatement, pun*

3. Make a list of headings like the one above, using one of your own future reading assignments from a textbook. Trade lists with another student and make up study questions for his or her list. After you get your list back, use the questions when you read your assignment, and report on their success or failure in helping you take notes and understand your reading.

Building Vocabulary as You Study

If you are a typical college student, your vocabulary could use enrichment. You are probably unfamiliar with the meanings of useful words like *esoteric, secular,* and *garish;* you can probably come up with just one meaning each for the words *pedestrian, sophisticated,* and *materialism.* And these are not oddball technical terms: they are used frequently in written English. Always follow the good advice in Chapter 3 about using your dictionary and thesaurus.

TIPS ON TAKING TESTS

Hardly anyone likes tests, and lots of intelligent people suspect that they do not even test what they claim to test; instead, they test how good you are at taking tests. But for many courses in college, your grades are likely to be determined by testing. In this section, we summarize some of the best advice we have heard, which can transform you into a calm, cool, and competent taker of tests.

Scoring High on an Objective Test

Objective tests consist of true-false statements, items to be matched, multiple-choice questions, fill-in-the-blank sentences, and any other grotesque devices teachers think up, so long as you are not required to write sentences. Often such tests involve writing A, B, C, or 1, 2, 3, or coloring in the right little stick with a number 2 pencil on a computer sheet.

Before the Test.   To prepare for an objective test, review the cleverly organized notes you took from your textbook and class lectures (see pages 239–243). There is no substitute for knowing the course material. You should have studied everything once already, before you begin to review for the test. If you have not, you need to work on your study habits. As you review, take notice of topics you do not remember clearly or in much detail; then reread the parts of your textbook that deal with those topics. Try making a list of special terms and their definitions. Making such a list, by the way, will help you on any kind of test.

One gimmick you can try is to squeeze the most important facts you need to know for the test onto both sides of *one* four-by six-inch index card. The process of choosing what to write on your card helps you to get all those pages of notes organized. Carry the index card around with you. You can stare sullenly at it while riding the bus or waiting in line at the grocery store or brushing your teeth.

Armed with a good night's sleep and a satisfied stomach (remember, these tests usually ask you to recognize fine distinctions, so you must be alert and keep your strength up), you are ready to take the test. Get to the testing place a little early, so you can sit and relax before the ordeal; you do not want your mind all muddled from rushing about. Be sure that you have a watch or that a clock is visible so you can schedule your time.

   During the Test.   When you get the test, look it over. Check out what kinds of questions there are and how many of each, so you can get an idea of how long you should spend on each part. Then go back to the beginning and read the instructions very carefully. Filling out your answer sheet incorrectly can make your best efforts worthless.

   Next go through the test and answer all the easy questions. This will help build your self-confidence and will get your mind in the right mood to tangle with the tough ones. Do not be too hasty, though. Read *all* the items in a matching list before you put down the answer to the first one. If you are doing multiple choice, with four possible answers, begin by eliminating the ones you know are wrong, and you will then have a better chance of choosing the right one.

   After you have finished the easy questions, estimate how much time you can spend on each of the hard ones. For instance, if you have twenty minutes left and sixteen unanswered questions, you should puzzle over each one for only about a minute. This planning will keep you from wasting time racking your brains over one answer that you will never get, while slighting another that you *can* think out.

   As you go through the test answering the hard questions, you may have the urge to change some of your earlier answers. One school of thought says you should always trust your first answer. But you may have a perfectly good reason to change it, like having misread the question the first time or finding your memory now sharper on that point. Do not change your answers on a shaky basis, like panic. And do not keep going over and over them looking for details you might have missed, or you will just get confused. In most cases, though, you will do better to guess at an answer than to leave one blank.

You are probably aware that not all teachers are skillful at making up objective tests, which are quite difficult to design. So you may encounter a test whose questions and answers you feel are ambiguous and confusing, even though you know the material. When you get the graded test back, discuss every ambiguous point with your teacher. You owe the effort to yourself and to the other students. If your grade is determined by tests, you must insist that the tests be clear and fair and that you are given the opportunity to learn from your mistakes.

Writing a Successful Essay Examination

The skills you need to write a good essay examination may seem irrelevant to life in the world outside college. But in other situations you will sometimes have to come up with impromptu, one-draft writing (like memos, on-the-spot job forms, teacher evaluations).

Before the Test.   To prepare for an essay test, study your text and your notes, as you would for an objective test. The index card gimmick works here too. But remember that this time you do not just have to *recognize* all those facts; you have to *recall* them. A little more memorization of details and definitions might be a good idea. In the process, ponder possible essay questions, and think about how you could organize your knowledge in writing.

During the Test.   When you get your test, survey it first. Look for instructions about how long each answer should be. Sometimes your teacher will ask for one- or two-sentence answers, sometimes for one well-developed paragraph, and sometimes for an essay of several paragraphs. These length differences are likely to be related to point distribution—for instance, on a mixed (both objective and essay) test, an essay may net a maximum of 30 points, while a short answer, no matter how clever, will provide a paltry 5 points.

If you have several short essays to write, immediately mark those questions that look most attractive (or least repulsive) to you.

The most unnerving thing about essay exams is lack of time. You can ease this problem a little by scheduling your time. Of course, you should distribute your time in proportion to the number of points assigned to each answer. Some teachers furnish a time schedule along with the test, but in other cases you are left on your own. If the written instructions do not assign points to questions, ask your instructor for the point distribution.

Here's a sample proportional schedule for an hour test worth 90 points on your grade:

$$\frac{90 \text{ points}}{60 \text{ minutes}} = 3/2 = \text{about 2 minutes for every 3 points}$$

	Points	Minutes	
5 short identification items, 5 points each	25	15	(3 minutes each)
1 short essay (paragraph)	15	10	
1 long essay	50	33	
	90	58	

This sample reveals how important time planning is. If you did not survey the test and make a schedule, you might be tempted to write for five minutes each on the identification items—and that extra ten minutes would really cut down on your time for the long essay, which has the most possible points.

After planning your time, plan your answers. Every test expert we consult agrees that the time you spend making a scratch outline of your essay is well worth it. Even though your answer may turn out shorter than it would be if you attacked the page immediately, your essay will be more pointworthy because of its clear organization and lack of sloppy repetition (which is sometimes suspiciously called *padding*).

As you plan, pay attention to the *verb* in the essay question: *list, explain, compare, evaluate, give examples.* Do what the verb tells you to do. If you are supposed to compare two kinds of cockroaches, a brilliant essay about cockroach habits simply won't do. And be careful not to miss a part of the instructions. If you are asked to *define* and *evaluate* five methods of cockroach extermination, and you just define them, you can expect only half credit for your answer.

In any course you may feel that you have a firm grasp of the general principles or trends or methods, but your teacher is not for a minute going to believe you do unless you follow up every general statement you make with a U-Haul full of specific details (names, dates, examples, quotations) that you have painstakingly memorized for this very purpose. Do not make the mistake of thinking that you need to know such "picky little stuff" only for objective exams. A mass of generalizations is boring and unimpressive to a teacher who is plowing through thirty essay exams over the weekend. A little life and color is certainly welcome (and likely to be rewarded) on those deadly Sunday afternoons.

In short, remember these three steps next time you must wrestle with an essay test:

1. Calmly survey the exam.
2. Schedule time according to point distribution.
3. Make a scratch outline of your essay.
   a. Do what the verb in the question tells you to do.
   b. Include lots of juicy details.

Sample Essay Exam Answers

To illustrate some common faults of essay exam writing, we are providing three sample answers (followed by analysis) to this question:

> In a short essay, discuss the placement of the topic sentence of a paragraph.

Answer A.   The topic sentence states the main idea of the paragraph. It serves as kind of an umbrella that covers all the ideas that will be included therein. It may be placed at the beginning or end of the paragraph, whichever makes the paragraph more clear and interesting. All the details, examples, and reasoning in the paragraph should be clearly related to each other and to the topic sentence. A short topic sentence may be used infrequently to emphasize a point; a long, balanced topic sentence may also be effective. The paragraph should not wander off the topic sentence. Sometimes a topic sentence is not necessary at all, in which case you should leave it out.

Answer B.   The topic sentence, or main point of the paragraph, is usually at the beginning in most writing. This placement makes the idea that the paragraph deals with clear to the reader right away. Then the supporting details and examples are easily understood, since the idea that unifies them is already in the reader's mind. This is why most topic sentences are near the opening of the paragraph. Closing with the topic sentence is a good idea too in certain situations. The supporting material may lead up to the main idea, or you may want to use the element of surprise that comes from not stating the point until the end. Placing the topic sentence at the end can also add variety to your paragraphs once in a while. A middle position may also add variety. Sometimes—not often—the center of the paragraph is just the right place for the topic sentence. You can also state the main idea twice if you want to, to emphasize and reinforce it. If no one could possibly miss the main point of the paragraph, you should not write in a topic sentence.

Answer C. The topic sentence of a paragraph usually appears at either the beginning or the end; in a few cases, it may appear in the middle, twice, or not at all. The main idea you intend to expand in the paragraph may be made clear, and the outline of your expansion made easy to see, if you open with the topic sentence, as I did in this paragraph. A paragraph that depends on a series of details or examples to lead inductively to a general conclusion (the main point) lends itself to a topic sentence at the end. For example, you could list a series of outrageous building costs and close with the topic sentence, "Clearly, the governor spent too much on his mansion." This final placement would emphasize the general statement. Putting the topic sentence in the middle of the paragraph may be appropriate for a paragraph that begins inductively and then reflects on the main point. Stating the topic in different ways both first and last may clarify and unify a paragraph with a complicated or abstract main idea. Finally, the main idea of a paragraph of description or narration may be best left unstated—it should be clear from the details.

Analysis of Answers

Answer A was written by a student who was not quite desperate, but close. It only addresses the question specifically in two sentences: the others give a flurry of all the student knows about topic sentences and paragraphs, in a way that is disunified and, ironically, has no topic sentence.

Answer B is a great improvement. The student does have a grasp of the information the question asks for. The answer does survey the possible placements and gives some semblance of reason for each one. Still, some of those reasons are too vague, and some of the development shows signs of padding or lack of planning.

Answer C is a good one. It is obviously well planned, since the order of the discussion is predicted in the first sentence. It gives examples and intelligent reasons for the various placements. It devotes more space to the major placements than it does to the minor ones. The student is clearly in control of the material.

EXERCISE   5-2

1. Figure out a time schedule for taking the following tests:
   a. Test time: 50 minutes

	Points	Total points
10 short definition items	5 each	50
5 short essays	10 each	50

   b. Test time: 2 hours (120 minutes)

	Total points
15 true-false questions	15
20 multiple-choice questions	40
2 short essays (30 points each)	60
1 long essay	50

2. Here's a sample half-hour essay examination based on Scheduling Your Study Time (pages 235–238). Read the section again. Then plan your time and take the test without looking back to the section.

Short-answer essays (10 points each)
a. List three advantages of setting up a study schedule.
b. Identify the best unit of time for most college study, and tell why it is good.
c. When should you review for a recitation class? When should you review for a lecture class? Why?

Longer essay (30 points)
Summarize the studying problems that the writer identifies. From your own experience, discuss whether that list of problems is true to life.

Analyze any difficulties you had with scheduling or planning your answers. Trade papers with other students, and see how they handled the answers.

GETTING EXTRA HELP: USEFUL REFERENCE BOOKS

Laird, D. A., and E. C. Laird. *Techniques for Efficient Remembering.* New York: McGraw, 1960.
Miller, L. L. *Increasing Reading Efficiency,* 4th ed. New York: Holt, 1977.
Morgan, C. T., and James Deese. *How to Study,* 3rd ed. New York: McGraw, 1979.
Robinson, F. P. *Effective Study,* 4th ed. New York: Harper, 1970.
Smith, G. L. *Spelling by Principles: A Programmed Text.* New York: Appleton, 1966.

Chapter Six
Researched Writing

At some time you may be asked to write a paper that does not spring entirely from your own mind. You may be expected to do research—to read fairly widely on a certain subject, to synthesize (to combine a number of different ideas into a new whole) and organize this accumulated information, and then to get your new knowledge down on paper in clear and coherent prose. The whole process may seem like busywork when assigned by your English instructor, but be assured: you will be learning a valuable skill, one that is essential in your advanced college classes and that will prove useful in compiling on-the-job reports after graduation.

Traditionally, research papers involve argument. You may be expected to choose a topic which is somewhat controversial, investigate the issues thoroughly on both sides, and take a stand. The writing process for a research paper is essentially the same as for any other, except that you begin with a thesis question which you later turn into a thesis statement. You still need to narrow the subject to a topic you can handle in the number of pages assigned. And the bulk of the writing in the paper should be yours, stating your evaluation of what you have learned from your sources. You will quote from and give credit to the authors you have read, but a cut-and-paste job (in which you merely string together ideas and quotations from your sources) will not do.

SCHEDULING YOUR RESEARCH PAPER

Writing a research paper is a time-consuming job. This is one paper that you simply cannot put off until the last minute. If you divide the project into units, you can keep the work under control.

Set Deadlines for Yourself

If your completed paper is due in, say, six weeks, you could put yourself on a schedule something like this:

1st week: Complete preliminary bibliography cards locating all your sources.
Try to narrow your topic down to a workable thesis question to investigate.

2d week: Read and take notes.
Settle on a preliminary thesis question.
Try to come up with a preliminary outline.

3d week: Continue reading and taking notes.

4th week: Complete reading and note-taking.
Turn your thesis question into a statement.
Wrestle the outline into shape.

5th week: Write the first draft.
Let it cool—rest yourself.
Begin revising and editing.
Get someone reliable to read your second draft and tell you whether every sentence is clear, every quotation properly introduced, and every paragraph nicely coherent.

6th week: Polish the paper.
Type the final draft.
Let it rest at least overnight.
Proofread it carefully.

That is a fairly leisurely schedule. You can, of course, do the work in a shorter time if required to. You will just have to be more industrious about the reading. Some instructors deliberately ask students to complete the project within a month in order to allow no chance for procrastination. Whatever your time limit, devise a schedule for yourself and stick to it.

Narrowing Your Topic

If you have an area of interest but no ideas about any way to limit that topic, your first step might be to consult a good encyclopedia. Perhaps your father recently underwent abdominal surgery; as a result of spending many hours with him, you have become interested in hospitals. An encyclopedia article on hospitals will briefly discuss their history, some specialized kinds, services provided, intern training, difficulties with sanitation, and cost of care, among other things. Remembering that your dad contracted a staph infection while recovering from his operation, you might decide to investigate the problem of infections in hospitals. Why have they become prevalent? What is being done about them? Or, as you read the article, you might encounter a new term and become interested in *hospices*—specialized hospitals that attempt to provide comfort and dignity for the dying. Are these proving successful? Should we have more of them in this country? Something in an encyclopedia article on your subject is likely to provide the spark needed to fire your curiosity and give you a focus for your research.

Expanding Your Associations

Once you have narrowed your topic, you may need momentarily to expand it again in order to locate all the relevant information in the library. As indexes and other reference tools do not necessarily classify information the way you do in your brain, you need to think of other headings under which your subject might be indexed. Before going to the library, you should make a list of topics related to your research subject. If you are planning to investigate hospices, your list might go like this:

Hospice
Dying
Death
Aging
Geriatrics
Health care
Old people
Euthanasia

EXERCISE   6-1

For each of the following subjects, list at least three related topics that you could look under in reference books.

1. No-fault divorce
2. High school students' legal rights
3. Fad diets
4. Detective fiction by women
5. Use of the word *ain't*
6. Tax shelters
7. Horror movies

TOPICS FOR RESEARCHED WRITING

If your mind remains a blank and your instructor will allow you to borrow a topic from us, here are some ideas that we think might be interesting to research.

For Writing an Informative Paper

1. Research the history of a familiar product or object, such as Coca-Cola, Mickey Mouse, the dictionary, the typewriter, the nectarine, black mass, black magic, vampire movies.
2. Research and analyze a fad, craze, or custom: fraternity initiation, pierced ears, "smile" buttons, any fad diet, punk fashions, Cabbage Patch dolls.
3. How can autistic children be helped?
4. How can alcoholics be helped?
5. How can rape victims be helped?
6. Why do people become alcoholics?
7. What is *anorexia nervosa* and can it be prevented?
8. What is *agoraphobia* and what can be done about it?
9. How can battered women be helped?
10. Why do women allow themselves to be beaten by their husbands?

For Writing about Literature

1. How effective is the ending of *Huckleberry Finn?*
2. Is the governess sane or insane in James's "The Turn of the Screw"?
3. What are the characteristics of the "Hemingway hero"?
4. What are the mythological implications of Eudora Welty's "Moon Lake"?
5. What was Zola's contribution to literary naturalism?

For Persuasion or Argumentation

After doing the appropriate research, defend either side of one of the following issues.

1. Is nuclear waste disposal safe—or suicidal?
2. The use of animals in research should (should not) be allowed.
3. Clear-cutting of forests should (should not) be stopped.

4. It is (is not) better for children if their incompatible parents get a divorce.

5. The children's toys now on the market often encourage (discourage) destructiveness and discourage (encourage) creativity.

6. The federal government does (does not) have the right to monitor activities of United States citizens whom it regards as possible terrorists.

7. The fashion industry does (does not) exploit consumers. Or substitute any area of business that interests you: the cosmetics industry, the funeral business, the car manufacturers, the oil industry, etc.

8. Having a working mother does (does not) harm a child's development.

9. Automation has (has not) hindered our culture more than it has helped.

10. Violence on children's TV shows is (is not) harmful to children.

11. Newspaper reporters should (should not) have the right to protect their sources.

12. Parents should (should not) have the right to censor the textbooks and literature taught in their children's schools.

13. Internment of Japanese-American families after the United States entered World War II was a grave injustice (was necessary for the national security).

14. Is sexual harassment in the workplace a serious problem—or a myth?

15. The government should provide more (fewer) benefits for single parents on welfare.

SOME CLUES ON USING THE LIBRARY

Once you have your deadlines set and your topic chosen, you need to get acquainted with your library. Most college libraries offer orientation courses to show students how to find things. If the course is not required, take it anyway. An orientation course is your surest bet for learning your way around a library. If no such course is offered, your library will at least have available a handbook explaining what's where. A few minutes spent studying these instructions may save you many hours of aimless wandering. After reading the handbook carefully, if you search and still fail to find what you need, ask for help. Librarians are seldom snarly about answering questions and will often take you in tow, lead you to the material you want, and give you valuable advice.

Locating the Major Resources

We can offer here some general instructions to help you find your way around your library.

The Card Catalog.   Somewhere near the entrance to the library you may see imposing rows of polished wood cabinets with small drawers in which are alphabetically filed cards listing all the books, periodicals, microfilm, and pamphlets available on the premises. These cards (listed by author, title, and subject) provide the *call number* that you need in order to track down the material. You can, in fact, sometimes decide whether to read or reject an item just by observing the information on the catalog card—date, author, publisher, bibliography, title and subtitle.

Some libraries use separate cabinets to house the subject cards. If you want to find a biography of Mark Twain, for instance, and look him up in the author/title section, you will be directed to try again under "Samuel Langhorne Clemens," his real name. When you locate the box with the Clemens cards, you may find only books *by* Mark Twain. If so, you must locate the cabinets containing subject headings. Here, under "Clemens," you will discover numerous books *about* Twain, i.e., books with Twain (or his work) as their subject matter.

The Computerized Catalog.   Your library may have a computer which will save you the trouble of leafing through the cards. If so, you will be able to call up the information needed to locate your material by the touch of a keyboard.

The Stacks.   Those seemingly endless numbered shelves on which books are stored are called the stacks (computer abbreviation: *stx*). In many libraries the stacks are open, and you are free to wander along the aisles, examine the books, and decide which ones you want to check out. If the stacks are closed, the library provides someone to do the finding for you.

The Circulation Desk.   In a closed-stack library, you present your call slips at the circulation desk and wait for a clerk to bring your books to you. (A *call slip* is a form provided by the library on which you write the call number, author, title, and possibly volume number of the item you want.) If the library has open stacks, you take your call slips, find the books yourself using the call numbers, and return to the circulation desk to check out the ones you want. Someone at the circulation desk can tell you if a book you could not locate is checked out or—worse luck—lost. If the book is simply out, you may put a "hold" on it, and when it is returned, you will be notified. If the book is lost, you can request a search. Should the librarians be able to find the book, you will receive notice. But if the book is genuinely lost—or, more likely, stolen—you are out of luck. Eventually the library will reorder the item, but probably not in time for you to use now.

The Reserve Desk.   Books (and sometimes copies of articles) being intensively used in courses may be put "on reserve" by faculty members and will be held at the reserve desk (or in the reserve room) where they are easily available to students. Materials on reserve are usually restricted for library use only—often by the hour. The card catalog will identify any item placed on reserve so that you need not exhaust yourself searching futilely in the stacks.

Reference Materials and Periodicals.   Libraries arranged according to types of material will have a separate *periodicals room* in which you may read recent copies of popular magazines and journals for all disciplines. A separate *reference room* will include bibliographical indexes, reference volumes, encyclopedias, and dictionaries for every area of research. These materials must be used where they are. You should not move them, and you are never allowed to check them out (i.e., they are *noncirculating*).

In many new libraries the materials are arranged by subject, divided floor by floor. All the resources—including reference tools and periodicals—for the social sciences, for instance, are collected on a single floor. Separate floors may be devoted to education, to the humanities, to the hard sciences, and to government documents. These *subject divisional libraries*, as they are called, also include on the main floor an easily accessible array of nonspecialized reference books and bibliographies, as well as a collection of the most often used books from every academic discipline. (This area is called the *general college library*, or GCL.)

HOW TO FIND WHAT YOU NEED IF YOU DON'T KNOW WHAT IT IS

When you begin compiling your preliminary bibliography— your list of books, articles, and chapters in books on your topic—you will not know what these are or where to find them. Do not despair. What sounds like a difficult task is actually fairly simple.

Begin with the Card or Computer Catalog

You will find the books available on your topic by looking it up by subject in the card catalog (or by using the handy computer). Remember also to look under related subjects if you fail to find enough material on your first try.

Consult Indexes and Bibliographies

The task gets a bit tricky when you move on to the next step, which involves finding out what articles and essays are available on your topic. The chief tools you need are mammoth sets of books which index, year by year, all the articles in a multitude of magazines.

You need to know first which indexes cover what type of magazines, or you could waste a lot of time scanning titles that have no potential usefulness. (Figure 6-2 provides a list of reference tools arranged by specialized areas.) The *Readers' Guide to Periodical Literature* (familiarly known as the *Readers' Guide*) will be of little value if your paper is on Edgar Allan Poe, for instance, because it indexes popular magazines, not scholarly ones. How often does *Mechanics Illustrated* come out with a big spread on Poe? But if you are investigating possibilities for cutting down pollution from automobile exhaust, *Mechanics Illustrated* may have just the article you want. Or if you are writing on some aspect of current events, the *Readers' Guide* will lead you to articles in *Newsweek, Time, U.S. News and World Report,* as well as to magazines which analyze current events, like *Harper's,* the *Atlantic,* and the *National Review*. A typical entry from the *Readers' Guide* is shown in Figure 6-1. Another useful index for any research involving current events is the *Public Affairs Information Service Bulletin* (PAIS). Here you will find indexed articles dealing with various topics of public interest.

For that Poe article, you would be better off consulting the *Humanities Index* (formerly part of the *International Index*), or, if you want the really scholarly articles, the *MLA Bibliography* (which works just like the other indexes, but you may

The symbols mean vol. 115, pages 106 through 107 and continued (+) in the back of the February 1982 issue.

Cross reference to an item listed under the name of a joint author.

This article includes a portrait (por).

This entry lists a short story, not an article.

The asterisk means this article is available as a talking book for the blind.

These articles are all illustrated (il).

Another cross reference.

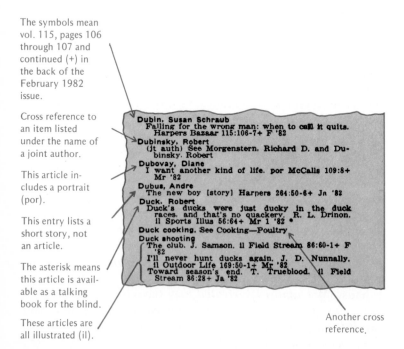

Dubin, Susan Schraub
 Falling for the wrong man: when to call it quits.
  Harpers Bazaar 115:106-7+ F '82
Dubinsky, Robert
 (jt auth) See Morgenstern, Richard D. and Dubinsky, Robert
Dubovay, Diane
 I want another kind of life. por McCalls 109:8+
  Mr '82
Dubus, Andre
 The new boy [story] Harpers 264:50-6+ Ja '82
Duck, Robert
 Duck's ducks were just ducky in the duck
  races, and that's no quackery. R. L. Drinon.
  il Sports Illus 56:64+ Mr 1 '82 •
Duck cooking. See Cooking—Poultry
Duck shooting
 The club. J. Samson. il Field Stream 86:60-1+ F
  '82
 I'll never hunt ducks again. J. D. Nunnally.
  il Outdoor Life 169:50-1+ Mr '82
 Toward season's end. T. Trueblood. il Field
  Stream 86:28+ Ja '82

Figure 6-1 An entry from the *Readers' Guide to Periodical Literature*.

have to troop off to the humanities area to find it). If you would like to find out what Poe's contemporaries thought of his writing, look him up in *Poole's Index to Periodical Literature*, which covers the major nineteenth-century magazines.

There are several other reference works of general interest. One of the most valuable is the *Essay and General Literature Index*. This treasure allows you to locate essays buried in books and to find chapters of books that may pertain to your topic, even though the title might give no clue. Then there is the *Book Review Digest*, which tells you briefly what various reviewers thought of a book when it came out (if it came out after 1905) and gives you informed guidance concerning the potential usefulness or possible partiality of a source you may be considering. All you need is the approximate year of publication in order to know which volume to consult. *The New York Times Index* will furnish you with the date of any noteworthy event since 1851, allowing you to look it up in the files of your local newspaper—or in the *Times* itself on microfilm. The *Social Sciences Index* (formerly part of the *International Index* and, until recently, combined with the *Humanities Index*) should prove useful if you are looking for articles related to sociology, psychology, anthropology, political science, or economics. Articles pertaining to history or literature are listed in the *Humanities Index*.

One more tip: just because some periodical index lists a magazine does not mean that your library will necessarily *have* that magazine. Before you tire yourself searching the stacks, spend a minute checking the list of periodical holdings for your library to find out whether the magazine will be there.

Also, just because a magazine or book is supposed to be in the library does not, in fact, guarantee that the item *will* be there. Theft is a major problem in libraries these days. You should report lost or ripped-out materials to someone at the circulation desk so that the missing items can be replaced.

Ask about the Others. If you plan to do some really high powered research, you may need more specialized indexes than the ones discussed here. There are countless more covering every conceivable field, some of which are listed in Figure 6-2. The indexes and bibliographies come first in bold type. In order to use these reference books, you may need to go to the section of the library where the books and magazines in the special field are located.

Remember: **The *Readers' Guide* index might well appear in almost every category.**

Figure 6-2 Specialized indexes and bibliographies (bold type) and reference volumes.

Applied science, technology, and agriculture
   Applied Science and Technology Index
   Bibliography of Agriculture
   *McGraw-Hill Encyclopedia of Science and
      Technology*

Art
   Art Index
   Guide to Art Reference Books
   Encyclopedia of World Art
   McGraw-Hill Dictionary of Art

Biography
   Biographical Dictionaries Master Index
   Biography Index
   Dictionary of American Biography
   Dictionary of National Biography
      (British)   } Dead notables
   Notable American Women,
      1607–1950

Biography, continued

> *Who's Who* (primarily British)
> *Who's Who Among Black Americans*
> *Who's Who of American Women*
> *Who's Who in America*

} *Living notables*

> *Twentieth Century Authors*
> *Webster's Biographical Dictionary*
> *World Authors, 1950–1970* (with supplements)

Business and economics

> **Business Periodicals Index**
> **Index of Economic Articles**
> **International Bibliography of Economics**
> **Journal of Economic Literature** (abstracts)
> **Public Affairs Information Service Bulletin**
> **Wall Street Journal Index**
> *Business Information Sources*
> *Poor's Register of Corporations, Directors, and*
>   *Executives of the U.S. and Canada*

Drama

> **Play Index**
> **Theatre and Allied Arts: A Guide to Books**
> *The Oxford Companion to the Theatre*

Education

> **Complete Guide and Index to ERIC**
>   **Reports** (1964 to 1969)
> **Current Index to Journals in**
> **Education**
> **Resources in Education**

} Guide to ERIC
(Educational
Resources
Information
Center)

Education, continued
> **Education Index**
> **Encyclopedia of Educational Research**
> *Encyclopedia of Education*

Government documents
> **Congressional Information Services**
> **Index to U.S. Government Periodicals**
> **Monthly Catalog of United States Government Publications**

History
> **America: History and Life**
> **Harvard Guide to American History**
> **Historical Abstracts**
> **Humanities Index**
> *An Encyclopedia of World History*
> *Encyclopedia of American History*

Literature
> **Book Review Digest**
> **Cambridge Bibliography of English Literature**
> **New Cambridge Bibliography of English Literature**
> **Essay and General Literature Index**
> **An Index to Black Poetry**
> **MLA International Bibliography**
> **Short Story Index**
> *Cambridge History of English Literature*
> *Encyclopedia of Poetry and Poetics*
> *Literary History of the United States* (includes bibliographies)

Mathematics
> **Mathematical Reviews**
> *Universal Encyclopedia of Mathematics*

Music
Music Index
Dictionary of Music and Musicians
International Cyclopedia of Music and Musicians
The New Oxford History of Music

Newspaper Indexes
Newspaper Indexes: A Location and Subject Guide for Researchers
The New York Times Index (1913 to date)
The Times Index (London: 1906 to date)

Philosophy and religion
Humanities Index
Religion Index One: Periodicals
Dictionary of the Bible
The Encyclopedia of Philosophy
Encyclopaedia of Religion and Ethics
Nelson's Complete Concordance of the Revised Standard Version Bible

Sciences
Bibliography of North American Geology
Biological Abstracts
Biological and Agricultural Index
Chemical Abstracts
General Science Index
Physics Literature: A Reference Manual
Van Nostrand's Scientific Encyclopedia

Social Sciences
Public Affairs Information Service Bulletin
Social Sciences Index

Social Sciences, continued
> *International Encyclopedia of the Social Sciences*
> > Political Science
> > **International Bibliography of Political Science**
> > Psychology
> > **Harvard List of Books on Psychology**
> > **Psychological Abstracts**
> > *Encyclopedia of Psychology*
> > > Sociology and Anthropology
> > **International Bibliography of Social and Cultural Anthropology**
> > **International Bibliography of Sociology**

Women's studies
> **Women: A Bibliography of Bibliographies**
> **Women in America: A Guide to Books**
> *The Book of Women's Achievements*
> *Woman's Almanac*
> *Women's Work and Women's Studies* (1972 to present)

Assorted useful reference books
> *Bartlett's Familiar Quotations*
> *Dictionary of Black Culture*
> *Dictionary of Slang and Unconventional English*
> *Facts on File*
> *Information Please Almanac*
> *New Larousse Encyclopedia of Mythology*
> *Oxford English Dictionary*
> *World Almanac and Book of Facts*

Specialized reference tools
> **Bibliography of Bibliographies**
> *Sheehy's* (formerly *Winchell's*) **Guide to Reference Books**

Get It All Down

Every time you consult a new source, *copy all the information necessary for documentation* (that is, for indicating the source to your readers). If you fail to record all the essential data, you may find yourself tracking down a book or article weeks later in order to look up an essential publication date or volume number that you neglected to record initially. The book may by this time be checked out, lost, or stolen, so get it all down the first time.

Use three- by five-inch or four- by six-inch note cards to keep track of the information. They should come out looking like the examples in Figure 6-3 (see page 272). Note the pertinent data and get it *all* down. For whatever documentation system you are using, you will need to record the following:

For books

1. Author or editor
2. Title
3. Place of publication
4. Publisher
5. Date of publication (plus date of edition, if the book has more than one)
6. Library call number

For articles

1. Author (or "Anonymous")
2. Title
3. Name of magazine or newspaper
4. Volume number (if a scholarly journal)
5. Date of issue
6. Pages the article covers

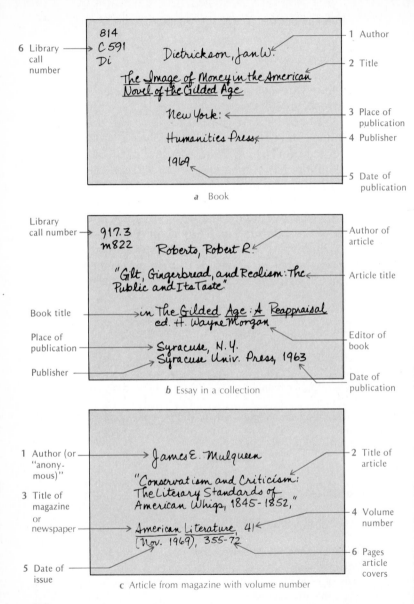

a Book

6 Library call number

814
C 591
Di

Dietrickson, Jan W.

1 Author

The Image of Money in the American Novel of the Gilded Age

2 Title

New York:

3 Place of publication

Humanities Press

4 Publisher

1969

5 Date of publication

---

b Essay in a collection

Library call number

917.3
m822

Roberts, Robert R.

Author of article

"Gilt, Gingerbread, and Realism: The Public and Its Taste"

Article title

Book title

in *The Gilded Age: A Reappraisal*
ed. H. Wayne Morgan

Editor of book

Place of publication

Syracuse, N.Y.

Publisher

Syracuse Univ. Press, 1963

Date of publication

---

c Article from magazine with volume number

1 Author (or "anony-mous)"

James E. Mulqueen

2 Title of article

"Conservatism and Criticism: The Literary Standards of American Whigs, 1845–1852,"

3 Title of magazine or newspaper

American Literature, 41

4 Volume number

5 Date of issue

(Nov. 1969), 355–72.

6 Pages article covers

Figure 6-3 (opposite) Sample bibliography cards.

/ **EXERCISE**   6-2 \

If you are unfamiliar with college libraries, this exercise will give you practice in using some of the most essential reference tools. (This exercise is adapted from one designed by the efficient and friendly librarians who manage our general college library collection.)

1. Use the author-title card catalog (or the handy computer) to locate *Mark Twain's Autobiography,* edited by A. B. Paine. Go find this work in the stacks. How many volumes are there? What color is the binding?

2. Articles from various magazines are grouped together by subject headings (as well as by author) in the *Readers' Guide to Periodical Literature.* Under what subject heading would you find articles about "ethnic jokes" in the 1982–1983 volume? Write this subject heading.

3. Abbreviations used in a periodical index are explained in the front of each volume. Here is an entry from the *Readers' Guide:*

   Food for thought in the elderly [nutrition linked to thinking and memory; research by James S. Goodwin and others] J. Arehart-Treichel. Sci News 123:358 Je 4 '83

   Use the *Periodical Directory* to find the call number of the magazine; then go find it in the stacks. What color is the binding?

4. Locate in *The New York Times Index* for 1982 the first announcement of comedian Marty Feldman's death. Write down the date that the article appeared in the *Times,* as well as the page and column number. Then, find the article on microfilm. What are the first four words?

List the library references you would use to find the answers to the following questions:

1. What is the address of the TV station in Peoria, Illinois?
2. Is there an alternative to root-canal work?
3. Did Ernest Hemingway have any brothers and sisters?
4. How long did it take to film *The Wizard of Oz*?
5. What was the major cause of death in the United States in 1970?
6. What are the recent discoveries about subatomic particles?
7. Is there a bibliography of articles and books about Spenser's *Faerie Queen*?
8. Did Joseph Heller's *Catch-22* get good reviews when it first came out?
9. Who is Artemis?
10. Are there articles that define what a *free school* is?
11. What do you call the architectural style of your county courthouse?
12. What effect does left-handedness have on learning to read?
13. Who was Machiavelli?
14. What are the roots of the Jewish religious laws of eating only kosher food?
15. What is the history of the word *boycott*?

ON TO THE READING

Using your bibliography cards, you next need to locate all the materials that look promising and try to decide which ones will be genuinely useful. As you are pondering what articles and books to study thoroughly and what ones to eliminate at this stage, you should give some thought to their reliability as well as their relevance to your thesis question. You have probably figured out by now that just because a statement appears in print, it is not necessarily honest or accurate. You need to become wary as you read.

Cultivate a Questioning Attitude

Published writers are not the only ones who have prejudices, biases, and quirks: we all have plenty, and we have to be vigilant as we read. The education process bogs down unless you keep an open mind. You should not reject a new idea just because it conflicts with an opinion you currently treasure. As Mark Twain observed in his *Notebook,* "One of the proofs of immortality is that myriads have believed it. They also believed that the world was flat." Be willing to consider new ideas, examine them, think about them, and decide on the basis of the available evidence what is and what is not valid. You will be bombarded by facts and opinions from all sides. In self-defense you must try to distinguish the truth from the tripe. It's not easy.

Be Suspicious of Slogans

As you form the habit of questioning statements, the first ones to examine are epigrams and slogans. These prepackaged ideas are all neat and tidy, easy to remember, pleasant to the ear. We have been brought up on epigrams and have Ben Franklin to thank for a sizable number, like "A stitch in time saves nine" and "Early to bed and early to rise, makes a man healthy, wealthy, and wise." An *epigram* usually states a simple truth in a short, witty statement—but often epigrams cleverly disguise opinion as fact. For instance, we have always heard that "Home is where the heart is," yet George Bernard

Shaw insisted, "Home is the girl's prison and the woman's workhouse." Clearly, the truth of both statements is debatable.

A *slogan* is a catchword or motto designed to rally people to vote for a certain party, agree with the opinions of a particular group, or buy a specific product. Bumper stickers reading "America—love it or leave it" or "America—change it or lose it" may inspire you, but do not consider them reasoned arguments. Your job as reader is to question opinionated statements: demand evidence and decide rationally which opinions are valid, which are empty propaganda, which are a mixture of both.

Consider the Connotations

More difficult to perceive than the bias of slogans is the subtle persuasion of *slanted writing.* But once you become aware of the emotional quality of many words—their connotations—you are less likely to be taken in by slanted writing.

Connotative language is not necessarily bad. In fact, without the use of emotional words, writing would be virtually lifeless. But you must be *aware* of connotations, both as you read and as you write. The rhetoric in the following passage by Theodore Roosevelt is first-rate. He is speaking of the U.S. entrance into the Spanish-American War. The utterance has impact, conviction, persuasion. Let's examine how much connotative words lend to the writer's effect:

> If we stand idly by, if we seek merely swollen, slothful ease and ignoble peace, . . . then bolder and stronger peoples will pass us by, and will win for themselves the domination of the world.

Note that he says not "stand by" but "stand *idly* by." He fears we may seek "ease"—but not a well-deserved ease, instead, "*swollen, slothful* ease." The word "peace" alone would not serve: it is "*ignoble* peace." Notice, too, that the people who are going to "pass us by" and leave us with no world to dominate are "*bolder* and *stronger* peoples": we are subtly asked to envision not invaders slaughtering innocent hordes, but rather clean-limbed, fearless people inspired by an admirable vision of world conquest. Surely the piece deserves high marks as effective propaganda. But you as reader must be able to detect that the chinks in Roosevelt's logic are effectively plugged with rhetoric. See the *either-or* fallacy on page 138 for help if the verbal trickery is still not clear. Your best protection against propaganda is your ability to think—to examine the language and the logic, to sort out the soundness from the sound effects.

WRITING EXERCISE 6-4

Find examples of writings that pretend to be objective, but are really biased, in one of your textbooks, a newspaper, or a news magazine. Write an analysis of how the writing is biased—slanted word connotation, sloganeering, dubious sources, logical fallacies, or simple omission of relevant material.

Consider Your Sources

You could be reasonably sure, even before reading it, that you would not get an unbiased comment from Theodore Roosevelt concerning the Spanish-American War. This does not mean, however, that you should ignore Roosevelt's statements if you are writing an appraisal of the reasons the United States entered that war. But you should be constantly wary when the sources you are reading could hardly be considered impartial.

You might expect an unprejudiced analysis of an event from journalists who were present, but again you must stay alert because not all publications achieve—or even *try* to achieve—objective reporting. You may be certain that the conservative *National Review* will offer an appreciably different appraisal from that of the ultraliberal *Mother Jones.* And the *Congressional Record,* which sounds like an unimpeachable source, is actually one of the least reliable, since any member of Congress can have any nonsense whatsoever read into the *Record.* You must sample several authorities so that you are able to weigh the matter and discount the prejudices. This is one reason that research papers require extensive bibliographies. You could probably scare up most of the facts from reading one *unbiased* source, but the problem is to discover a source that is unbiased—if one exists.

Do not make the mistake of embracing what you consider a reliable source and then placing your trust in it till death do you part. Too many of us do just this: we put our faith in the Bible, the *National Lampoon,* the *Wall Street Journal,* or *Time* magazine, and never bother to think again. You will discover writers and publications whose viewpoint is similar to yours. These will naturally strike you as the most intelligent, perceptive, reliable sources to consult. But be careful that you do not fall into the comfortable habit of reading these publications exclusively. And remember that book reviews can provide the most reliable help if you are trying to evaluate a book-length source.

The date of a publication often makes a difference in its value or reliability. If you are doing a paper analyzing the relative safety of legal and illegal abortions, you will find an article written in 1936 of little use. If, on the other hand, you are writing a paper on the *history* of the long struggle to legalize abortion, a 1936 article could be quite important. In general, we place the highest value on recent articles simply because the latest scholar or scientist has the advantage of building on all that has gone before.

WRITING EXERCISE   6-5

Find, photocopy, and read an article in *Newsweek* on some timely and controversial subject (some recent decision of the Supreme Court, for instance). Then, find, photocopy, and read an article on the same subject in the *National Review*. Next, find, photocopy, and read an article on the same subject in the *Nation*. Look over the photocopies again, and make a list of any differences you discover. What can you say about the slant or the objectivity of each article from observing those differences? Which article do you consider the most objective? Why?

Making the Outline Easier

Keeping your thesis in mind, you can get started on the reading. Have your note cards handy. At the same time you are doing research, you will be working out an outline. The note cards, each containing information related to a single idea, can be shuffled around later and slipped into appropriate sections of your outline. Taking notes consecutively on sheets of paper makes this handy sorting of ideas difficult.

Use Subject Headings.   Chances are that your outline may not really take shape until you are well along with your reading—possibly not until you have finished it. As you take notes, put subject headings indicating in a word or two what each note is about in the upper-right-hand corner of your note cards. Eventually these subject headings probably will correspond to sections of your outline. As you collect more and more cards, leaf through them occasionally to see if they can be arranged into three or four main categories to form the major headings of an outline. The sooner you can get the organization worked out, the more efficient your research becomes. You know exactly what you are looking for and avoid taking notes that would eventually prove off the point and have to be discarded.

If an idea sounds potentially useful, copy it down whether it fits exactly or not. If the idea recurs in your reading and gathers significance, you may decide to add a section to your outline or to expand one of the existing sections. Later, at the organizing stage, if you have cards with ideas that just do not seem to fit in anywhere, let them go. Let them go cheerfully. Do not ruin the focus and unity of your paper by trying to wedge in every single note you have taken. Unless you are an uncommonly cautious notetaker, you will have a number of cards that you cannot use.

Tips on Note-Taking

Of necessity you will do a considerable amount of reading for your research paper. If you remember that most published articles are put together according to the same advice we have given you in this book, you can summarize more efficiently. Read the introductory paragraphs of an essay quickly to discover the writer's thesis. If that main idea is relevant to your own thesis, continue reading carefully and jot down any useful ideas on note cards. Pay special attention to beginning and ending sentences of paragraphs; these will likely be topic sentences conveying or summarizing major ideas.

If you are examining a book, the author's thesis will appear in the preface. You can thus get a quick clue concerning the usefulness of the volume. Usually a book will have a broader scope than your paper. You can tell from the table of contents which chapters may be pertinent to your investigation, and you need only consult those sections. If the book has an index, try to locate your topic there. You will then be directed to precisely the relevant pages and can treat yourself to a coffee break in the time saved.

Again, do not forget to record *on each card:*

1. Author's last name
2. Abbreviated title
3. Page number or numbers

If you get in the habit of writing down these essentials before you take notes, there is less chance of forgetting an item.

Summarize the ideas in your own words, except when you think you might want to quote directly (verbatim) in which case copy the author's exact words and *enclose them in quotation marks*. If you carelessly forget the quotation marks and use those words in your paper, you will have committed a serious literary offense, *plagiarism* (see page 285). Do not simply omit the specific examples when you summarize, because you are going to need some yourself. Remember that you must give credit for these examples, as well as for the ideas they illustrate, even if you put them in your own words when you incorporate them into your paper. Otherwise you will lapse into plagiarism. Your note cards should look something like the one shown in Figure 6-4.

The Photocopying Option. If the time you can spend in the library is limited and your finances are not, you might want to photocopy articles or pertinent portions of books in order to have these materials available to study at your convenience. You can then underline and make marginal notes

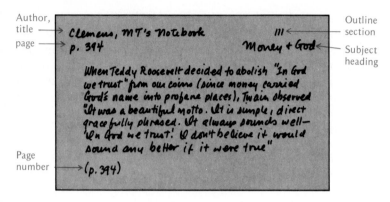

Author, title page ————→
page ————→

Outline section ←————
Subject heading ←————

Clemens, MT's Notebook III

p. 394

Money + God

When Teddy Roosevelt decided to abolish "In God we trust" from our coins (since money carried God's name into profane places), Twain observed "It was a beautiful motto. It is simple, direct gracefully phrased. It always sounds well—'In God we trust!' I don't believe it would sound any better if it were true"

Page number ————→ (p. 394)

Figure 6-4 Sample note card.

without defacing the library's copy. And if later you want to check the accuracy of a quotation in your rough draft, you will be spared making yet another trip to the library to do so. But do not fail to note the source of the material directly on the photocopy.

HOW TO WRITE A QUALITY SUMMARY

Another kind of summary—much more exacting—is called a *précis* (pronounced *práy-see*). Précis writing is a valuable and challenging craft, highly useful in business and government work. Busy executives and top-level officials need precise summaries of the endless piles of papers that daily cross their desks. You would not take the trouble to write an actual précis when taking notes for a documented paper, but learning how to write a précis will sharpen your skills for summarizing in general. After mastering the art of the précis, you will be able to take ordinary notes more carefully and accurately. You cannot skim a passage and hope to produce a good précis, because you are expected to include all the important ideas from the original passage in your shortened version. Furthermore, you are expected to mention these ideas in the same *order* and in the same *tone*, using your own words. You may quote an impressive phrase or two, but *do not forget the quotation marks*.

Retain Only the Main Ideas

While you must write clear, coherent sentences in your précis, nobody expects the summary to be as stylistically pleasing as the original: the point is to make it considerably shorter. You need to eliminate all nonessential information by reading each paragraph carefully and setting down in your own words the main ideas that you remember. If you have not had much practice in summarizing, you should begin by working on a sentence at a time. Consider this one from Pete Axthelm's "A Really Super Bowl" (*Newsweek*, 22 Jan. 1979):

> In an effort to keep everyone buying tickets and watching television as far as possible into this elongated sixteen-game season, the NFL juggled its schedule so that strong teams faced the toughest tests and weaker members were able to kindle local hopes while playing fellow stragglers. [46 words]

Now ask yourself: What did he say? You might jot down something like this:

> To keep fans interested through the long season, the NFL scheduled teams against others of equal strength. [17 words]

Now, reread the sentences to see if you left out any important ideas. There is the bit at the beginning about buying tickets that is not included in the summary. Since finances no doubt provided the motivation for the unusually long season, the idea *is* important. You would do well to substitute *buying tickets* for the single word *interested*. Accuracy is more important than brevity.

After you have finished summarizing all the sentences in the passage, go back over your first draft and prune it down even more by combining sentences and dropping any unnecessary words. (See page 188 for further help.) How much you can shorten a passage depends upon the style and substance of the original. Naturally you can condense the information in a paragraph by Ralph Waldo Emerson in fewer words than you can a passage of the same length by Ernest Hemingway. Most expository prose can be greatly reduced— usually by half, at least. You must, of course, resist the temptation to add comments of your own. Remember, you are *summarizing, not analyzing*, in a précis.

Here is a paragraph from Christopher Hitchens's article about the peculiarities of the Nobel Prize awards ("The Faded Laurel Crown," *Harper's*, Nov. 1977), followed by a précis of the passage.

> There are further ironies in the way the Peace Prize is awarded. On several occasions it has gone to institutions rather than to individuals, but more often than not these recipients only serve to emphasize the element of futility in the donor. The International Red Cross, which won the prize in 1917, 1944, and 1963, is, after all, an organization which accepts war as inevitable and tries to palliate its effects. The same can be said of the Office of the United Nations High Commissioner for Refugees (1954). And it comes as a surprise to see some laureates, such as Theodore Roosevelt or Austen Chamberlain, on a list of peace crusaders. [111 words]

Ironically, the Peace Prize has been given to institutions whose function underlines the futility of the award. The International Red Cross (winner in 1917, 1944, and 1963), and the United Nations High Commissioner for Refugees (1954), rather than working to prevent war, merely try to relieve the suffering. And some winners, like Theodore Roosevelt and Austen Chamberlain, appear strange choices as peacemakers. [62 words]

TIPS ON AVOIDING PLAGIARISM

Plagiarism means using somebody else's writing without giving proper credit. Most teachers consider plagiarism close to a criminal offense. In some schools students may be expelled for plagiarism. The most lenient penalty is an F in the course. Deliberate plagiarism is, after all, a form of cheating. You can avoid accidental plagiarism by using a moderate amount of care in taking notes. Put quotation marks around any material—however brief—that you copy verbatim. As you leaf through the note cards trying to sort them into categories, circle the quotation marks with a red pencil so you cannot miss them. There remains the necessity of avoiding the author's phrasing if you decide not to quote directly but to paraphrase. This obligation is not so easily met. You naturally tend to write the idea down using the same phrasing, changing or omitting a few words. *This close paraphrasing is still plagiarism.* To escape it you must not even look at your source as you take notes that are not direct quotations. We suggest that you use both methods—verbatim notes and summarizing notes—and let the summaries condense several pages of reading onto a single card. You will scarcely be able to fall into the author's phrasing that way. Or if your writer uses an eye-catching

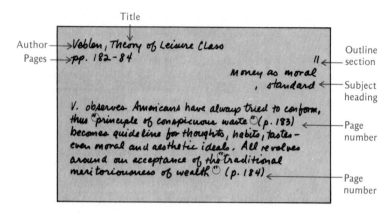

Figure 6-5 Sample summary note card.

phrase—something like Thorstein Veblen's *code of pecuniary honor*—get that down in quotation marks in the middle of your summary. A summarizing note card will look something like the card in Figure 6-5.

Paraphrase Carefully

Sometimes, of course, you must do fairly close paraphrasing of important ideas. Since plagiarism is often accidental, we will give you a couple of examples to show you exactly what plagiarism is. Here is a passage from Marvin Harris's *Cows, Pigs, Wars, and Witches: The Riddles of Culture*, which, we will assume, you need to use in making a point in your paper:

No one understood better than Gandhi that cow love had different implications for rich and poor. For him the cow was the central focus of the struggle to rouse India to authentic nationhood.

If you incorporate that material into your paper this way, you have plagiarized:

> Gandhi understood the different implications of cow love for rich and poor. He saw the struggle to rouse India to authentic nationhood focused on the cow (Harris 21).

The fact that the source is cited suggests that this plagiarism might have resulted from ignorance rather than deception, but it is plagiarism nonetheless. Changing a few words or rearranging the phrases is not enough. Here is another version, somewhat less blatant but still plagiarism:

> Gandhi well knew that rich and poor were affected differently by cow love, which he saw as a means of inspiring his people to authentic nationhood (Harris 21).

There are still two phrases there that are distinctly Harris's: *cow love* and *authentic nationhood*. It is quite all right to use those phrases but *only if you put them in quotation marks*. We also think you should acknowledge your source in the text of your paper—as well as in your note—whenever possible, like this:

> According to Harris, Gandhi well knew that rich and poor were affected differently by "cow love," which he saw as a means of inspiring his people "to authentic nationhood" (21).

Notice, by the way, that the phrase *rich and poor* in the original does not appear in quotation marks in this acceptable version. The phrase is so simple, so commonly used—and so nearly impossible to replace without using many more words—that quotation marks are unnecessary. Here is another acceptable version in which none of the original phrasing is used:

Harris suggests that Gandhi well knew that rich and poor were affected differently by reverence for the sacred cow but saw this symbol as a means of uniting his people (21).

Remember: **If you are paraphrasing, put the passage into your own words; if you are quoting directly, put the passage in quotation marks.**

WRITING THE FIRST DRAFT

After you have read all the material you feel is necessary to cover your topic thoroughly, gather up your note cards and shuffle them to fit the sections of your outline. If your outline is still a flabby hulk, now is the time to whip it into shape and turn your thesis question into a thesis statement. The actual writing of the paper is the same as writing any other paper, except that you incorporate the material from the note cards into your text (either in your own words or through direct quotations) and give credit at the end to the original authors both for ideas borrowed and for actual passages quoted. Quickly review Chapter 1 if you are still having difficulty at this stage.

To Quote or Not to Quote

Never quote directly unless (1) the material is authoritative and convincing evidence in support of your thesis or (2) the statement is extremely well phrased or (3) the idea is controversial and you need to assure your readers that you are not slanting or misinterpreting the source. You would want, for instance, to quote directly an observation as well put as this one:

> Bernard Rosenberg defines pragmatism as "a distinctly American philosophy whose only failing is that it does not work."
>> —"A Dictionary for the Disenchanted," *Harper's,* Nov. 1970.

There is no need, however, for the direct quotation in the following sentence:

> The ICC, in an effort to aid the rail industry, has asked for a "federal study of the need and means for preserving a national passenger service."

You could phrase that just as well yourself. But remember, even after you put the statement into your own words, you still need to indicate where you got the information.

Quoting Quotations

Sometimes in your reading you will come across a quotation that says exactly what you have been hoping to find. If the quotation is complete enough to serve your purpose, and if you honestly do not think you would benefit from tracking down the original, then do not bother. Instead, include that quotation in the usual way. But notice that your citation will include "qtd. in" before the source and page number:

> George Cukor once told Scott Fitzgerald, "I've only known two people who eat faster than you and I, and they are both dead now" (qtd. in Latham 39).

> Mark Twain relates that he once knew a Miss Sexton, who pronounced her name "Saxton to make it finer, the nice, kindhearted, smirky, smily dear Christian creature" (qtd. in Wecter 103).

Indenting Long Quotations

If you are writing on a topic in the humanities, you are expected to set off quotations longer than four typewritten lines by indenting them ten spaces. Omit the quotation marks (since the spacing indicates that the material is quoted), and give the citation in parentheses two spaces *after* the period:

```
    In Life on Earth David Attenborough

describes the three-toed sloth this way:

            It spends eighteen out of

            twenty-four hours soundly asleep.

            It pays such little attention to

            its personal hygiene that green

            algae grow on its coarse hair and

            communities of a parasitic moth

            live in the depths of its coat,

            producing caterpillars which graze

            on its moldy hair.  (248)
```

If your quotation includes more than one paragraph, indent the paragraph three spaces (instead of the usual five).

Notice that if you want to quote conversation, indenting the whole passage is a handy way of avoiding an untidy clutter of quotation marks within quotation marks.

Working Quotations in Smoothly

If you want your research paper to read smoothly, you must take care in incorporating quotations into your own writing. You must have ready a supply of introductory phrases with which to slide them in gracefully—phrases like "As Quagmire discovered," "Professor Clyde Crashcup notes," and "According to Dr. Dimwit." If you run through the examples in this section on quoting, you will find a generous assortment of these phrases. Borrow them with our blessing.

Notice, please, that the more famous the person, the less likely we are to use Mr., Miss, Mrs., or Ms. in front of the name. "Mr. Milton" sounds quite droll. If the person has a title, you can use it or not, as you think appropriate: Dr. Pasteur or Pasteur, Sir Winston Churchill or Churchill, President Lincoln or Lincoln.

Introduce Your Quotations.   Most of the time you will introduce a quotation before beginning it, like this:

As Mark Twain observed, "Heaven for climate, hell for society."*

But you may want to break one up in the middle every so often for variety, this way:

"But if thought corrupts language," cautions George Orwell, "language can also corrupt thought."

Or you can make most of the sentence yours and quote only the telling phrases or key ideas of your authority, like this:

Lily B. Campbell considers King Henry's inability to fight "a saintly weakness."

* We have omitted many citations in this book to save space. But remember, you do not have this option in a documented paper. Whenever you quote directly, you *must* cite the source.

Or this:

> The play's effectiveness lies, as E. M. W. Tillyard points out, in "the utter artlessness of the language."

But do introduce your quotations, please. The standard MLA (Modern Language Association) documentation style suggests identifying the source within the citation immediately following the quotation. But we find that identifying the source before presenting the borrowed material allows the readers a clearer understanding of which ideas are yours and which come from sources.

If you have difficulty introducing your authorities gracefully in the text of your paper, perhaps you are using too many direct quotations.

Make the Grammar Match. When you integrate a quotation into your own sentence, you are responsible for making sure that the entire sentence makes sense. You must adjust the way your sentence is worded so that the grammar comes out right. Read your quotations over carefully to be sure they do not end up like this one:

> When children are born, their first reactions are "those stimuli which constitute their environment."

"Reactions" are not "stimuli." The sentence should read this way:

> When children are born, their first reactions are to "those stimuli which constitute their environment."

What a difference a word makes—the difference here between sense and nonsense. Take particular care when you are adding someone else's words to your own; you get the blame if the words in the quotation do not make sense, because they *did* make sense before you lifted them out of context.

Use Special Punctuation.   When you write a documented paper, you probably will need to use some rather specialized marks of punctuation: *ellipsis dots* (to show that you have omitted something from a quotation) and *brackets* (to make an editorial comment within a quotation). You will find both of these useful devices discussed fully in our alphabetized "Revising Index," Chapter 3.

To Cite or Not to Cite

The main purpose of documentation—of citing sources used in a research paper—is to give credit for ideas, information, and actual phrasing that you borrow from other writers. You cite sources in order to be honest and to lend authority to your own writing. You also include citations to enable your readers to find more extensive information than your paper furnishes, in case they become engrossed in your subject and want to read some of your sources in full.

We are all troubled occasionally about when a citation is necessary. We can say with authority that you must include a citation for:

1. All direct quotations
2. All indirect quotations
3. All major ideas that are not your own
4. All essential facts, information, and statistics that are not general knowledge—especially anything controversial

The last category is the one that causes confusion. In general, the sort of information available in an encyclopedia does not need a citation. But statements interpreting, analyzing, or speculating on such information should be documented. If you say that President Warren G. Harding died in office, you do not need a citation, because that is a widely known and undisputed fact. If you say that Harding's administration was one of the most corrupt in our history, most people would not feel the need for a citation, because authorities agree that the Harding scandals were flagrant and enormous. But if you say that Harding was sexually intimate with a young woman in the White House cloakroom while President of the United States, we strongly suggest that you cite your source. Because such information is not widely known and is also debatable, you need to identify your source so that your readers can judge the reliability of your evidence. Then, too, they might want further enlightenment on the matter, and your citation will lead them to a more complete discussion. Probably it is better to bother your readers with too many citations than to have them question your integrity by having too few.

Accuracy Is the Aim

After years of being told to be original, to be creative, to think for yourself, you are now going to be told—on this one matter, at least—to fall into line and slavishly follow the authorities. What you might consider a blessed bit of variety will not be appreciated in the slightest. If you put a period after the first citation, put a period after every one. Get the form correct every time, right down to the last comma, colon, and parenthesis.

The information (date, publisher, place of publication) necessary for completing a citation is located on the title page and on the back of the title page of each book. For magazines you usually can find it all on the cover.

When in Doubt, Use Common Sense

Keep in mind that the purpose of documentation is dual:

1. To give credit to your sources
2. To allow your readers to find your sources in case they want further information on the subject

If you are ever in doubt about documentation form (if you are citing something so unusual that you cannot find a similar entry in the samples here), use your common sense and give credit the way you think it logically should be done. Be as consistent as possible with other citations.

You will find instruction on the documentation styles for the MLA used in the humanities beginning on page 308 and the APA (American Psychological Association) used by the social sciences beginning on page 326.

REVISING THE PAPER

Since a research paper requires the incorporation of other people's ideas and the acknowledgment of these sources, you need to take special care in revising.

Check the Usual Things

1. Be sure the introduction states your thesis.
2. Be sure each paragraph is unified, coherent, and directly related to your thesis.
3. Be sure the transitions between paragraphs are smooth.
4. Be sure your conclusion evaluates the results of your research; if the paper is argumentative, be sure the last sentence is emphatic.

Check the Special Things

1. Be sure that you have introduced direct quotations gracefully, using the name and, if possible, the occupation of the person quoted.
2. Be sure each citation is accurate.
3. Be sure that paraphrases are in your own words and that the sources are clearly acknowledged.
4. Be sure to underline the titles of books and magazines; put quotation marks around the titles of articles and chapters in books.
5. Be sure that you have written most of the paper yourself; you need to examine, analyze, or explain the material, not just splice together a bunch of quotations and paraphrases.
6. Be sure always to separate quotations with some comment of your own.
7. Be sure to use ellipsis dots if you omit any words from a quotation that your readers would not otherwise know were missing; never leave out anything that alters the meaning of a sentence.
8. Be sure to use square brackets, not parentheses, if you add words or change verb tenses in a quotation.
9. Be sure that you have not relied too heavily on a single source.
10. Be sure to indent long quotations ten spaces—without quotation marks.

Before you work on your final draft, give your entire attention to the following instructions on form.

Preparing the Final Draft

1. Provide margins of at least one inch at the top, bottom, and sides.
2. Double-space throughout.
3. Do not put the title of your paper in quotation marks.
4. Insert corrections neatly in ink *above the line* (if allowed by your instructor).

5. Put page numbers in the upper-right-hand corner. But do not number the title page or the first page of the paper. After the title page and the outline, count all pages in the total as you number. Note correct page numbering on the sample student paper, which follows.

6. Proofread. You may well be close to exhaustion by the time you finish copying your paper, and the last thing you will feel like doing is rereading the blasted thing. But force yourself. Or force somebody else. But do not skip the proofreading. It would be a shame to allow careless errors to mar an otherwise excellent paper.

DOCUMENTATION STYLES

We provide complete instruction for documenting papers according to the two most widely used academic styles:

1. MLA (Modern Language Association) for the humanities
2. APA (American Psychological Association) for the social sciences

If you are writing a paper using library sources for any of the remaining academic disciplines, you should identify a leading journal in that field and follow the style used there.

SAMPLE RESEARCH PAPER FOR THE HUMANITIES

The following research paper was written by Steve Sobotta, a student at Illinois State University. We have added comments in the margin of his paper, pointing out pertinent particulars about style (in regular type) and content (in italic type).

USES OF THE SEMICOLON AND COLON:

A BRIEF HISTORY OF CHANGES

Stephen C. Sobotta

Center each line. Space information attractively. If no title page is required, put your name, course, and section number in upper right-hand corner of first page (single-spaced); skip four lines before the title.

English 101, Section 13

Ms. Susan Day

Outline

Thesis: The uses of the semicolon and colon have changed considerably during the past 300 years.

   I. The uses of these two marks have changed dramatically since the seventeenth century.

  II. The eighteenth century provided several further changes.

 III. The nineteenth century dictated a slightly different use of the semicolon and colon.

 IV. The rules of the twentieth century have changed little since the late nineteenth century.

Center title; leave 4 spaces to first line; indent paragraphs 5 spaces.

→ Uses of the Semicolon and Colon:

A Brief History of Changes

The proper, use of punctuation; is essential: in writing!

Author begins with This statement is correct; the punctuation, however, is not
attention-getting first correct. The accepted use of punctuation is essential when using
sentence; then offers the colon and semicolon, two marks important in establishing
general information sentence boundaries. The period and comma, our most widely used
about importance of forms of punctuation, are also crucial, but are more generally
topic. understood since teachers in elementary school concentrate on
these two. The colon and semicolon often do not receive equal
emphasis. Yet these two marks can prove most useful in achieving
style and fluency, as they serve to add emphasis, to offer

Author states thesis in explanations, or to introduce examples→ These valuable marks of
last 2 sentences of first punctuation also have an interesting history. Their use in
paragraph. writing has changed over the past few hundred years--in some
ways dramatically.

In the seventeenth century, punctuation in general was

Title makes clear that used far more casually than today. The abundance of marks used
Simpson is a linguist— and their sometimes strange placement has been blamed on the
thus not necessary to printers, who were often illiterate (and served by apprentices
give occupation. who knew even less about the written language)→ Percy Simpson,
in Shakespearean Punctuation, mentions that scholars have often

Raised note number surmised that these unskillful printers tossed in punctuation
indicates information- simply to fill in spaces?¹ But he questions whether the printers
al note. First citation could have been this inept. Could a printer, he wonders, have
appears on page 2. randomly placed punctuation in a text and have that text still

2

appear admirable? "Would he print the beautiful lines of Donne in
this form--

> For love, all love of other sights controules,
> And make one little roome, an every where.--

as a sheer freak in typography?" asks Simpson (8). A printer
may have left out stops now and again because of laziness, but it
seems unlikely that printers should be blamed for the lack of
consistency in Elizabethan punctuation.

Actually, no one was in charge of punctuation in those
days; there were not set rules. As Simpson points out, "Modern
punctuation is, or at any rate attempts to be, logical; the

Author provides major transition from background material about punctuation to history of semicolon and colon.

earlier system was mainly rhythmical" (8). English punctuation
has developed through a series of sometimes radical changes over
the past three hundred years. In order to observe these changes,
let us now take a short journey through the world of punctuation
beginning with the seventeenth century and ending somewhere
close to the middle of the twentieth century.

Author indicates that paraphrased material comes from Simpson.

In Shakespeare's time, Simpson observes, the semicolon was
of value for heavy stopping, both to mark emphasis and to make
the structure of the sentence clear. It was used to provide a
rhythmic flow and to add pauses where the author deemed
necessary (58). The semicolon was also used to mark a dependent
clause at the beginning of a sentence. 2 Shakespeare provides an
example of this use in Measure for Measure, 4.2.115-16:

Quoted lines of poetry indented 10 spaces.

> When Vice makes Mercie; Mercie's so extended,
> That for the faults love, is th' offender friended.
> (qtd. in Simpson 59)

3

In much seventeenth-century writing, the function of the comma
and semicolon seems to be interchangeable. Both are used
randomly and in places in which the opposite mark should or could
appear. The main difference between them appears to be a longer
stop provided by the semicolon for emphasis (Simpson 56-64).

The colon, which is used in almost the same way as the
semicolon, commands an even stronger stop to mark emphatic
pauses. Shakespeare's Henry the Sixth, Part I offers a clear
distinction between the semicolon and the colon:

> She's beautifull; and therefore to be Wooed:
> She is a woman; therefore to be Wonne. (qtd. by
> Simpson 65)

The colon, besides providing a longer and more complete stop
here, also supplies a way to divide two main ideas. The semicolon
divides the main ideas into two secondary ideas. Both work
together to achieve maximum emphasis (Simpson 65-69).

In A Treatise of Stops, Points, or Pauses, published in
1680, two formal and two informal rules are set forth regarding
the semicolon and colon. (Spelling and capitalization are
reproduced here exactly as in the seventeenth-century text.
Underlining indicates italic type.) The formal rules are these:

> 1. A Semi-Colon; viz, A Point abov, with a Comma under
>   it; thus, [;]. It is a Note of an imperfect
>   distinction in the middl of the member of a
>   Sentence, as it were between the parts of a
>   composed Speech, and Notes a longer Stop than
>   a Comma.

Author reproduces Shakespearean spelling.

Text having no known authors introduced by title and date.

Long quotation indented 10 spaces.

4

> 2. A Colon; <u>viz</u>, Two Points, One under ano<u>the</u>r,
> <u>thus</u>, [:]. It is a Note of perfect Sens, but not
> of a perfect Sentence, and <u>that</u> becaus,
> ei<u>ther</u> <u>the</u> preceding, without <u>the</u> following;
> or <u>the</u> following, without <u>the</u> preceding, cannot
> well be understood. And it Notes a longer Stop than
> a Semi-Colon. (4)

After a long, indented quotation, page number (in parentheses) goes outside the period.

Considering the abundance of published writers following the
advent of printing and the heavy emphasis on the English
language in seventeenth-century schools, it seems strange that
these were the only main rules distributed to school teachers in
London. There were, of course, these two informal rules also
mentioned in the <u>Treatise</u>:

> 1. Where a Semi-Colon placed is; there you,
> May pleas to make a Stop, while you tell Two.
> 2. A Colon is a longer Stop; Therefore,
> Stop at each Colon, While you may tell Four. (4)

School children were thus instructed to count to two after each
semicolon and to four after each colon. This idea of punctuating
according to breathing pauses was certainly not new. According
to the <u>Oxford English Dictionary</u>, the earliest English
punctuation was used to mark pauses in the reading of English
psalms, in which a colon ''placed in the middle of a verse . . .
expresses this <u>mediatio</u> or breath-place.''

Three spaced periods indicate an omission.

In the eighteenth century we begin to see more precise
rules laid down concerning punctuation and some modifications
in the guidelines regarding semicolons and colons. The chief

No page number necessary for dictionary, which is alphabetized.

5

work influencing the formation of these rules was <u>An Essay on Punctuation</u>, published in 1785 by Joseph Robertson. The semicolon seems to be given a more definite purpose here. Robertson states that it is to be used for dividing a "compounded" sentence into two or more parts, not so closely connected as those which are separated by a comma, yet not so independent of each other as those which are distinguished by a colon. It still requires a longer pause than a comma. "The colon is now [in the eighteenth century] used when the preceding part of a sentence is complete in its construction; but is followed by some additional remark or illustration" (Robertson 84). This last use of the colon has regained popularity today. But modern writers are seldom concerned by Robertson's rule that the colon "still requires an even longer pause than a semicolon" (88).

During the late nineteenth and early twentieth centuries, the rules governing punctuation began to be strictly codified. In 1949 linguist George Summey observes in <u>American Punctuation</u> that the semicolon has become "the most clearly specialized balancing and coordinating mark" among all punctuation (98). The semicolon has clearly gained precision since the seventeenth century when it was used only as a pause between thoughts. Summey cites several instances when the semicolon should be favored over the comma: in the absence of a connective between independent clauses, in setting off long and complex word groups, and in the case of a shift of grammatical subjects (97–99). The colon, in Summey's words, is "usually a mark of expectation, with emphasis on a following explanation, list,

Explanation inserted into a quotation is enclosed in brackets.

Note transitional sentence.

When it's obvious something's left out (because quotation's not a complete sentence), no spaced periods needed.

6

table, or quotation'' (104). No other mark of punctuation performs such an array of tasks. Summey makes no mention of either the semicolon or colon being used as a pause. Both marks have by this time lost their function of providing ''breath-places.''

> Archaic term, "breath-places," picked up from earlier quotation from the *Oxford English Dictionary*, goes in quotation marks.

Only minor changes have occurred during the latter half of the twentieth century. According to The Way to Punctuate by William Drake (1971), the semicolon should now be used between sentences in place of a comma, mainly to provide a clear sentence division. The semicolon may also substitute for a comma and a conjunction between sentences (19-20). The colon, on the other hand, Drake reminds us, is not related to the semicolon--in spite of its name. As he says, it has more in common with the single dash, in that it serves to anticipate or announce something to follow. But the colon can also stand between two sentences when the second explains the first more fully or adds details to illustrate the first (55-57), a usage first appearing in the eighteenth century.

> Conclusion reiterates ideas on language and punctuation change stated in introduction.

As the rules governing the use of colons and semicolons have changed in various ways over the centuries, writers have adapted to these changes--and in many ways contributed to them. The evolution of the language is accompanied by the evolution of its punctuation. And the language does change, whether we like it or not--commas, colons, semicolons and all.

Notes *like P5* [7]

[1] It was thought for a time that these printers placed extra punctuation in texts simply because the marks were in abundance on their shelves (Simpson 8).

[2] Some clauses that are now considered independent were then considered dependent. The clause preceding the semicolon in this line from Milton's Areopagitica--"Suppose we could expell sin by this means; look now . . ." (qtd. in Simpson 58)-- was at that time treated as dependent.

Three spaced periods indicate an omission.

Summary note card
(used for note 1 above and for material on p. 1)

Source ———
Page ———

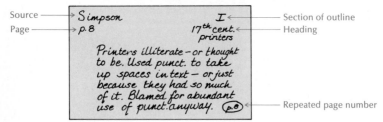

Section of outline
Heading

Simpson   I
p. 8   17th cent.
                    printers

Printers illiterate – or thought
to be. Used punct. to take
up spaces in text – or just
because they had so much
of it. Blamed for abundant
use of punct. anyway. (p.8)

Repeated page number

8

                    Works Cited

Drake, William D. The Way to Punctuate. London: Chandler, 1971.

"Punctuation." The Compact Edition of the Oxford English
    Dictionary. 1971 ed.

Robertson, Joseph. An Essay on Punctuation, 1785. No. 168.
    English Linguistics 1500-1800: A Collection of
    Facsimile Reprints. Ed. R. C. Alston. Menston, England:
    Scholar, 1969.

Simpson, Percy. Shakespearean Punctuation. Oxford: Clarendon,
    1969.

Summey, George, Jr. American Punctuation. New York: Ronald,
    1949.

A Treatise of Stops, Points, or Pauses, 1680. No. 65. English
    Linguistics 1500-1800: A Collection of Facsimile
    Reprints. Ed. R. C. Alston. Menston, England: Scholar,
    1968.

Entries alphabetized; hanging (reverse) indention used after first line of each entry; double space between entries.

Entry for dictionary begins with word defined. No editors, publishers, or pages needed: only date of edition.

Cite city of publication only: this is an exception.

Abbreviate publisher's names.

Work with no known author entered by title (*a, an, the* don't count when alphabetizing).

THE MLA DOCUMENTATION STYLE FOR THE HUMANITIES

The simplified new MLA documentation style resembles those used in other academic disciplines. It works like this:

A. Mention your source (author's last name and page number) within the text of your paper in parentheses, like this:

One of the great all-time best-sellers,

Uncle Tom's Cabin, sold over 300,000 copies

in America and more than 2 million copies

worldwide (Wilson 3).

B. Your readers can identify this source by consulting your "Works Cited" list at the end of your paper (see items I through N). The entry for the information above would appear like this:

Wilson, Edmund. Patriotic Gore: Studies in

the Literature of the American Civil

War. New York: Oxford UP, 1966.

C. If you are quoting directly or if you want to stress the authority of the source you are paraphrasing, you may mention the name of the source in your sentence. Then include just the page number (or numbers) at the end in parentheses, like this:

In Patriotic Gore, Edmund Wilson tells us

that Mrs. Stowe felt "the book had been

written by God" (5).

D. If you must quote indirectly—something quoted from another source not available to you—indicate this in your parenthetical reference by using "qtd. in" (for "quoted in"). The following example comes from a book written by Donald Johanson and Maitland Edey:

Richard Leakey's wife, Maeve, told the
paleoanthropologist David Johanson, "We
heard all about your bones on the radio
last night" (qtd. in Johanson and Edey 162).

E. If you are using a source written or edited by more than three people, use only the name of the first person listed, followed by "et al." (meaning "and others"):

Blair et al. observe that the fine arts were
almost ignored by colonial writers (21).

F. If you refer to more than one work by the same author, include a shortened title in the citation in your text:

(Huxley, <u>Brave</u> 138).

G. If the author's name is not given, then use a shortened title instead. In your abbreviation, be sure to use at least the first word of the full title to send the reader to the proper alphabetized entry on your Works Cited page. The following is a reference to a newspaper article entitled "Ramifications of Baboon Use Expected to Become an Issue":

The doctor observed that some people
objected to the transplant on grounds that

```
were emotional rather than rational
("Ramifications" A23).
```

H. If you are quoting more than **four** typed lines, you should indent the quotation ten spaces and omit the quotation marks. Cite the page number in parentheses two spaces after the period:

```
About Nora in Ibsen's A Doll's House, Liv

Ullman writes,

          She says goodbye to everything

          that is familiar and secure.  She

          does not walk through the door to

          find somebody else to live with

          and for; she is leaving the house

          more insecure than she ever

          realized she could be.  But she

          hopes to find out who she is and

          why she is.  (263)
```

I. On your last page, a separate page, alphabetize your Works Cited list of all sources mentioned in your paper. Use **hanging indention**: that is, after the first line of each entry, indent the other lines five spaces.

J. In your Works Cited list, in citing two or more works by the same author, give the name in the first entry only. Thereafter, in place of the name, type three hyphens and a period, skip two spaces, then follow with the usual information. Alphabetize the entries by title.

Lewis, C. S. <u>The Dark Tower and Other</u>

      <u>Stories</u>. Ed. Walter Hooper. New York:

      Harcourt, 1977.

---. <u>The Screwtape Letters</u>. New York:

      Macmillan, 1976.

K. Omit any mention of *page* or *pages* or *line* or *lines*: do not even include abbreviations for these terms. Use numbers alone.

L. Abbreviate publishers' names. See the list of abbreviations suggested by the MLA on pages 323–325.

M. Use regular (not roman) numerals throughout. Exception: James I, Elizabeth II. Use *lowercase* roman numerals for citing page numbers from a preface, introduction, or table of contents. You may use roman numerals to indicate act and scene in plays: "In *Hamlet* III.ii, the action shifts. . . ."

N. Use raised note numbers for *informational notes* only (i.e., notes containing material pertinent to your discussion but not precisely to the point). Include these content notes at the end of your paper on a separate page just before your Works Cited list, and entitle them "Notes."

O. If you are writing about literature, you should cite the edition of the novel, play, short story, or poetry collection you are using in an informational note. Thereafter, include the page numbers in parentheses in the text of the paper. The note should read like this:

    [1] Joyce Carol Oates, "Accomplished

Desires," in <u>Wheel of Love and Other</u>

<u>Stories</u>. Greenwich: Fawcett, 1970: 127. All further references to this work appear in parentheses in the text.

Your subsequent acknowledgments in the text will be done this way:

Dorie was not consoled, although Mark "slid his big beefy arms around her and breathed his liquory love into her face, calling her his darling, his beauty" (129).

Note the placement of the quotation marks—before the parentheses, which are followed by the period. *But* if the quotation is a long one that you need to indent without quotation marks, the period comes *before* the parentheses as shown in item "H" above.

SAMPLE ENTRIES FOR A "WORKS CITED" LIST

The following models will help you write Works Cited entries for most of but not all the sources you will use. If you use a source not treated in these samples, consult the more extensive list of sample entries found in the new *MLA Handbook* or ask your instructor.

Books

1. Book by one author

   Abernathy, Charles F. <u>Civil Rights: Cases
       and Materials</u>. St. Paul: West, 1980.

2. Two or more books by the same author

   Gould, Stephen Jay. <u>The Mismeasure of Man</u>.
       New York: Norton, 1981.

   ---. <u>The Panda's Thumb: More Reflections
       in Natural History</u>. New York: Norton,
       1980.

3. Book by 2 or 3 authors

   Brusaw, Charles, Gerald J. Alfred, and
       Walter E. Oliu. <u>The Business Writer's
       Handbook</u>. New York: St. Martin's,
       1976.

   Ciardi, John, and M. Williams. <u>How Does a
       Poem Mean</u>? Rev. ed. Boston: Houghton,
       1975.

4. Book by more than three authors

   Sheridan, Marion C., et al. <u>The Motion

       Picture and the Teaching of English</u>.

       New York: Appleton, 1965.

   [The phrase "et al." is an abbreviation for "et alii," meaning "and others."]

5. Book by an anonymous author

   <u>Beowulf</u>. Trans. Kevin Crossley-Holland.

       New York: Farrar, 1968.

6. Book with an editor

   Zaranka, William, ed. <u>The Brand-X

       Anthology of Poetry</u>. Cambridge:

       Apple-Wood, 1981.

   [For a book with two or more editors, use "eds."]

7. Book with an editor and an author

   Shakespeare, William. <u>Shakespeare: Major

       Plays and the Sonnets</u>. Ed. G. B.

       Harrison. New York: Harcourt, 1948.

8. Work in a collection or anthology

Firebaugh, Joseph J. "The Pragmatism of
Henry James." Henry James's Major
Novels: Essays in Criticism. Ed. Lyall
Powers. East Lansing: Michigan State
P, 1973. 187-201.

Pirandello, Luigi. Six Characters in Search
of an Author. The Norton Anthology of
World Masterpieces. Ed. Maynard Mack,
et al. 5th ed. 2 vols. New York:
Norton, 1985. 2:1387-1432.

9. Work reprinted in a collection or anthology

Sage, George H. "Sport in American Society:
Its Pervasiveness and Its Study."
Sport and American Society. 3rd ed.
Reading: Addison-Wesley, 1980. 4-15.
Rpt. in Physical Activity and the
Social Sciences. Ed. W. Neil
Widmeyer. 5th ed. Ithaca: Movement,
1983. 42-52.

[First give complete data for the earlier publication; then give the
reprinted source.]

10. Multivolume work

> Blom, Eric, ed.   Grove's Dictionary of
>
> > Music and Musicians.   5th ed. 10 vols.
> >
> > New York: St. Martin's, 1961.

11. Reprinted (republished) book

> Malamud, Bernard.   The Natural.   1952.
>
> > New York: Avon, 1980.

12. Later edition

> Gibaldi, Joseph, and Walter S. Achtert.
>
> > MLA Handbook for Writers of Research
> >
> > Papers.   2nd ed.   New York: MLA, 1984.

13. Book in translation

> de Beauvoir, Simone.   The Second Sex.   Trans.
>
> > H. M. Parshley.   New York: Knopf,
> >
> > 1971.

> [Alphabetize this entry under *B*.]

Newspapers

14. Signed newspaper article

Krebs, Emilie. "Sewer Backups Called No

    Problem." <u>Pantagraph</u> [Bloomington,

    IL] 20 Nov. 1985: A3.

[If the city of publication is not apparent from the name of the newspaper, give the city and state in brackets after the newspaper's name.]

Weiner, Jon. "Vendetta: The Government's

    Secret War against John Lennon."

    <u>Chicago Tribune</u> 5 Aug. 1984, Sec. 3:1.

[Note the difference between "A3" in the first example and "Sec. 3:1" in the second. Both refer to section and page, but in the first the pagination appears as "A3" in the newspaper, whereas in the second the section designation is not part of the pagination.]

15. Unsigned newspaper article

"Minister Found Guilty of Soliciting

    Murder." <u>New York Times</u> 2 Aug. 1984:

    A12.

16. Letter to the editor

Kessler, Ralph. "Orwell Defended."

    Letter. <u>New York Times Book Review</u>

    15 Dec. 1985: 26.

17. Editorial

> "From Good News to Bad." Editorial.
>
>   Washington Post 16 July 1984: 10.

Magazines and Journals

18. Article from a monthly or bimonthly magazine

> Foulkes, David. "Dreams of Innocence."
>
>   Psychology Today Dec. 1978: 78-88.

> Lawren, Bill. "1990's Designer Beasts."
>
>   Omni Nov. 1985: 56-61.

19. Article from a weekly or biweekly magazine (signed and unsigned)

> Adler, Jerry. "A Voyager's Close-Up of
>
>   Saturn." Newsweek 7 Sept. 1981:
>
>   57-58.

> "Warning: 'Love' for Sale." Newsweek 11
>
>   Nov. 1985: 39.

20. Article from a magazine with continuous pagination

Potvin, Raymond, and Che-Fu Lee.

   "Multistage Path Models of Adolescent

   Alcohol and Drug Use." <u>Journal of</u>

   <u>Studies on Alcohol</u> 41 (1980):

   531-542.

21. Article from a magazine that paginates each issue separately or that uses only issue numbers

Terkel, Studs.   "The Good War: An Oral

   History of World War II." <u>Atlantic</u>

   254.1 (July 1984): 45-75.

[That is, volume 254, issue 1.]

Other Sources

22. Review (of a book)

Langer, Elinor.   "Life Under Apartheid: The

   Possible and the Real." Rev. of

   <u>A Revolutionary Woman</u>, by Sheila

   Fugard. <u>Ms</u>. Nov. 1985: 26-27.

23. Personal or telephone interview

Deau, Jeanne. Personal interview. 12 Mar.

    1983.

Vidal, Gore. Telephone interview. 2

    June 1984.

[Treat published interviews like articles, with the person being interviewed as the author.]

24. Published letter

Tolkien, J. R. R. "To Sam Gamgee." 18

    Mar. 1956. Letter 184 in The Letters

    of J. R. R. Tolkien. Ed. Humphrey

    Carpenter. Boston: Houghton, 1981.

    244-245.

25. Unpublished letter

Wharton, Edith. Letter to William

    Brownell. 6 Nov. 1907. Wharton

    Archives. Amherst College, Amherst.

Isherwood, Christopher. Letter to the

    author. 24 Apr. 1983.

26. Anonymous pamphlet

    How to Help a Friend with a Drinking Problem.
        American College Health Association,
        1984.

    Aaron Copland: A Catalogue of His Works.
        New York: Boosey, n.d.

    ["n.d." means "no date given."]

27. Article from a specialized dictionary

    Van Doren, Carl. "Samuel Langhorne
        Clemens." DAB. 1958 ed.

    [Some commonly used resources, such as the *Dictionary of American Biography*, have accepted abbreviations.]

28. Encyclopedia article (signed and unsigned)

    Martin, William R. "Drug Abuse." World
        Book Encyclopedia. 1983 ed.

    "Scapegoat." Encyclopaedia Britannica:
        Micropaedia, 1979 ed.

    [The micropaedia is volumes 1–10 of the *Britannica*.]

29. Bible

The Holy Bible.   Revised Standard Version.

    Cleveland: World, 1962.

The Jerusalem Bible.   Trans. Alexander

    Jones et al.   Garden City: Doubleday,

    1966.

[Do not list the Bible unless you use a version other than the King James. Cite chapter and verse in parentheses in the text of your paper this way: (Rom. 12.4–8). Underline only the titles of bibles other than the King James version.]

30. Film

Wyler, William, dir.   Wuthering Heights.

    With Merle Oberon and Laurence Olivier.

    Samuel Goldwyn, 1939.

[If you are citing the work of an actor or screenwriter, put that person's name first.]

31. Lecture

Albee, Edward.   "A Dream or a Nightmare?"

    Illinois State University Fine Arts

    Lecture.   Normal, 18 Mar. 1979.

Note: For any other sources (such as television shows, recordings, works of art), you should remember to include enough information to permit an interested reader to locate your original source. Be sure to arrange this information in a logical fashion, duplicating so far as possible the order and punctuation of the entries above. To be on safe ground, consult your instructor for suggestions about documenting unusual material.

Standard Abbreviations of Publishers' Names

Allyn	Allyn and Bacon, Inc.
Appleton	Appleton-Century-Crofts
Ballantine	Ballantine Books, Inc.
Bantam	Bantam Books, Inc.
Basic	Basic Books
Bobbs	Bobbs-Merrill Co., Inc.
Bowker	R. R. Bowker Co.
Cambridge UP	Cambridge University Press
Clarendon	Clarendon Press
Columbia UP	Columbia University Press
Cornell UP	Cornell University Press
Crown	Crown Publishers, Inc.
Dell	Dell Publishing Co., Inc.
Dial	Dial Press, Inc.
Dodd	Dodd, Mead, and Co.
Doubleday	Doubleday and Co., Inc.
Dover	Dover Publications, Inc.
Dutton	E. P. Dutton
Farrar	Farrar, Straus, and Giroux, Inc.
Feminist	The Feminist Press
Free	The Free Press
GPO	Government Printing Office
Grove	Grove Press, Inc.
Harcourt	Harcourt Brace Jovanovich, Inc.
Harper	Harper & Row Publishers, Inc.
Harvard UP	Harvard University Press

Heath	D. C. Heath and Company
Holt	Holt, Rinehart and Winston, Inc.
Houghton	Houghton Mifflin Company
Indiana UP	Indiana University Press
Information Please	Information Please Publishing, Inc.
Johns Hopkins UP	The Johns Hopkins University Press
Knopf	Alfred A. Knopf, Inc.
Larousse	Librairie Larousse
Lippincott	J. B. Lippincott Co.
Little	Little, Brown and Company
Macmillan	Macmillan Publishing Co., Inc.
McGraw	McGraw-Hill, Inc.
MIT P	The Massachusetts Institute of Technology Press
MLA	The Modern Language Association of America
Morrow	William Morrow and Company, Inc.
NAL	The New American Library, Inc.
National Geographic Soc.	National Geographic Society
NCTE	The National Council of Teachers of English
NEA	The National Education Association
New Directions	New Directions Publishing Corporation
Norton	W. W. Norton and Co., Inc.
Oxford UP	Oxford University Press
Penguin	Penguin Books, Inc.
Pocket	Pocket Books
Prentice	Prentice-Hall, Inc.
Princeton UP	Princeton University Press
Putnam's	G. P. Putnam's Sons
Rand	Rand McNally and Co.
Random	Random House, Inc.
Ronald	Ronald Press
St. Martin's	St. Martin's Press, Inc.
Scott	Scott, Foresman, and Co.
Scribner's	Charles Scribner's Sons

Sierra	Sierra Club Books
Simon	Simon and Schuster, Inc.
State U of New York P	State University of New York Press
Straight Arrow	Straight Arrow Publishers, Inc.
Swallow	The Swallow Press
UMI	University Microfilms International
U of Chicago P	University of Chicago Press
U of Illinois P	University of Illinois Press
U of Nebraska P	University of Nebraska Press
U of New Mexico P	The University of New Mexico Press
UP of Florida	The University Presses of Florida
Viking	The Viking Press, Inc.
Warner	Warner Books, Inc.
Yale UP	Yale University Press

EXERCISE   6-6

In order to practice composing entries for a Works Cited list, complete an entry for each of the works described below. You need to supply underlining or quotation marks around titles. We'll write the first one for you to show you how.

1. The author of the book is Charles K. Smith.
   The title of the book is Styles and Structures: Alternative
      Approaches to Student Writing
   It was published in 1974 by W. W. Norton and Co., Inc.

   Smith, Charles K. <u>Styles and Structures</u>:

   <u>Alternative Approaches to Student</u>

   <u>Writing</u>. New York: Norton, 1974.

2. Author: Robin Lakoff
   Title of the book: Language and Woman's Place
   Published by Harper & Row in New York in 1975

3. Author: Max Spalter
   Title of the article: Five Examples of How to Write
      a Brechtian Play That Is Not Really Brechtian
   Periodical: Educational Theatre
   Published in the 2nd issue of 1975 on pages 220 to 235
   Note: this periodical has continuous page numbering.
4. Author: Daniel S. Greenberg
   Title of the article: Ridding American Politics of Polls
   Newspaper: Washington Post
   Published on September 16, 1980, in section A, on page 17
5. Authors: Clyde E. Blocker, Robert H. Plummer, and Richard
      C. Richardson
   Title of the book: The Two-Year College: A Social Synthesis
   Published in Englewood Cliffs, New Jersey, by Prentice-Hall in
   1965
6. How would your textbook, *The Writer's Rhetoric and Handbook,*
   appear in a Works Cited list? Include the exact data.
7. In which order would the publications from 1 to 6 above appear in
   your list? Write the correct answer.

   a) 5 4 2 6 1 3   b) 1 2 3 4 5 6   c) 4 3 6 1 5 2   d) 6 4 3 5 1 2

THE APA DOCUMENTATION STYLE FOR THE SOCIAL SCIENCES

You use the APA style this way:

A. Always mention your source within the text of your paper in parentheses, like this:

```
The study reveals that children pass through

identifiable cognitive stages (Piaget, 1954).
```

B. Your readers can identify this source by consulting your "References" list at the end of your paper. The entry for the information above would appear like this:

> Piaget, J. (1954).   <u>The construction of</u>
>
>   <u>reality in the child</u>.   New York: Basic
>
>   Books.

[Note the use of sentence capitalization for titles in the references section.]

C. If you are quoting directly or if you want to stress the authority of the source you are paraphrasing, you may mention the name of the source in your sentence. Then include just the date in parentheses, like this:

> In <u>Words and Women</u>, Miller and Swift (1976)
>
> remind us that using the plural is a good way
>
> to avoid "the built-in male-as-norm quality
>
> English has acquired. . ." (p. 163).

D. If you are using a source written or edited by more than two people and fewer than six, cite all authors the first time you refer to the source. For all following references cite only the surname of the first person listed, followed by "et al." (meaning "and others"):

> Blair et al. (1980) observe that the fine
>
> arts were almost ignored by colonial
>
> writers.

When there are only two authors, join their names with an "and" in the text. In parenthetical materials, tables, and reference lists, join the names by an ampersand (&).

```
Hale and Sponjer (1972) originated the Do-
Look-Learn theory.

The Do-Look-Learn theory (Hale & Sponjer,
1972) was taken seriously by educators.
```

E. If the author's name is not given, then use a shortened title instead. In your abbreviation, be sure to use at least the first word of the full title to send the reader to the proper alphabetized entry in your "References" section. The following is a reference to a newspaper article entitled "Ramifications of Baboon Use Expected to Become an Issue":

```
The doctor observed that some people
objected to the transplant on grounds that
were emotional rather than rational
("Ramifications," 1979).
```

F. If you are quoting more than *forty* words, begin the quotation on a new line and indent the entire quotation five spaces, but run each line to the usual right margin. Omit the quotation marks. Do not single-space the quotation.

```
In Language and Woman's Place (1975) Lakoff
observes that

        men tend to relegate to women things
        that are not of concern to them, or do
```

not involve their egos. . . . We might

rephrase this point by saying that

since women are not expected to make

decisions on important matters, such as

what kind of job to hold, they are

relegated the noncrucial decisions as a

sop (p. 9).

G. On your last page, a separate page, alphabetize your "References" list of all sources mentioned in your paper. Use *hanging indention:* that is, after the first line of each entry, indent the other lines five spaces.

H. In your "References" section, in citing two or more works by the same author, put the earliest work first. When more than one work has been published by the same author during the same year, list them alphabetically, according to name of the book or article and identify them with an "a," "b," "c," etc., following the date:

Graves, D. (1975). An examination of the

writing processes of seven-year-old

children. Research in the Teaching of

English, 9, 227-241.

Graves, D. (1981a). Writing research for

the eighties: What is needed. Language

Arts, 58, 197-206.

Graves, D. (1981b). <u>Writers: Teachers and</u>

<u>children at work</u>. Exeter, NH:

Heinemann Educational Books.

l. Use the following abbreviations: Vol., No., chap., trans., ed., Ed., rev. ed., 2nd ed., p., pp. (meaning Volume, Number, chapter, translated by, edition, Editor, revised edition, second edition, page, and pages). Use official U.S. Postal Service abbreviations for states: IL, NY, TX, etc.

SAMPLE ENTRIES FOR A LIST OF "REFERENCES"

The following models will help you write entries for your References list for most of the sources you will use. If you use a source not treated in these samples, consult the more extensive list of sample entries found in the *Publication Manual of the American Psychological Association* or ask your instructor.

Alphabetize your list by the author's last name. If there is no author given, alphabetize the entry by the title. Use hanging indention; that is, after the first line of each entry indent the other lines five spaces.

Books and Journals

1. Book by one author

Abernathy, C. F. (1980). <u>Civil rights:</u>

<u>Cases and materials</u>. St. Paul: West.

2. Two or more books by the same author (list in chronological order)

Gould, S. J. (1980). <u>The mismeasure of man</u>. New York: Norton.

Gould, S. J. (1981). <u>The panda's thumb:</u> <u>More reflections on natural history</u>. New York: Norton.

3. Book by two or more authors

Brusaw, C., Alfred, G. & Oliu, W. (1976). <u>The business writer's handbook</u>. New York: St. Martin's.

Cook, M. & McHenry, R. (1978). <u>Sexual</u> <u>attraction</u>. New York: Pergamon.

[Note that in your list of references you use the ampersand sign instead of writing "and."]

4. Book by a corporate author

White House Conference on Children and Youth. (1970). <u>The becoming of</u> <u>education</u>. Washington, D.C.: U.S. Government Printing Office.

5. Book with an editor

> Zaranka, W., Ed. (1981). <u>The brand—X
> anthology of poetry</u>. Cambridge:
> Apple—Wood.

[For a book with two or more editors, use "Eds."]

6. Article in a collection or anthology

> Emig, J. (1978). Hand, eye, brain: Some
> basics in the writing process. In C.
> Cooper & L. Odell (Eds.) <u>Research in
> composing: Points of departure</u> (pp.
> 59—72). Urbana, IL: National Council
> of Teachers of English.

7. Multivolume work

> Asimov, I. (1960). <u>The intelligent man's
> guide to science</u>. (Vols. 1—2). New
> York: Basic Books.

8. Later edition

Gibaldi, J. & Achtert, W. (1984). <u>MLA</u>
<u>handbook for writers of research</u>
<u>papers</u> (2nd ed.). New York: MLA.

9. Article from a journal

Emig, J. (1977). Writing as a mode of
learning. <u>College Composition and</u>
<u>Communication</u>, <u>28</u>, 122–128.

Other Sources

10. Personal or telephone interview, letter, lecture, etc.
Not cited in Reference list, only in text citation.

11. Article from a specialized dictionary or encyclopedia
Treat as an article in a collection (number 6 above).

Chapter Seven
Practical Career Writing

Almost everything we have said about theme writing applies to writing in general. You should always say clearly what's on your mind in the most effective way. The difference between the writing you do in college and the writing you will do on the job is mainly a difference in form. Instead of writing essay examinations, you will write memos to people you work with. Instead of writing a term paper on the life cycle of platypuses, you will write case studies, lesson plans, law briefs, or drilling reports. Instead of just writing letters to your Aunt Helen, you will also write letters to people in industry—often people who are strangers to you.

Professional success often depends on successful communication. Letters must be written clearly and concisely so that the people who receive them can quickly understand exactly what the writer had in mind. Writing that is not clear or leaves out essential information invariably leads to extra work, extra memos, extra letters—hence extra cost—to straighten out the confusion caused by the original unclear message.

People who do the hiring understand these hard facts. They are second in line—right after English teachers—to point out the value of writing skills. Howard W. Blauvelt, chief executive officer of the Continental Oil Company, attests that "Business needs skilled communicators. . . . The ability to listen, digest, distill, and further communicate information is fundamental."[1] Most professional people, whether employed in private industry or a government agency, spend much of their working time writing. By learning to write well, you have gone a long way toward preparing yourself for a promising career.

[1] Quoted by Elizabeth M. Fowler, "Careers: Practical Skills for Graduates," *New York Times:* D.17.3.

WRITING EFFECTIVE LETTERS

Letter writing is the most useful writing skill that people practice after finishing school. More of us convey information,
ideas, suggestions, thanks, complaints, and requests in letters
than in any other productive way. Everyone needs to be able
to write them well. For those taking jobs in business, industry,
or the governmental bureaucracy, effective letter writing is
essential for a successful career.

Cultivate the "You" Attitude

The best way to write a really persuasive letter is to show
you, the reader, what the writer can do for *you*—how *you* will
profit and why. As Robert L. Shurter observes, "Nothing related to business correspondence is more important than this
point of view, known for years as the *you attitude:* we can
most readily persuade others to do what we want them to do
by demonstrating that it is to their advantage to do it."[2] You
have to be honest about it, of course. If you dream up some
phony reason or resort to shameless flattery, your reader will
reject your letter at once. Observe the *you attitude* in operation in the examples on the next page, which we have borrowed from Shurter. The first one (Figure 7-1) illustrates the
wrong way to make a request.

Figure 7-2 shows the same request, improved by incorporating the *you attitude*. Notice how the first letter focuses on
the needs of the writer: *I* need, *I* selected, *I* have to, *I* hope. In
the second letter the focus shifts to *you* and *your*. No one
would doubt that the second letter is more effective.

---

[2] Donald J. Leonard, *Shurter's Communication in Business,* 4th ed. (New
York: McGraw, 1979): 84.

Dear Sir:

I need a lot of information on the way in which
business people react to the current crises in
our colleges, and I selected you and some
others to send this questionnaire to because
your names were mentioned in the newspapers.

I have to have this information in two weeks,
because my paper is due then, and I hope you will
help me by returning the questionnaire promptly.

                              Sincerely yours,

Figure 7-1 Typical request letter that exhibits the *I attitude*.

Dear Mr. Jones:

You and several other prominent business people
were recently quoted in The Record concerning
the present crises in our colleges--and your
comments so interested me that I decided to write
my term paper on "Business's View of Today's
Colleges."

Your answers to the enclosed questionnaire--all
you need to do is check yes or no--will be kept
completely confidential. If you wish, I will
send you a summary of the results based on my
survey of 50 prominent business people in this
area.

You will recognize that I am attempting, in a
small way, to open communication between education and business by means of a realistic survey.
You can help by checking the answers and returning the questionnaire in the enclosed, self-
addressed envelope.

                              Sincerely yours,

Figure 7-2 Request letter that incorporates the *you attitude*.

The *you attitude* is easier to adopt with some types of letters than with others. It's difficult, for instance, when requesting a letter of recommendation, but easier—and more essential—when writing a letter applying for a job. Try to incorporate the *you attitude* into your thinking when you plan what to write. Use it when it works. When it will not, settle for a graceful compliment.

EXERCISE   7-1

Rewrite the following letter of request more effectively.

Dear Ms. Leonardo,

I am writing an article about the checking account plans of our local banks. I intend to publish my work in the local community newspaper, <u>The Post-Amerikan</u>. I need the following information from you:

> checking charges
> returned check policies
> interest rate, if any
> minimum balance, if any

Please respond within two weeks.

Sincerely,

Phoebe Caulfield
Phoebe Caulfield

Organize Before You Write

A good letter is lean; it sticks to the point. In order to write a lean letter, you must organize your thoughts. Jot down the things you must say (just as you would in outlining an essay), and consider how the ideas are logically related. Put the points in order, then write one short, clear paragraph for each main item, making sure that you include all necessary information. Wind up politely, perhaps with a word of thanks.

Organization is important in all writing. It is especially important in the writing you do on the job, because time is money: clarity is essential. If you write a long, rambling letter that fails to focus on your purpose, the reader may just toss your letter in the nearest wastebasket. At the very least, you are not likely to get the response you want if you tax your readers' minds with vagueness and tire their eyes with excess words.

Consider Tone and Level of Usage

Just as you must adopt a tone appropriate to your purpose in writing essays, so should you match tone to purpose in a letter. Try to strike a balance between being formal and being friendly. Since you are usually trying to get your reader to do something (whether it's buying from your company or granting you a job interview), do not be sarcastic or too aggressive. Be confident, not slavish: "I beg you to consider me for this job" is too servile. Be courteous but not stuffy. Using the impersonal *one* often sounds stilted: "One hopes that the Magnum Oil Corporation will consider one's credentials." You can use *I* and *you* and sound natural without becoming too chummy. Try to adopt the tone that you would find most appealing in a stranger's letter to you.

While most letter writers do not use strictly formal language, neither do they use colloquial or slangy language. In most cases, try to be temperate and use informal language. (You can review usage levels on pages 191–192.) Instead of high-sounding phrases like *due to the fact that,* use the plainer *since* or *because*. Avoid old-fashioned business phrases like *pursuant to, be advised that, enclosed herewith,* and *in receipt of*. Avoid clichés like "I'll give it the old college try" and "We'll give them a run for their money." Arranging plain English words in concise sentences that say clearly what you mean will leave a favorable impression.

One last piece of advice: give bad news gently. If you should decide to turn down a prospective job, say "I was pleased to receive your offer, but . . ." instead of "Fortunately, I got a better offer." Your meaning will be the same, but you will not offend someone you may need to contact later in your new job. A callous attitude might get you to the top quickly, but it's more likely to land you among the unemployed even faster.

Follow the Standard Format Faithfully

When you write to your Aunt Helen, you probably pick up any handy piece of paper and jot down a message. You never give a thought to format because you are writing a personal note. Auntie loves you and is unlikely to be offended by the casual appearance of your letter.

Such casualness will seldom be appropriate for business letters for a couple of reasons. First, the person you are writing to is likely to be a stranger or someone you know only slightly. Generally, correspondence between strangers is fairly formal. Then too, the person you are writing is likely to respond on the basis of the way your letter looks, as well as to what you say in it. If your letter is sloppy, your reader might justifiably decide you are a slob and ignore you.

Since most business correspondence follows a standard format (as shown in Figure 7-3), you will do well to follow it.

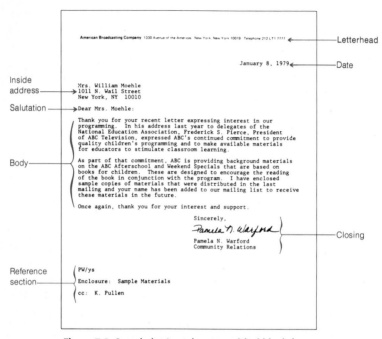

Letterhead

Date

Inside address

Salutation

Body

Closing

Reference section

Figure 7-3 Sample business letter, modified-block format.

Letters are usually typed in one of two standard formats. In the *full-block* format all lines begin at the left margin. In the *modified-block* format, which is the most popular, both the heading and the closing are set on the right side of the page. Although your margins will vary so that the letter is centered, all letters should have margins of at least 1 1/4 inches on all sides. Center the letter vertically as well as horizontally.

Aside from appearance, the main reason for using a standard format is that it always places important information in the same easy-to-find places. As you read the following explanation of each part, refer to Figure 7-3 to see how it should be typed.

1. The ***heading*** supplies the name and address of the sender, which is you. Naturally, letterhead stationery includes all this information. All you need to add is the date, with the month spelled out first, then the day and the year. If you do not use letterhead stationery, type the heading, single-spaced, with your own address this way in the upper-right-hand corner:

   3818 18th Street
   San Francisco, CA 94114
   July 12, 1982

2. The ***inside address*** contains the full name, business title, company name, and address of the person to whom you are writing. Notice that before the person's name you use a courtesy title, like Ms., Mr., or Dr. The inside address is used in case the envelope is separated from the letter in a company's mail room.

3. The ***salutation*** is a polite greeting. Usually it is followed by a colon. If possible, ***try to address an individual by name:***

   Dear Ms. [or Mr. or Dr.] Wakoski:

If you do not know the person's name, find it. On pages 347–349 we explain how. If you are unable to locate the person's name, you can open this way:

   Dear Personnel Manager:
   Dear People in the Credit Department:

Dear Sir and ***To Whom It May Concern*** are now considered too impersonal to be effective. You may, however, use simply ***Ladies*** or ***Gentlemen***, if you are sure that the people you are addressing are all of one sex. **_Dear Joan_** (or **_John_**) is appropriate if you are on friendly terms with the person you are addressing.

4. The **_body_** is the heart of a letter. The message must be clearly written and well organized. Note that the paragraphs are single-spaced and begin at the left margin. A double space separates paragraphs. You may indent the first line of each paragraph, but many people do not.

5. The **_closing_** is a polite way of ending a letter. The first line, or complimentary close, is followed by a comma. You can use one of the old standbys:

Formal	Informal
Yours truly,	Warmly,
Very truly yours,	Cordially yours,
Sincerely yours,	Best regards,
Yours sincerely,	With best wishes,

Avoid being too offbeat or too cute. Your signature and typed name complete the closing. If you are representing a firm, your title appears directly under your name.

6. The **_reference section_**, which is used as needed, may include enclosure or copy notations. The reference notation lists the writer's initials and, if you are lucky enough to have one, the typist's initials. The enclosure notation simply calls the reader's (or the mail room's) attention to the inclusion of other items with the letter (and tells how many inclusions there are) like this:

Enclosure

Enc. 3

Enclosure: one set of blueprints

The copy notation indicates that copies were sent to other people.

cc: Ms. Wakoski

As you probably guessed, cc means carbon copy; pc means photocopy.

TYPES OF CORRESPONDENCE

The majority of letters ask the reader to *do* something, to supply information or support some worthy cause. But different purposes require different approaches. Three common types are letters of request, letters of persuasion, and letters of complaint.

Letters of Request

Organize requests like this: (1) explain exactly what you want and give any specific information that is necessary, (2) explain why you want what you want, and (3) thank your reader for the expected help. See the sample in Figure 7-4.

1228 Spruce Street
Bloomington, IL 61701
July 10, 1983

High Blood Pressure Information Center
120/80 National Institutes of Health
Bethesda, MD 20014

Dear Friends:

    Would you please send me your Public Affairs Pamphlet No. 483A, entitled ''Watch Your Blood Pressure!'' by Theodore Irwin?

    You are performing a valuable public service by distributing this free information. Thanks for the good work.

Yours sincerely,

Mary Beth Marlow

Mary Beth Marlow

Figure 7-4 Sample letter requesting information.

Notice that the message states the request clearly and politely, and that it gives the exact title of the catalog, all in one paragraph. Virtually every item of merchandise has a number (with other numbers for every part) for easy identification. So always include the necessary numbers. If your letter requests several separate things, like three or four booklets, consider numbering them and listing them on separate lines to make it easier for your readers to fill your requests. Address your request to a specific person or department if possible.

Requesting a Reference. A particular kind of request letter that you are likely to write sooner or later is a request for a reference. The same rules apply in this case, but you should also take care to identify yourself and to supply some extra information that will help the reader compose a useful reference letter for you (see Figure 7-5).

Besides the self-addressed postcard, you may want to include other personal information, such as grade point average, honors and scholarships, and activities, memberships, or offices. Be sure to give specific guidelines for writing the recommendation, if there are any. Many college placement services provide special, easily duplicated forms for letters, which you should be sure to include.

Letters of Persuasion

Certainly job application letters must be persuasive since you are, in effect, selling yourself, but we discuss these important letters in a separate section (see pages 352–358). The kind of persuasive letters that we are talking about here are the ones you may want to write to editors, members of Congress, cabinet members, or even the President, in order to express your viewpoint on matters of public policy that affect your life.

310 Darby Drive
Colfax, IL 61728
June 17, 1983

Dr. Lucia Getsi
Department of English
Illinois State University
Normal, IL 61761

Dear Professor Getsi:

I am applying for a proofreading job at <u>The</u> <u>Daily</u> <u>Deluge</u>
in Colfax, Illinois (my hometown), and I would be grate-
ful if you would write a letter of recommendation for me.

In the fall semester of 1981 I took your course in "The
American Short Story, 1860-1920," and wrote my term paper
on "Mythological Implications in Eudora Welty's 'Moon
Lake.'" I received an A in the course, which I found
informative and enjoyable.

If you are willing to write a letter for me, please
address it to

                    Ms. Patricia Gilbey
                    Managing Editor
                    <u>The</u> <u>Daily</u> <u>Deluge</u>
                    110 South Main Street
                    Colfax, IL 61728

It should arrive before July 1. If you feel unable to
recommend me, would you please return the enclosed postcard to let me know?

Thank you for doing me this favor.

With warm regards,

Margie Sanford

Margaret Sanford

Figure 7-5 Letter requesting a reference.

418 Fairview Avenue
Bloomington, IL   61761
March 14, 1983

Editor, The Daily Pantagraph
201 West Washington Street
Bloomington, IL   61701

To the Editor:

I am alarmed by the Agriculture Department's plan to use
the pesticide mirex--which kills birds and marine life--
in a new attempt to eliminate the fire ant. Mirex also
has been shown to cause cancer in mice and birth defects
in rats.

Mirex is one of the chlorinated pesticides, like DDT and
dieldrin, which spread through the environment and remain
active for many years. DDT, for instance, is found in
Antarctic seals, although it was never used in Antarctica.

Dieldrin is in the milk of Illinois mothers at a concentration 5.6 times that considered safe for infants by the
Food and Drug Administration. Once these chemicals enter
a human body, they tend to stay there.

Spraying pesticides over wide areas is expensive, ineffective, and alarmingly dangerous. The money used to spread
mirex could be more judiciously spent. Other insects
have been controlled by using hormones to lure them into
traps and by introducing relatively harmless natural
enemies into infested areas. These and other possibilities should be fully explored before the Agriculture
Department again spreads a damaging and long-lived pesticide over millions of acres of farmland where it almost
certainly will enter our food and water.

                              Sincerely yours,

                              Dan LeSeure

                              Dan LeSeure

Figure 7-6 Example of a persuasive letter.

When you write such a letter, you really are writing a brief persuasive essay. Choose your tone carefully. Keep your audience (that is, your reader or readers) constantly in mind. Present your arguments clearly, concisely, and logically. At the end, offer your solutions to the problems discussed, if possible. Your persuasive letter might come out something like the one shown in Figure 7-6. You can increase the effectiveness of your letter by sending copies to the Secretary of Agriculture, your senators, and the President.

Letters of Complaint

Just as you want to avoid being sarcastic when you write a letter of persuasion, you want to remain reasonable when you write a letter of complaint. Calling your reader names is not the way to solve your problem, whether it is a new car that refuses to start or a computer that likes to add other people's bills to your account. Unless your goal is simply to let off steam, try something like the letter shown in Figure 7-7 when you write to a consumer relations manager. This letter is reasonable, despite the writer's annoyance at the hair dryer's frailty. Notice also how the letter expresses confidence in the manufacturer's fairness (third paragraph) instead of speculating on whose fault the failure was.

Find a Person's Name.   If possible, direct your letter of complaint to a specific person: it's the best way to get speedy results. If you are having trouble with a local business, call and get the owner's or the manager's name first. If you are dealing with a large business, you may want the name of the person who has responsibility for consumer complaints or the person in charge of a specific department, like the service manager, customer relations manager, or credit manager. If

216 West Boyd St.
Gilman, IL 60938
September 7, 1983

Mr. Leon White
Consumer Affairs
Persis Products, Inc.
312 State Street
Chicago, IL 60637

Dear Mr. White:

 I have been having trouble with my new
Hot'N'Heavenly hair dryer (model 1040c, no.
6737). It no longer heats properly.

 I bought the dryer at Meyer and Frank's
in Eugene, Oregon (see enclosed copy of receipt), and was quite satisfied with it at
first. Now that it is not working, I can
not find a store in Gilman, Illinois, that
carries your dryers.

 Since it is only two months old, I am
sure you will want to replace or repair my
hair dryer, but I do not know where to send
it.

 I will appreciate hearing from you concerning this problem at your earliest convenience.

Yours sincerely,

Russ Finley

Russell Finley

Figure 7-7 Sample letter of complaint.

you are dealing with a large corporation, write to the president, the vice president in charge of pubic relations, or a specific division manager. You can get the names of corporate officials at your library from *Thomas' Register of American Manufacturers* or *Poor's Register of Corporations, Directors, and Executives*. Chambers of commerce and better business bureaus may also provide names or assistance.

Once you have the name, get busy. But remember these four things:

1. Be reasonable.
2. Give exact details about your problem.
3. Give all information (like model or serial numbers, amount paid) that may be needed.
4. Thank your reader in advance for the assistance.

It matters not what your complaint is—poor service in a store or on a plane or train, gadgets that refuse to work, promises that are not kept, pollution that stifles you and your dog, or food that is inedible—you will get more action for your effort by following these four rules than you would with pages of obscenity or sarcasm.

On the Other Hand . . .

Most people in business expect and appreciate a fairly impersonal, informative standard letter. However, a polite business letter will not always get results. A letter with an unusual approach—humorous, for example, or anecdotal—may get more careful attention in certain situations. Whether to risk a nonstandard approach (and no doubt have more fun writing the letter) is up to you. If you believe that your standard letter may be one among many just like it, perhaps an offbeat piece of correspondence will set you off from the crowd.

POSTAL POINTERS

Return address →

Sue LeSeure
500 W. Main St.
Normal, IL 61761

Ms. Maria Valdez
Personnel Manager
Great Western Publishing Corp.
7777 State St., Room 456
Chicago, IL 60606

← Mailing address

a

Alabama AL	Kentucky KY	Ohio OH
Alaska AK	Louisiana LA	Oklahoma OK
Arizona AZ	Maine ME	Oregon OR
Arkansas AR	Maryland MD	Pennsylvania PA
California CA	Massachusetts MA	Puerto Rico PR
Colorado CO	Michigan MI	Rhode Island RI
Connecticut CT	Minnesota MN	South Carolina SC
Delaware DE	Mississippi MS	South Dakota SD
District of Columbia DC	Missouri MO	Tennessee TN
Florida FL	Montana MT	Texas TX
Georgia GA	Nebraska NB	Utah UT
Guam GU	Nevada NV	Vermont VT
Hawaii HI	New Hampshire NH	Virginia VA
Idaho ID	New Jersey NJ	Virgin Islands VI
Iilinois IL	New Mexico NM	Washington WA
Indiana IN	New York NY	West Virginia WV
Iowa IA	North Carolina NC	Wisconsin WI
Kansas KS	North Dakota ND	Wyoming WY

b

Figure 7-8 Postal pointers: (*a*) sample envelope, (*b*) postal service abbreviations.

A Word About Envelopes

The envelope should include your return address, typed in the upper-left corner, and the mailing address, typed as shown in Figure 7-8*a*. Since the postal service uses clever machines to read the mailing address from the bottom up, make sure that city, state, and zip code (in that order) are on the last line and the street address (or box number) is on the line above that. If there is an apartment number or room number, it should go directly after, and on the same line as, the street address. Names, titles, and any other information must appear on lines *above* these last two. The postal service has also supplied convenient two-letter abbreviations for the states. Use them without periods. (See Figure 7-8*b*.)

EXERCISE   7-2

In each of the following exercises, use a standard business-letter format (block or modified block) and remember to be clear, concise, and polite.

1. Write a letter requesting:
   a. A reference from one of your professors or employers
   b. An instruction manual and repair booklet for an electric toaster
   c. Information on how your favorite beer is brewed
   d. Information from your local agricultural extension office on how to have your garden soil analyzed.
2. Write a persuasive letter to your local newspaper or to the politician you like the least about:
   a. Conflicts of interest in Congress (or state legislatures)
   b. Preserving our wilderness areas (wildlife, clean air or water, Victorian architecture, or whatever)
   c. The high cost of housing (or apartments)
   d. The social responsibility of corporations
   e. Improvement of the mass transit system in your town

3. Write a reasonable letter of complaint about:
    a. An electric can opener that snarls at you but refuses to open cans
    b. A new leather coat that split at the shoulder seam and that the store refuses to take back
    c. A telephone bill that lists eleven calls to Perth, Australia
    d. A new stereo speaker that has been "repaired" twice but still has a surly growl
    e. Police officers who were rude and overbearing when they came to ask you to keep the noise down at a party

WRITING APPEALING JOB APPLICATIONS AND RÉSUMÉS

Now that you have mastered the general techniques of letter writing, it is time to move on to the type of letter that will probably be crucial to you soon: the job application letter. Your letter could make the difference between getting a job and remaining unemployed. It also could mean the difference between spending half your waking hours doing something relatively satisfying and spending those endless hours doing something you actively dislike.

Practical Advice About Application Letters

We have badgered you again and again about keeping your reader in mind when you write. In your job application letter, you must studiously cultivate the *you attitude* discussed on pages 335–337. Your letter must say more than "I need a job." It must say instead: "This is what I can do for your organization if you hire me." You want to match your qualifications to the job requirements as closely as possible.

There are three other things you should keep in mind while writing your letters of application. *First, your tone should be polite and confident.* You want to present your best qualifications—your education and experience—in the most favorable light. But if you appear too aggressive, too confident, employers may fear that you will be unable to get along with the mere mortals they already employ. Nor should you go to the other extreme and beg for a job because you have a family or an aging parent to support. Such appeals simply do not work. *Second, you should always use a standard business-letter format,* like the one in Figure 7-9 (page 355). Many people in business judge job applicants as much on the way their letters look as on what they say. *Finally, your letter should be brief and to the point*—no longer than one type-written page, possibly three or four short paragraphs.

Since you must accomplish a great deal in a brief space, we have broken the body of a basic job application letter into three parts: *effective opening, presentation of qualifications,* and *arrangement for interview.* The following sections will show you what to concentrate on in each of the parts.

Write an Effective Opening.   Often the best way to begin your letter is the most direct way, like this:

My training and experience as a proofreader and copy editor should be useful to your firm.

This opening makes clear *what* kind of job you want, *why* you are qualified for it, and *how* your skills can be valuable to a particular business (the *you attitude*). Naturally, if you are applying for a job that was advertised, you will say so. If you know someone in the organization who will agree to speak well of you, by all means mention that person's name. When you apply for your first full-time job after college, however, you may have to write to a number of large companies that employ people with your skills. In that case, you will be fishing for an opening and will have to generalize your qualifications and incorporate the *you attitude* as imaginatively as possible. You may prefer a copyediting job, but mention proofreading also to increase your chances of getting some job—one that could lead to the job you really want.

Another way of opening your application letter is to ask a question: "Do you need a good, experienced copy editor?" That catches the reader's attention and gets right to the point. You must be sure, however, that you back up your claim in the next paragraph.

Present Your Qualifications.   The heart of your application letter is the proof that you can do for a prospective employer what you say you can do. Creating a good impression is important, but proof that you are qualified is the clincher. You need not be long-winded about it, because you will include a résumé supplying the details. Your letter should mention only those things that *best* qualify you for the job. These days that usually means experience, like this:

> For two summers I worked as a proofreader on the *Daily Deluge* in Colfax, Illinois, and for three years as a part-time advertising copywriter for radio station WXYZ in Normal. As the enclosed résumé indicates, I majored in English and minored in journalism at Illinois State University.

If you do not have much work experience, you can emphasize your training (and your grades, if they are good). Or ransack your past for other useful experience. Many jobs require you to deal with the public. If you sold tickets at the college theater or were a member of a club that raised money for charity, mention those volunteer jobs to show you have had experience in dealing with people. Another common skill that business needs is organizational ability. If you planned activities at a summer camp or organized church socials, you can list those things as examples of your ability to organize. Be as resourceful as you can when considering your skills, but do not exaggerate them.

500 West Main Street
Normal, IL   61761
March 15, 1978

Ms. Maria Valdez
Personnel Manager
Great Western Publishing Corp.
7777 State Street, Room 456
Chicago, IL   60606

Dear Ms. Valdez:

Do you need a good, experienced proofreader or copy editor?

For two summers I worked as a proofreader at The Daily Deluge in Colfax, Illinois, and for three years as a part-time advertising copywriter for radio station WXYZ in Normal. As the enclosed resume indicates, I majored in English and minored in journalism at Illinois State University.

My experience with various writing and proofreading assignments could prove useful to your firm. I know a position with your nationally known firm would be satisfying to me, as it would further my ambition to become a professional editor.

May I come in for an interview at your convenience? Thank you for your consideration.

Sincerely,

Sue LeSeure

Sue LeSeure

Enclosure: Resume

Effective opening →

Presenting qualifications }

Summarizing experience }

Setting up interview →

Figure 7-9 Sample job application letter.

If you know what your long-range career goal is, you might mention it as an indication of your commitment.

> My experience with various writing and proofreading assignments could prove useful to your firm. I know that a position with your nationally known firm would be satisfying to me, as it would further my ambition to become a professional editor.

Employers like employees who are devoted to their work. They also prefer employees who have a high opinion of the company they work for, so, in keeping with the *you attitude*, try to work in an indirect compliment ("your nationally known firm"). Just be careful not to overdo it. You might also want to refer to your present status.

> When I finish school in June . . .

or

> A position in your accounting department would offer me more opportunity for advancement than I have with my present excellent, though smaller, firm.

Notice that you should explain your desire to change jobs in a positive way. Employers take a dim view of employees who change jobs because of personal disagreements or disputes over how to run the place. Salary is a subject that should not be dealt with in application letters. If an advertisement asks for your requirement, suggest that the matter be discussed in your interview.

Set Up an Interview. The real object of your application letter is to obtain an interview, since few good jobs are handed out without one. Conclude your letter by offering to be interviewed at the company's convenience, and add a polite word of thanks.

> May I come in for an interview at your convenience? Thank you for your consideration.

If you gain an interview, more than likely you will be notified by telephone rather than by letter. You want to avoid frustrating your caller. If there are limitations on your availability (if, for example, you will be away from your phone during part of the day), be sure to say what are the best times to call. If the limitations are very restrictive, offer an alternative:

> I will be at home (309-828-6473) before 10 a.m. and after 5 p.m. on weekdays. I realize that my hours are inconvenient, so I will call you on Tuesday the 14th to discuss my application if you have not reached me.

Allow two weeks, though, to give the prospective employer ample time to contact you by mail before you call. In today's tight job market, you may possibly be expected to pay your own expenses if the job you seek is out of town. Try to go, because without the interview, you have little chance of getting the job. If you are applying to a large company, you might ask to be interviewed at a regional office near your home. But certainly you should make every effort to appear for an interview if offered one.

Other Things to Consider. You must try to direct your letter to a specific person, usually the head of the department you are interested in or perhaps the company's personnel manager. This personal touch shows you are serious, knowledgeable, and sufficiently energetic to locate the name. (Try *Thomas' Register of American Manufacturers* or *Poor's Regis-*

ter of Corporations, Directors, and Executives.) If you absolutely cannot find a name, "Director of Personnel" will do in a pinch. You should type each letter of application individually. Form letters with blanks filled in may be faster, but they are not likely to be considered seriously. (Your résumé may be commercially duplicated, however.)

Make Your Letter Perfect.   Finally, take the time to prune your letter down to the essentials. Ask a loved one to read it and make suggestions. Use correct spelling, grammar, and punctuation. Proofread the final typed version at least twice. Call on your loved ones again. Typos and spelling mistakes will kill your chances.

Write a Follow-Up.   After you have had your interview, you should write a brief follow-up letter to the interviewer. In this letter you could comment on some feature of the company which impressed you, but primarily you should thank your interviewers for their time and consideration. Since your purpose is merely to keep your name in the interviewer's mind, a few *brief*, friendly lines will do. If, however, the interview ended on a "Don't call us, we'll call you" note, no follow-up letter will help.

DISCUSSION EXERCISE   7-3

We have reprinted here two drafts of Laurie Dahlberg's application for an internship. After collecting her information and deciding what she needed to say, she wrote the first draft. Then she took it to a friend, who gave her some advice for rewriting the letter more effectively. Read both of Laurie's drafts carefully. What advice did her friend give her? What would you say are two major changes in the letter, and why did she make them? What are two minor changes, and what reasons do you see for those?

October 27, 1984

Curator of Paintings
Museum of Fine Arts
Boston MA 02115

Dear Sir:

Although I have not yet completed my master's degree in Art
History, I am submitting my application for your internship
on the advice of one of my professors, Harold Gregor.

The focus of my studies here at Illinois State University
was originally in Chinese and Japanese art, but because this
university does not offer oriental language courses, I have
changed my concentration to Modern European art to complete
my degree.

I intend to seek another degree in museum studies in the
fall of 1985. As I am planning a career in museum work, an
internship at the museum of Fine Arts would be a wonderful
opportunity and a challenge which I am confident I could
meet.

I am enclosing a list of pertinent graduate and
undergraduate courses. Of course, I haven't received final
grades in my current courses. I need nine hours to complete
my master's degree, and my grade point average is 4.0.

Thank you for considering my application. I know I would
enjoy working with the staff and collections of the Museum
of Fine Arts.

Sincerely,

Laurie V. Dahlberg

Laurie V. Dahlberg

915 W. Grove St.
Bloomington IL 61701
October 27, 1984

Jessica Carmine
Curator of Paintings
Museum of Fine Arts
Boston MA 02115

Dear Ms. Carmine:

On the encouragement of my professor Harold Gregor, I would
like to submit my application for the internship which is
offered in the Department of Paintings.

Presently, I am working on my master's degree in art
history, with a concentration in modern European art. As

you will notice from my list of courses, I also have a
special interest in Oriental art.

Next fall I intend to seek a further degree in museum
studies. Since I am planning a career in museum work, an
internship at the Museum of Fine Arts would be a wonderful
opportunity and a challenge which I am confident I could
meet.

My grade point average in graduate school has been excellent
at 4.0. I am enclosing a list of my pertinent graduate and
undergraduate courses. Of course, I haven't yet received
final grades for those classes which I am currently taking,
but my present grade is A in each of them.

Thank you for considering my application. In September I
had the pleasure of visiting your museum for the first time
to see your splendid Oriental collection. I am certain I
would enjoy working with the staff and collections of the
Museum of Fine Arts.

Sincerely,

Laurie V. Dahlberg

Laurie V. Dahlberg

Tips for Creating an Effective Résumé

A résumé (or *vita*) is a listing, in easy-to-read form, of
everything about you that might be useful to an employer:
your work experience, your education and technical training,
personal details, and a list of references—at least three people
who will testify to your sterling character and considerable
capabilities.

When and How to Use a Résumé. Always include a résumé with your application letter. Your résumé is your representative—a personal record of your accomplishments. It
should be as attractive and informative as you can make it.
Since your résumé need not be written in full sentences and
since there is no standard form for headings, you have a lot of
leeway to present your best points effectively. *Try to fit every-*

thing on one typed page. Two pages is the limit. Brevity is just as important as an attractive format. Limiting yourself to one page forces you to stick to the essentials. Be sure it looks appealing. Once it is perfect, you may want to have your résumé duplicated commercially. The sample résumés in Figure 7-10 (pages 363–367) show several ways to organize and type the information.

What to Say: Developing the Form.   Begin with your name, address, and telephone number. Make each of the four parts—education, experience, personal data, and references—a separate heading. List either experience or education first, depending on which is stronger in your case. Refer to Figure 7-10 while reading this explanation of the four parts:

Experience.   List your jobs in reverse order: the present one first, then the job before that, and so on, since employers are most interested in what you have been up to lately. If you have not had much work experience, be sure to list all jobs, no matter how unimportant they seem. Explain briefly what you did instead of merely listing a job title that may not convey the full scope of your duties. If you have had many jobs, downplay the ones that are irrelevant to your career goals in order to save space. For example, you may have a summarizing entry like this:

Summers 1980–1985   Worked as counterperson at three fast-food restaurants in the Chicago area.

Education.   List all your formal education and degrees, at least back through high school. Again, start with the most recent. You can use separate subheadings for scholastic honors or scholarships and for technical or management training that you received with a private company or in the armed services.

Personal Data. This category includes information like age, height, weight, health, and marital status. Since federal and some state laws prohibit discrimination on the basis of race, religion, and sex, you may omit that information if you wish. You may want to mention your military service record, membership in clubs, and offices held.

References. List at least three people who have agreed to write reference letters for you. Give their complete business addresses (and telephone numbers, if they do not object). Never list anyone who has not agreed to give you a reference or anyone you think may not give you a wholehearted recommendation. If you are using your college placement service, you need only list the names (with titles) and add "References available upon request from the University of _____ Placement Service."

Matching Your Cover Letter to the Job

Every résumé you send out should be accompanied by an application letter tailored especially for the job you are seeking. Following are Dan Linneman's résumé and the cover letters he sent along for two different jobs. Notice how he alters his emphasis to fit the job requirements. See Figure 7-11 (pages 368–371).

EXERCISE 7-4

Go through the help-wanted advertisements or your local newspaper, and choose a job that sounds like one you might like. Write a letter of application and a résumé. Do not mail them unless you want the job, but do not throw them away either. You can use the letter as a model when you write the real thing. If you keep your résumé, you will need only to update it.

Figure 7-10 Sample résumés.

Sue LeSeure
500 W. Main St.
Normal, IL 61761
Telephone: 309/452-9999

Experience

Oct. 1976 to present (during school term)	Station WXYZ, Normal IL Part-time, 20 hours per week. Wrote advertising copy and solicited ads.
June-August 1979/ June-August 1978	The Daily Deluge, Colfax IL Full-time proofreader (substituted for head proofreader, 1979)
June-August 1977	Gilbey's Variety Store, Colfax IL Sales clerk (with stocking and pricing duties). Also made deliveries and called in supply orders.
June-August 1976	Unemployed
Jan. 1974-Aug. 1975	Alice's Restaurant, Colfax IL Waitress and cashier

Education

Sept. 1977-June 1980	Illinois State University Will receive B.A. in English, June 1980.
Sept. 1976-June 1977	Baskerville Community College
Sept. 1972-June 1976	Octavia High School
Scholastic honors:	Earned a 3.46 grade point average (on a 4.0 scale). George Canning Scholarship in English Literature, 1979-80. Illinois State Scholarship, 1976-80.
Technical training:	Attended a two-week seminar on "Advertising in Today's Marketplace," sponsored by College of Business and McLean County Association of Commerce and Industry.

Personal Data

Age:	24		Married, no children
Health:	Excellent		Willing to relocate
Memberships:	Student Association for Women; Journalism Club (President, 1979-80)
Hobbies:	photography, swimming

References

Ms. Mary Gilbey, Owner Gilbey's Variety Store 555 S. Fifth Street Colfax IL 61763 Phone: 309/723-9999	Dr. Charles Harris Assoc. Prof. of English Illinois State University Normal IL 61761 Phone: 309/436-9999	Mr. Waldo Withersnorp Advertising Manager Radio Station WXYZ 112 Beaufort Avenue Normal IL 61761

Figure 7-10 *Cont.*

TOM LONG   604 1/2 N. Main St.
                                                      Bloomington, IL 61701
                                                      (309) 829-1505

Experience: The Pantagraph September 1981-present
               Bloomington, Illinois
               Reporter covering government and politics in
               state, local, national and international
               issues; feature stories, courts and general
               assignment.

               St. Louis Post-Dispatch Jan.-July 1981
               Springfield, Illinois
               Political reporting intern, second member of
               Illinois Statehouse Bureau covering all
               aspects of state government.

               The Daily Vidette Oct. 1978-May 1980
               Illinois State University
               Normal, Illinois
               Reporter, editor, photographer

               Freelance articles published in The
               Progressive (Feb. 1985), Arab Studies
               Quarterly (Spring 1985), The Washington Star
               (May 31, 1981), Illinois Issues (August
               1981), Illinois Times (July 1981). Reporting
               for Time (Jan.-Aug. 1981) and Chicago Lawyer
               (April 1981).

Other
background: Travel to the Middle East (Israel, West Bank,
               Gaza Strip and Jordan) in 1983 and 1984,
               resulting in articles and photos published in
               The Pantagraph, The Progressive, Arab Studies
               Quarterly.

               1984 Associated Press Illinois Editors
               feature writing award for newspaper series on
               West Bank.

               Experienced photographer.

Education: M.A. in Public Affairs Reporting, 1981
               Sangamon State University
               Springfield, IL
               Robert P. Howard-Chicago Tribune Scholar

               B.S. in Journalism, 1980
               Illinois State University, Normal, IL

               References available upon request.

Figure 7-10 *Cont.*

Laurie L. Haag

703 N. School St.
Normal, Illinois
61761
(309) 452-0269

Birth date:
November 7, 1958

Career Objective:

To use my communications background in a socially
responsible profession.

Education:

B.S. in Communications, Illinois State University (emphasis
in journalism and public relations, minor in art),
1981. Completed 9 hours toward Masters in Speech
Communication, 1985.

Parkland Community College, 1976-1978.

Work Experience:

Aug. to Dec., 1984 Sir Speedy Printing Center, Bloomington.
Duties included customer service, lay-out and paste-up,
and graphic design.

Aug., 1982 to May, 1984 Kinko's Copies, Normal.
Assistant Manager. Duties included customer service,
employee training, bookkeeping, operation and maintenance of
machinery, lay-out and paste-up, and design and
implementation of advertising.

July, 1978 to Dec., 1980 Kay Campbell's Casuals,
Bloomington.
Sales clerk.

Related Activities:

Taught swimming and tennis lessons to students ranging from
pre-school to adult during summers while in high school;
worked as a life-guard for seven summers; did volunteer work
at a community center in Champaign from 1976 to 1977;
and was a member of the Parkland College women's basketball,
volleyball, and softball teams.

References available from Illinois State University
Placement Service.

Figure 7-10 *Cont.*

ROBERT D. HARPER

ADDRESS
408 West Locust Street
Apartment #2
Bloomington, IL 61701
(309) 828-6726

PERSONAL DATA
Birthdate: 9/14/62
Height: 5'10"   Weight: 140 lbs.
Single
Excellent Health

CAREER OBJECTIVE

To obtain an entry level assembler, PL/I, or COBOL
programming position with an established company.

EDUCATION

B.S. August 8, 1984, Illinois State University, Normal,
   Illinois
Major course of study: Applied Computer Science
                 G.P.A. in major: 3.56 out of 4
Minor course of study: Business Administration

RELEVANT COURSE WORK

Four years of programming in an IBM 370/MVS environment at
Illinois State University from 1980 to 1984.

At least two classes requiring programming in each of the
following languages: PL/I, COBOL, and 370 Assembler.

Three classes in structured design.

Classes in Operating Systems, Micro Computers, Internal and
External Data Structures, and FORTRAN.

Previous experience with IBM utilities and accessing
methods, including VSAM.

EXPERIENCE

9/80 - 8/82   Drastic Plastic Records, Inc.
              Board of directors.

6/79 - 5/80   Bloomington Normal Computer Works
              Sales person and BASIC programmer.

Figure 7-10 *Cont.*

ACTIVITIES

Co-founder and president of the Normal Community High School
Computer Club from 1979 to 1980.

Member of the McLean County Computer Club from 1978 to 1981.

Instructor of a BASIC programming course for students of
Normal Community High School in Spring, 1980.

INTERESTS

Micro computer hobbyist since 1978.

Electronics hobbyist (especially musical and digital
electronics).

Amateur musician/recording engineer.

References available upon request.

2

Figure 7-11 Sample résumé and cover letters.

R. Daniel Linneman
R.R. 2 Box 96
Danvers, IL 61732
Telephone: (309) 963-4010

Experience

Fall 1978-present   Farmer, Danvers, Illinois
Management and operation of 190-acre cash grain farm. Corn,
soybean, dry bean and small grain production, grain handling
and marketing, machinery operation and maintenance,
machinery repair, financial management.

Oct. 1984-June 1985   McLean County Association for
                        Retarded Citizens (MARC) Center,
                        Bloomington, Illinois
                        Home Individual Program Manager
Professional foster care for adult developmentally
disabled/mentally ill males. Managed budget, developed and
implemented behavior programs, coordinated extensive
medical services, developed and implemented training for
activities of daily living, served as advocate, participated
in interdisciplinary team.

March 1983-Oct. 1984   MARC Center, Bloomington, Illinois
                        Work Floor Supervisor
Supervised and trained employees in subcontract work,
coordinated production of subcontract work, participated in
time studies, designed and built jigs and fixtures to
facilitate production.

Jan. 1981-March 1983   MARC Center, Bloomington, Illinois
                        Cook
Prepared morning, noon, and evening meals Saturday and
Sunday for 24 people in MARC Center-supported apartments;
supervised 3 assistants.

June 1976-June 1977   Linneman and Associates, Valley
                        Forge, Pennsylvania
                        Research Assistant
Did library research, prepared audio-visual materials, and
wrote briefs on marketing and strategic planning.

Education

June 1977-1978   Pennsylvania State University
                        Graduate Research Assistant,
                        Agronomy Department
Collected and organized tissue samples from corn research
plot, analyzed samples for glucose content, assisted
professor in crop physiology laboratory, began course work
towards M.S. Degree in Agronomy.

Figure 7-11 *Cont.*

Sept. 1974-May 1976	Illinois State University, Normal, Illinois Received B.S. in Agricultural Science
Sept. 1972-May 1974	Windham College, Putney, Vermont
Aug. 1969-May 1972	Phoenixville, Pennsylvania Area High School
Scholastic Honors	Graduated with High Honors (3.65 on a 4.0 scale) from Illinois State University Dean's List / Honors List at Windham College (three out of four semesters)

Continuing Professional Training

Illinois Cooperative Extension Service:
    Crop Protection Workshop, 1985
    Crop Scouting Workshop, 1984
    Vegetable Production Workshop, 1983
Institute for the Study of Developmental Disabilities:
    Anger Control Workshop, 1985
    Behavior Modification Training for Developmentally Disabled Persons, 1985

Personal Data

Birth date: April 10, 1954
Health: Excellent

References

Dr. Daniel P. Knievel
Pennsylvania State University
Agronomy Department
State College, PA 16802

Dr. Wilbur Chrudimsky
Illinois State University
Agriculture Department
Normal, IL 61761

Dr. Frederick Fuess
Illinois State University
Agriculture Department
Normal, IL 61761

Marilea White, M.S.W.
MARC Center
108 E. Market Street
Bloomington, IL 61701

Figure 7-11 *Cont.*

1009 W. Monroe Street
Bloomington, IL 61701
July 10, 1985

Bambridge Peterson
County Administrator
McLean County
Room 204 Courthouse
202 N. Main St.
Bloomington, IL 61701

Dear Mr. Peterson:

I am writing in response to your Pantagraph advertisement for
Parks and Recreation Director for Comlara Park.

As you will see from the enclosed resume, I have successfully
operated and managed a farm in McLean County for the past seven
years. The experience has yielded a broad range of management
skills including market analysis, budget planning,
bookkeeping, and supervising assistants. Throughout this
period, I have served in several positions with McLean County
Association for Retarded Citizens (MARC). This work has also
required supervisory and management expertise, as well as close
cooperation with other workers and administrators of
interrelated programs.

I have always enjoyed camping, boating and swimming, and I feel
that the Parks and Recreation Director position would be a
unique opportunity to promote these activities and serve the
community.

Please review the enclosed resume in light of your needs for this
position. I live in Bloomington and would be happy to interview
at your convenience.

Sincerely,

Dan Linneman

Dan Linneman

enclosure: resume

Figure 7-11 *Cont.*

R.R. 2 Box 96
Danvers, IL 61732
October 6, 1985

Box R-45
Pantagraph
301 W. Washington
Bloomington, IL 61701

Dear People:

I am writing in response to your Pantagraph advertisement to
fill the position of soil scientist to assist on the McLean
County Soil Survey.

As you will see from the enclosed resume, I have a strong
agricultural background both in the field and in the classroom.
I have been a farmer in this county for the past seven years and
have my B.S. degree in Agricultural Science with some work
completed toward my M.S. degree. My social service work at MARC
Center has required me to function as part of a team, a skill that
will be important in the soil survey job. My transcript, also
included here, reflects my strong interest in and aptitude for
soil science and subjects related to agriculture in general. Dr.
Chrudimsky, my soil science professor for three semesters, will
attest to my skill in this area.

I have been interested in a McLean County soil survey since 1975,
when I discovered the lack of consolidated information on the
soils of our county in comparison with other counties in
Illinois. I followed with great interest the debate in county
government over soil survey funding. I would consider it a
privilege to work on the survey myself.

Sincerely,

R. Daniel Linneman

R. Daniel Linneman

Appendix A
Using Microcomputers in
Your Writing

If you're lucky enough to get a chance to use a word processor, by all means do it. You'll find writing more fun, revising easier, and your printed pages more beautiful. We have found that even people with severe computer-phobia convert to word processors with remarkable enthusiasm. The advantages of writing on a microcomputer come from several nifty features that all the word processing programs we know of share.

THE NOVELTY FACTOR

Writing on a computer can boost your skills just because you may sit down at the keyboard more willingly than you'd sit down at your desk. Writers at any level can benefit from mere practice—more than they do from instruction, in many cases. Once you've gone through the initial frustration of learning your program, you'll enjoy snatching a session at the computer in your free time.

One of the new things you'll be getting used to is working with a *program*. A program, which is a set of rules and directions that the computer memorizes, makes the computer operate according to built-in instructions. For example, in a word processing program there's always a button (or buttons) on the keyboard that, when pushed, set the margin where you want it. There's also a button (or buttons) to push to center a title—no more tiresome counting and backspacing. The keyboard operations that you do to make the computer obey you are called *commands*.

You don't have to memorize the commands (though you'll probably know the most-used ones by heart very soon). You can make command lists appear on the screen, so you can choose the one you want. These lists are called *menus*. Learning to find the right menu and get it on the screen is half the battle of mastering your program. If you're a bit old-fashioned, you can always look up the commands in the manual that comes with your program.

THE FIRST ONE'S FREE—AND THE SECOND, AND THE THIRD . . .

You'll notice right away when you use a word processor that, for once, you don't have to pay for your mistakes. While you write at the keyboard, letters, words, and even whole lines can be erased with a couple of keystrokes. Your typos, awkward phrasing, repetitive word choice—all those embarrassing flaws—can disappear without anyone's ever knowing you had them. Your letters to the folks back home will suddenly become correct and stylish.

Those letters will also become more organized, to everyone's admiration. Of course, when we write letters home by hand or typewriter, we're likely to have sections like this one:

```
Oh, and I forgot to mention, back when I was
```

```
telling you about Leah's new baby, did you

know that Leah and Steve bought a new house?

It's got an extra bedroom, and it's right

close to Ben and Ginny's, so Ginny can just

go baby-sit real easy.
```

When you write on the computer, you can skip the apologetic transition and just go back and put the new house by the new baby, where it belongs. Word processing programs have *insert* modes as well as delete methods. You can make additions and revisions anywhere in your piece; the program doesn't confine you to the end.

There's a marker (the *cursor*) on the screen that shows you where you're working. You can move the cursor to the point where you want to put in new stuff and just type it in. The old stuff will keep moving over to make room for it. The screen may look quite strange during this process, as the old stuff slithers over, but you should stay calm. After you have made your insertion, there's a command that will *re-form* the section, making it look okay again. Some word processors re-form automatically as you insert.

The ease of inserting new stuff makes your outlining work neater: as you think of new categories that belong under I.A., for example, you can put those in the right place even though you are currently working on II.B.

And admit it. There have been times when you knew you needed another example, detail, or explanation in a paragraph and said to yourself, "I can't bear retyping that page. I'll just let it go the way it is." With the insert mode, you can do what you know in your heart is right.

KEEP ON MOVIN'

You may admit that there have also been times when you read over a paper and realized that one whole section should have come earlier in the paper—for example, that your conclusion actually would serve much better as the introduction. In the old days, only saintly people would sigh, roll fresh paper into the Remington, and start all over.

In the new age, you don't have to be a saint to move a block of text (a section of writing). Word processing programs have commands to deal with that on-screen. Using the cursor and keyboard commands, you can mark the section that you want moved, show the computer where you want it, hit a key, and blip! the section will be gone from the old place and appear magically in the new place. If you read it there and realize that it was better off before, you can just blip it back to its original location. This feature is super. It lets you take a quick peek at, say, how your conclusion would look as an introduction, instead of just trying to picture it in your mind.

The program also has commands to mark and delete a whole section, mark and copy a whole section (so that it will appear in both places), or mark and move a whole section to a separate place of its own, outside the paper you're working on, so you can use it later.

With inserting and deleting so easily done, your laziness won't limit the quality of your writing. You can save a rough draft, let it age, and come back to revise it without retyping. You can even try bizarre and unusual structures and sentences, just to see whether they work, without wasting much time—perhaps discovering new terrain in the process.

You can also discover new terrain, as you know, by using free writing in the invention process. Your computer will help you free-write without having your unconscious editor keep popping in to check your spelling and punctuation—and meanwhile ruining your flow of thought. Just turn off the monitor, so you can't see what you're writing while you're doing it. The blank screen will force you to let your ideas flow without blockage.

GOODBYE TO ALOT AND EXAGERATE

Many word processors will work together with other programs that check your spelling and find typos. These programs read through your essay and point out every word they don't recognize. Each program has a dictionary (really, just a word list). When a word in your essay is flagged, that means it's not in the program's dictionary. You have a choice of moving on (for instance, if your name is LaShonda, that will get flagged every time, but it's not wrong) or correcting the error. Some programs will even suggest a spelling: if you wrote *spagetti*, the program would display the word *spaghetti* and ask you if that's really what you meant. Most programs also let you add words to the dictionary—for instance, if you add your name to the dictionary, it will recognize the word and not flag it every time.

These spelling checkers make our lives easier, but some of the proofreading still has to be done by hand. The program recognizes *their, there,* and *they're* as correct—but you may have written the wrong one for your context. Matters of usage like this one are still your responsibility. If you make a typo that just happens to form a real word, the program won't find that typo. For example, in the previous sentence, we could have mistakenly typed "work" and "type" instead of "word" and "typo," and the program would not tell us that we'd written a mighty weird sentence. It won't catch mechanical problems, like capitalization and spacing errors. And finally, it won't catch words left out or repeated. Careful proofreading of the final copy by a human is still a necessity, and probably it always will be.

THE BEAUTY OF IT ALL

Imagine this nightmare: you get to class on Friday with a five-page, single-spaced, narrow-margined masterpiece hot off the typewriter. While collecting the papers, your instructor casually says, "And I hope you all remembered that these must be double-spaced, with one-inch margins all around, so I have room for my comments."

Your heart sinks. First you have to grovel before your instructor, asking for an extension, and then cancel your plans for a weekend in Colorado to stay home and retype your paper—unless you've written it on a word processor. If you have, there are commands to redesign the whole thing without retyping. You can change margins, line spacing, page length, the placement of the page number, and (sometimes) even the size of the type without retyping a word. If your word processor has *on-screen formatting*, the changes will show on the screen as you redesign, and you can check the appearance as you go.

You can also make title pages, tables of contents, and Works Cited lists look professional with a word processor. The program lets you know what line of the page your cursor is on, so you can center a line vertically as well as horizontally on your title page. For example, a normal page has fifty-four or fifty-five lines of type on it, so you would skip to twenty-seven to type the paper's title; then you'd use the centering command to automatically put the title in the middle of the page. If your teacher has an exact format, you'll be able to follow it precisely; if your teacher is less particular, you can bounce the required material around on the page until you achieve a look *you* like.

COMPOSE AT THE KEYBOARD

You may insist that you can't write perfectly polished prose except with your favorite felt-tip pen on wide-lined, legal-sized paper. You may be certain that inspiration will fail you if you're facing a keyboard and a screen instead. But do try it anyway. Force yourself, if necessary, to try composing a few pieces of writing from start to finish on a word processor. Then consider the ease with which you can revise. Consider the time saved by not having to retype the last draft. Consider the handsome appearance of your final copy. Probably you will never willingly go back to pen and paper (except to take notes and make lists) if you can lay hands on a word processor.

Appendix B
Spelling

In the past, people were considerably more relaxed about correct spelling than we are today. William Shakespeare, demonstrating his boundless creativity, spelled his own last name at least thirteen different ways. John Donne wrote "sun," "sonne," or "sunne," just as it struck his fancy. But along about the eighteenth century, Dr. Samuel Johnson decided things were out of hand. He took it upon himself to establish a standard for the less learned and brought out his famous dictionary. The language has refused to hold still, even for the stern-minded Dr. Johnson, but people have been trying to tame it ever since.

Today, educated people are expected to be able to spell according to the accepted standard. Nobody encourages a lot of creativity in this area. So if you failed to learn to spell somewhere back in grade school, you now have a problem.

TRY PROOFREADING

Spelling is intimately tied up with proofreading. A quick read-through will not catch careless spelling errors, and it will not make you stop and look up words that just do not look right the way you wrote them. It will do you no good to shrug and say, "Oh, I'm a terrible speller," as though it were the same as "Oh, I'm a hemophiliac." If you know your spelling is weak, leave it alone on the rough draft—worrying about it could really cramp your style—but do look up all those words before you type the finished copy or hand in your in-class theme.

SPELLING BY RULES

Memorizing and applying spelling rules can be almost as challenging as remembering the spelling of individual words. But many people profit by knowing at least a few spelling rules, so four groups of common spelling rules follow. Three of these groups concern suffixes (endings like *-s*, *-ing*, *-able*), since those rules are a little more consistent than most.

Doubling or Not Doubling

Pattern A. Double the final consonant if it's in an accented syllable with a short vowel sound.

> forgot, forgotten, forgettable
> fog, foggy
> pad, padding
> regret, regretted

Pattern B. Do not double the final consonant if the vowel sound in its syllable is long

> write, writer, writing
> eat, eaten
> relate, related
> rail, railing

Pattern C. Do not double the final consonant if its syllable is unaccented.

> counsel, counselor
> question, questionable

Dropping or Not Dropping

Pattern A.   Drop the final -*e* before -*ing*, -*able*, or other suffixes beginning with vowels.

> please, pleasing
> store, storage
> sense, sensible

but:

> hoe, hoeing

Pattern B.   Retain the final -*e* before suffixes beginning with consonants.

> awe, awesome
> hope, hopeful
> live, lively
> tone, toneless

Pattern C.   If the final -*e* is preceded by a *u*, the *e* is usually dropped.

> true, truly
> argue, argument

Pattern D.   If the final -*e* makes a *c* or *g* before it soft (makes the *c* sound like *s* or makes the *g* sound like *j*), it's usually retained.

> outrage, outrageous
> notice, noticeable

Changing or Not Changing

Pattern A. The final -*y* after a consonant changes to *i* before all suffixes except -*ing*.

> fly, flies, flying
> forty, forties
> apply, applied, applying

Pattern B. The final -*y* after a vowel stays *y*.

> play, played
> alloy, alloys
> trolley, trolleys

but:

> lay, laid
> pay, paid
> say, said

Pattern C. The final -*y* stays *y* in proper nouns.

> two Marys
> the Raffertys

EI or IE

Pattern A. When *i* and *e* are used together, put the *i* before the *e* in most cases.

> friend   fierce
> believe   niece
> thief

Pattern B. When the *i* and *e* combination follows the letter *c*, put the first *e* first.

> deceit
> conceive
> receive

Pattern C. When the *i* and *e* combination sounds like a long *a* (as in *day*), put the *e* first.

> vein
> freight
> heir

This jingle is one way many people remember the rules about *ie* and *ei:*

> **i** before **e**, except after **c**,
> Or when sounded as **a**
> As in **neighbor** and **weigh**.

One of the problems with this spelling rule is that there are many exceptions, and several of them are common. Memorization seems to be your only recourse. Here is a list of some common exceptions to the preceding *ei*/*ie* rules:

Pattern A Exceptions		Pattern B Exceptions
counterfeit	seize	financier
either	sleight	species
foreign	sovereign	
forfeit	stein	
height	surfeit	
leisure	weird	
neither		

The Apostrophe Problem

Some people classify the myriad misuses of the apostrophe as spelling errors. Remember that apostrophes show possession (dog's puppies) or contraction (can't), but they don't belong in plain old plurals (pigs, radishes, submarines). Look up *Apostrophe* in the "Revising Index" and study its proper use.

SPELLING BY ROTE

Reading the preceding section on spelling rules may have led you to a conclusion: you cannot spell most English words by sounding them out. *Sensible or sensable? Independant or independent? Desperate or desparate?* The truth is you'll just have to memorize how most words are spelled. Here are some methods you can use to help you identify problem words and learn them by heart:

1. Learn the differences between similar words. Lots of people have trouble with pairs like *accept* and *except, affect* and *effect, loose* and *lose.* We explain these differences in the "Glossary of Usage," so if you feel shaky on which of two similar words is right, look there.
2. Make a list of words you misspell. Make it up from the errors you find while proofreading and the spelling mistakes your instructors mark. Neatly print some of these words, spelled correctly, on a piece of paper and tape it to your mirror. Maybe looking at it every morning will make the correct spellings as familiar as your own face.
3. Once you have looked up the correct spellings of your problem words, you can sometimes make up little devices to help you remember them. It helps some people to think, "You can't believe a lie," to remind themselves that *believe* has the word *lie* in it. And

once you got that one down, all you have to remember is that **receive** is the other way. If you have trouble remembering whether to write **their** or **thier,** try remembering that all three words that sound like that—**there, they're,** and **their**—begin with the word **the.** Some of these devices can get more elaborate than the spelling of the words themselves, but if devices do the trick for you, use them.

4. You may feel that you are a hopeless case. There are dozens of learn-to-spell books written just for people like you. Ask at the local bookstore or check out some of the study guides listed at the end of "Reading and Writing in College Classes," and work through whichever one suits you best.

EXERCISE   A-1

1. In each of the following groups, one word is misspelled. Find that word and look in the dictionary for its correct spelling.
   a. sandwich, tradgedy, hallucination, forever
   b. precede, proceed, superceed, recede
   c. predict, perform, personal, prespective
   d. managable, flying, tries, allowable
   e. February, experience, suprise, library
   f. dependant, arrangement, irresistible
   g. livelihood, maintainence, pronunciation
   h. desparate, separate, marriage
   i. disappear, accomodate, occurrence
   j. deceive, believe, recieve, inveigle
   k. malice, catagory, experience
   l. familiar, suspicious, athelete
   m. lonliness, management, mischief
   n. sacrifice, freindly, original
   o. ingrediant, successful, rhythm
   p. pathetic, dismal, wierd
   q. perceive, strict, writting
   r. restaraunt, conscious, neighbor

2. Add two suffixes each (*-ing, -able, -s, -er, -ance, -ful, -ness,* etc.) to the following words and then check your spelling with a dictionary.

a. fog	i. rebel	q. manage
b. ignore	j. battle	r. hope
c. change	k. plan	s. rally
d. advise	l. travel	t. play
e. happy	m. pad	u. thought
f. practice	n. prefer	v. write
g. hate	o. ponder	w. focus
h. alley	p. occur	

Acknowledgments

David Attenborough, excerpt from *Life On Earth, A Natural History.* Copyright © 1979 by David Attenborough Productions Ltd. By permission of Little, Brown and Company and William Collins Sons & Co., Ltd., London.

Hugh Drummond, M. D., excerpt from "Power, Madness and Money," *Mother Jones,* Jan. 1980. Copyright © 1980 Foundation for National Progress. Reprinted with permission from *Mother Jones* magazine.

Marvin Harris, excerpt from *Cows, Pigs, Wars and Witches: The Riddles of Culture.* Copyright © 1974. Reprinted by permission of Random House, Inc.

Christopher Hitchens, excerpt from "The Faded Laurel Crown," *Harper's Magazine,* Nov. 1977. Copyright © 1977 by *Harper's Magazine.* All rights reserved. Reprinted from the November 1977 issue by special permission.

Donald J. Leonard, excerpt from *Shurter's Communication in Business,* 1979. Reprinted by permission of McGraw-Hill Book Company, Publisher.

Casey Miller and Kate Swift, excerpt from *Words and Women: New Language in New Times,* 1976. Copyright © 1976 by Casey Miller and Kate Swift. Reprinted by permission of Doubleday & Company, Inc.

Index